BUILD A Philadelphia Chippendale DRESSING TABLE

A COMPLETE
STEP-BY-STEP GUIDE

Tony Kubalak

SCHIFFER
PUBLISHING
4880 Lower Valley Road • Atglen, PA 19310

Other Schiffer books by the Author:
Carving 18th-Century American Furniture Motifs, ISBN 978-0-7643-5236-2

Other Schiffer books on Related Subjects:
Home Woodworker Series: Home Workshop Setup —the Complete Guide, Jim Harrold, ISBN 978-0-7643-4418-3
New Woodturning Techniques and Projects, Helga Becker, ISBN 978-0-7643-5018-4
Home Woodworker Series: 14 Wooden Boxes You Can Make, Jim Harrold, ISBN 978-0-7643-4243-1

Library of Congress Control Number: 2020952777

Edited by Ian Robertson
Designed by Justin Watkinson
Type set in Academy Engraved LET/Minion Pro/Optima LT Std

ISBN: 978-0-7643-6233-0
Printed in India

Published by Schiffer Publishing, Ltd.
4880 Lower Valley Road
Atglen, PA 19310
Phone: (610) 593-1777; Fax: (610) 593-2002
E-mail: Info@schifferbooks.com
Web: www.schifferbooks.com

To my wife, Barb, and our son, Peter;
you make the bad bearable and the good great.

Thanks to Ross Coyle for reviewing my text from a woodworker's viewpoint and making suggestions and corrections. Another big thanks for his repeated finishing advice over many years. That advice was instrumental to my finishing success with this piece.

Thanks to my wife, Barb, and our son, Peter, for reviewing my text from a nonwoodworker's perspective. If my sentences make sense to them, maybe they are okay.

Thanks to the Minneapolis Institute of Arts for allowing me to study, measure, and photograph the original reference model. Without their access, my reproduction would not be as accurate and my job would have been more difficult.

Preface

This is my first book dedicated to one piece of furniture. It is a Philadelphia Chippendale dressing table—a.k.a. lowboy—dated 1760–1780. The carvings are attributed to the Garvan carver, an unknown craftsman who has been identified by stylistically similar carvings on other pieces. It is the most elegant example of the form that I have seen. The carvings are voluminous, stunning, and masterfully executed. The knee carving is especially beautiful and captivating.

One of my goals with this book is to help aspiring woodworkers build a piece they might have admired but never dreamed they could build, for a variety of reasons. I understand the aspiration because there was a time not so long ago when my desire to build a piece was way ahead of my skills. I was fortunate that I had someone with whom to work to guide me. My hope is that this book can be that guide for someone else.

This is also the first time I have incorporated 3-D computer model drawings. I hope that they will be helpful and clear. They look good to me, and I think that they will be useful to the reader. They seem especially useful in communicating case information, including dimensions, construction sequencing, and joinery.

Finally, it is my intent to break down this complex piece into its individual parts and then sufficiently describe each one in step-by-step detail so the diligent and serious reader will be able to complete each part. Your successful completion of the various subprojects will then be combined to become your version of this magnificent piece.

My hope is that this book will help you in some small way achieve something you did not think possible, and build a project you didn't think you could. Your successful completion of this piece will be a source of pride for you, and a legacy you can pass to future generations.

Tony Kubalak
January 2020

Contents

Introduction and Overview

The dressing table, or lowboy, was a common form in eighteenth-century American furniture. Most of them had four drawers: one long one over three shorter ones. Many times the central, lower drawer would be carved. In the Queen Anne and Chippendale periods, these tables predominantly had cabriole legs that terminated in a variety of foot styles, including slipper, trifid, and ball and claw.

The example this book will describe is from the Chippendale period, circa 1760–1780, and is the most elegant example of the form that I have seen. The carving is in the rococo style and is voluminous and exceptionally executed. **Figure 1-1** is the original, and **figure 1-2** is my version.

Look closely at the lower vines on the central carved drawer front of the original. You will notice that the leaf tips are missing. When I made my version, I added them back. There are witness marks on the original that indicate there was something there in the past. It is not clear exactly what was there, so I made an educated guess. Mine are probably not exact, but they certainly could have been something very similar.

The original is currently in the Minneapolis Institute of Arts, and the carving is attributed to the Garvan carver. The Garvan carver is an unknown individual and is so named because his work is stylistically consistent with pieces in the Mabel Brady Garvan Collection at Yale University. This individual was highly skilled, and his work is exquisite.

When I first saw this piece I was initially captivated by the knee carving. It was visually stunning and technically impressive. I counted five layers and marveled at how integrated and alive all the elements were. I told myself that I had to give this a try. As a first step I thought it would be invaluable if I could examine the piece up close and in detail.

With apprehension, I contacted the museum curator and asked if I could come by and take some measurements and photographs. To my very pleasant surprise, he graciously said yes. He also volunteered that part of the museum's charter was to provide educational opportunities to the public and serious students. I told him I was delighted to hear that, and I made an appointment to go measure the piece.

After collecting measurements and numerous photographs, I started to collate and organize the info I had gotten. I made some drawings and studied the pictures. As these things go, I was highly motivated in the beginning, but the initial excitement wore off before I completed the drawings, so it sat for awhile. Fifteen or so years later, with intermittent work along the way, I finally got it done.

In that time interval, I evolved the way I draw plans and sketches. I no longer use pencil and paper, but Sketchup and Inkscape. I have found that making a 3-D computer model is my preferred method now. By making the model I am building the piece virtually. It forces me to think through the joinery and other construction details. Several of the graphics in this book are various views from the model. I think the 3-D computer model is a great way to convey construction details. The drawing capability of Inkscape provides the line drawings that are the carving templates and rail profiles.

The intent of this book is to be comprehensive and cover every detail of construction, carving, and finishing. My goal is that the serious reader will be able to build their version from the descriptions in the book.

Most of the drawings are not full scale, but the dimensions are. There are full-size drawings of carved elements and profiles from which the reader can make templates (*see* insert).

Before one begins this piece, I would recommend studying the drawings and order of operations to familiarize yourself with the sequencing. Some parts are independent of others and can be worked on separately and concurrently, but some are closely related, and good sequencing will work better and make the job easier.

Another recommendation is to cut all the case joints while the component stock items are square. This will make cutting and fitting the joints and subassemblies easier because all the reference surfaces will be intact. Once the joints are cut, shape and carve the pieces that require it. Now, when the carved pieces are joined together, you know they will fit.

As a final cautionary note, make sure all the dimensions you use from this book make sense on your version. Make parts to fit your piece and adjust sizes as needed. Not only will yours be better for this, but you will better understand the construction details and be able to make better judgment calls as you progress.

Case Construction Overview

On a macroscale, the case is four sides with drawer supports and guides in between. The sides are a single board each. The back is three pieces of wood: two legs and a back board. The

FIG. 1-1. The original reference model is currently at the Minneapolis Institute of Arts.

FIG. 1-2. My reproduction. The lower vines of the applied middle-drawer carving are missing on the original. I put them back on my reproduction.

front is the most complicated, where good sequencing will make things easier.

Once the case is together, add the quarter columns, top, cove molding, and Greek key molding, in that order. Finally add the drawers. That's all there is to it! Conceptually it is relatively straightforward. As always, though, the challenge is in the details.

I am being a little facetious, but only a little. You want and need to think of this complicated piece as a series of smaller and much more manageable subprojects. As I have told my son many times, "No one solves a big problem. One solves many small problems that add up to the big one." With that mindset you will be able to get through this project and understand how to attack other complicated projects by breaking them into smaller ones.

Let's start from the finished piece and work backward. **Figure 1-2** shows my finished piece. **Figure 1-3** shows a model view without the top. The red attachment bars are my additions that are used to attach the top. The bars are dovetailed to the back board and top front rail. Screws from the bottom of the bars connect the top to the case.

Figure 1-4 is the completed case without any of the embellishments. Visualize the four sides of the "box": the front, the back, and two sides. The pieces in the middle are the drawer supports and guides. The yellow pieces are secondary wood—pine in this case. The red ones are my additions and are made from pine. The top three are the top attachment bars. The other three are kickers for the top and lower middle drawers. Without these kickers, the drawers would tend to increasingly angle down as they are pulled out farther. The kickers force the drawers to remain mostly horizontal.

Figure 1-5 shows the four sides. The front face frame is constructed as a subassembly, as is the back subassembly. The sides are one piece each, so the only preparation is the tenons and the bottom profile.

Figure 1-6 shows the sequence for the front face frame. The lower front face frame is put together as a subassembly, and then it and the top rail are attached to the two front legs. **Figure 1-7** shows the components of the lower front face frame. This subassembly consists of two rails and two stiles. This is one of the subassemblies to begin with.

Figure 1-8 shows the back subassembly. It consists of one solid-pine back board and two legs. The mortises in the back board support the central drawer runners, guides, and kicker.

To recap, build the front and back subassemblies. When these are complete, attach the two sides and the internal drawer supports.

I use hot hide glue, so putting all these pieces together at one time is a significant challenge because there are so many parts, and the open time of the glue is short. To make this simpler and get a better result, glue only a few pieces at one time, and then only to either the front or back. For purposes of discussion, glue pieces to the front subassembly first. Clamp the whole case together when only a few pieces are glued, to help keep everything square and aligned. When a set of glued items has sufficiently dried, take the case apart, being careful not to disturb the glued items. Glue a few more pieces, clamp the remaining parts together to keep everything in its relative position, and let it dry. Repeat this until all the parts are glued to the front. The last step is to glue all the pieces to the back in one operation. These all have to be done at once, because once one part is glued to the back and front, the case cannot be pulled apart. **Figures 1-9**, **1-10**, and **1-11** show this gluing sequence.

Next, add the remaining drawer guides and kickers as shown in **figure 1-12**. These are nailed to the legs, so mortises are not needed. Finally, glue in the top attachment bars. The case is now fully constructed.

After the case is constructed, attach the carved top with three screws through each attachment bar. **Figure 1-13** shows the attachment bars dovetailed to the front and back. Be careful that the screws are short enough so they do not punch through the top. Try to size them so that there is about ⅛" remaining to the top surface. Drill pilot holes so the screws will be easier to drive and the chance of splitting the top board is minimized.

Recall that these are some of my additions and are not on the original. The original used glue blocks around the inside of the case to attach the top.

When the top is attached, fit the cove molding immediately beneath the top. Then fit the Greek key molding beneath the cove. Add the three-part quarter columns with glue. Finally, build and fit the drawers.

FIG. 1-3. The red top attachment bars are my addition. Screws from the bottom of the bars into the top hold it in place.

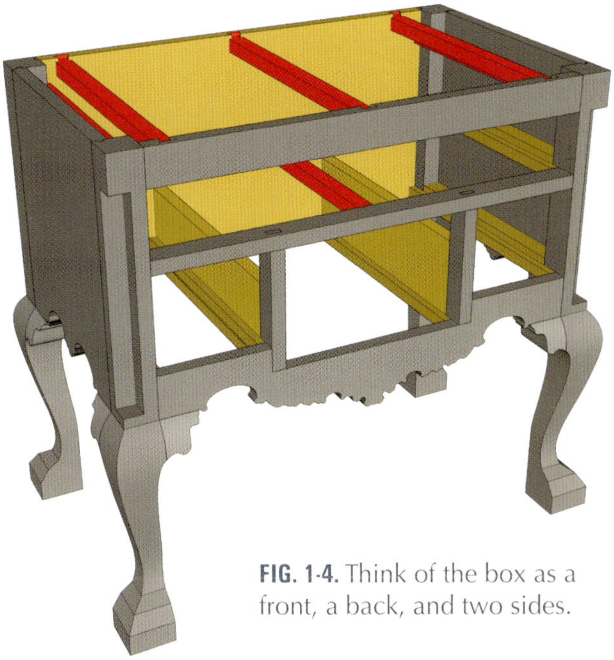

FIG. 1-4. Think of the box as a front, a back, and two sides.

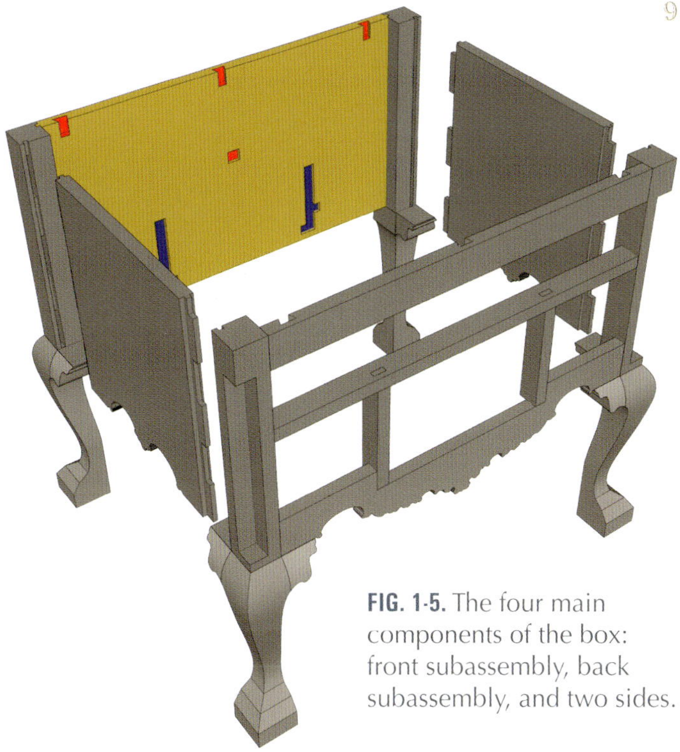

FIG. 1-5. The four main components of the box: front subassembly, back subassembly, and two sides.

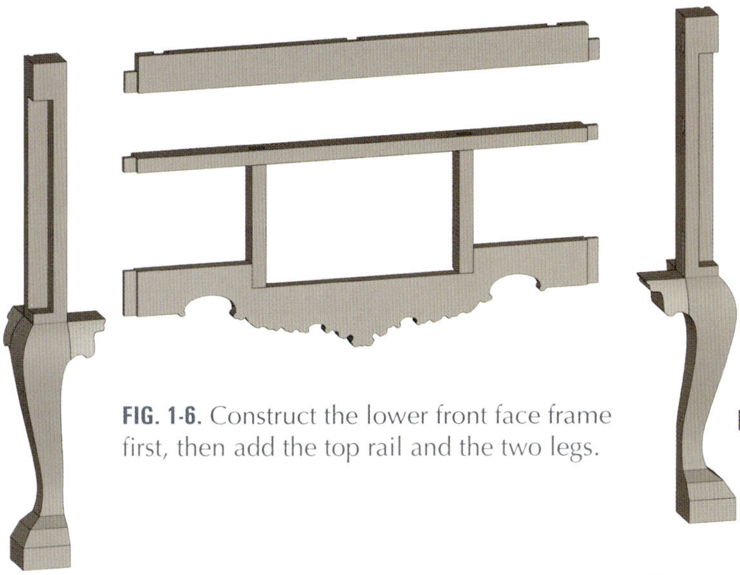

FIG. 1-6. Construct the lower front face frame first, then add the top rail and the two legs.

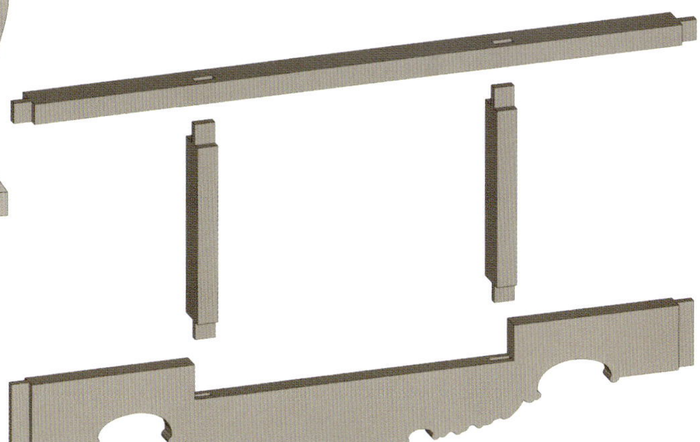

FIG. 1-7. The lower front face frame consists of the lower and middle rails and the two stiles.

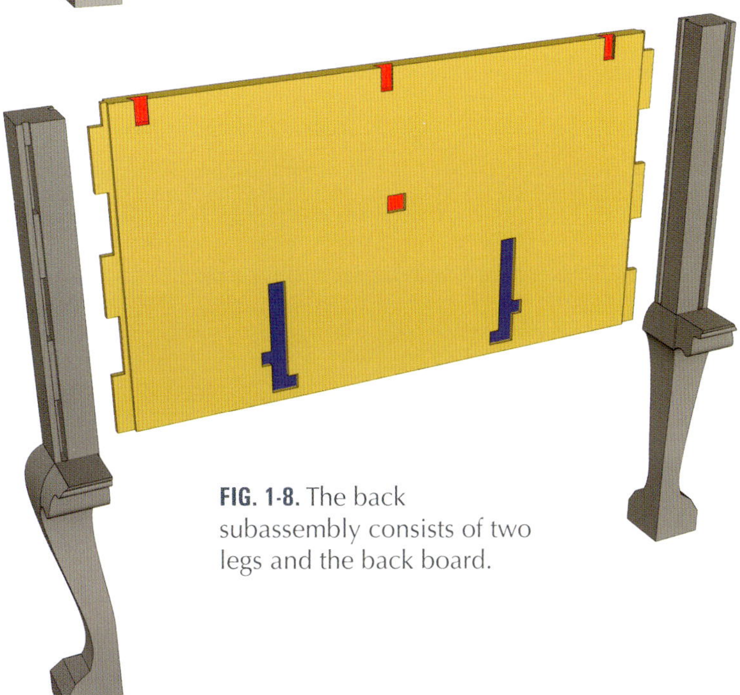

FIG. 1-8. The back subassembly consists of two legs and the back board.

FIG. 1-9. After the front subassembly is together, glue the side boards to the front. Clamp with the back subassembly to keep the case square. When the glue is dry, remove the back subassembly.

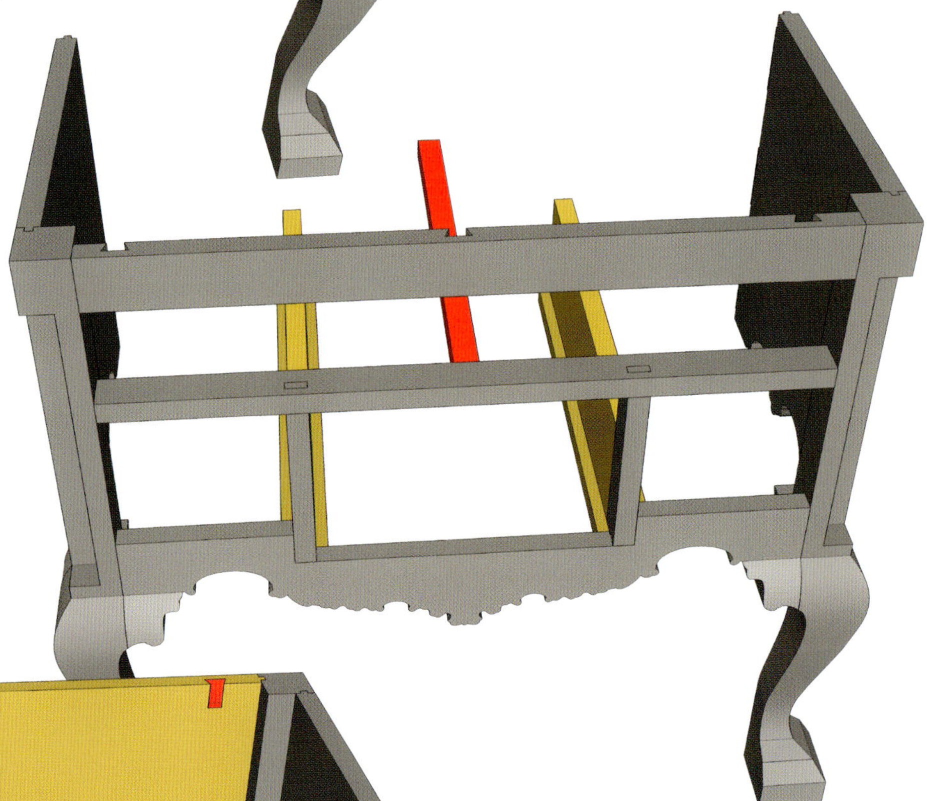

FIG. 1-10. Glue the middle-drawer supports and the red middle-drawer kicker to the front. Clamp with the back subassembly.

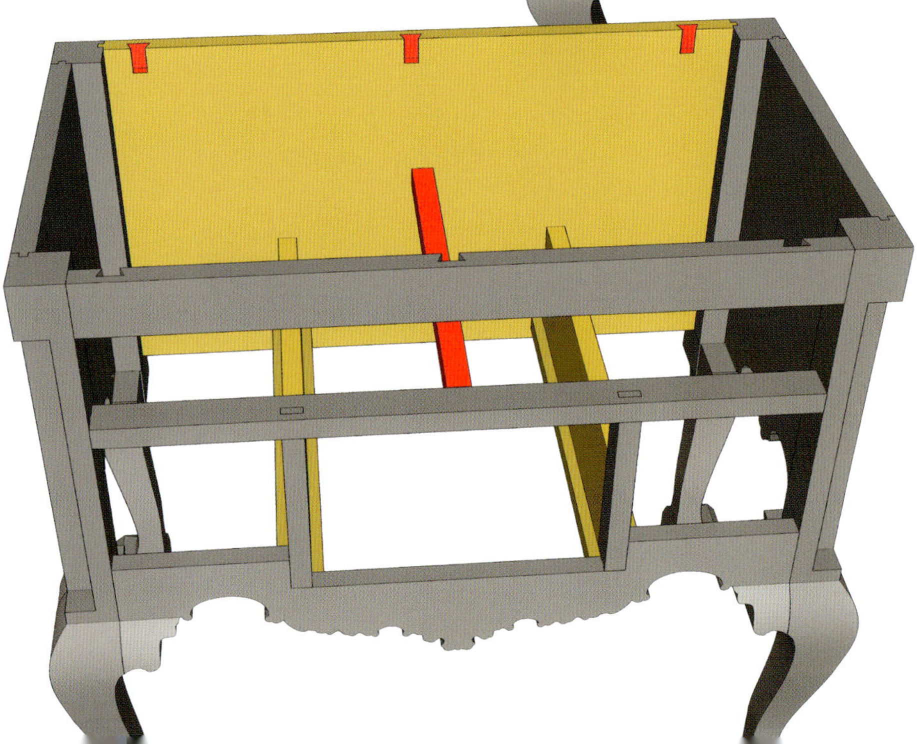

FIG. 1-11. Glue the back subassembly.

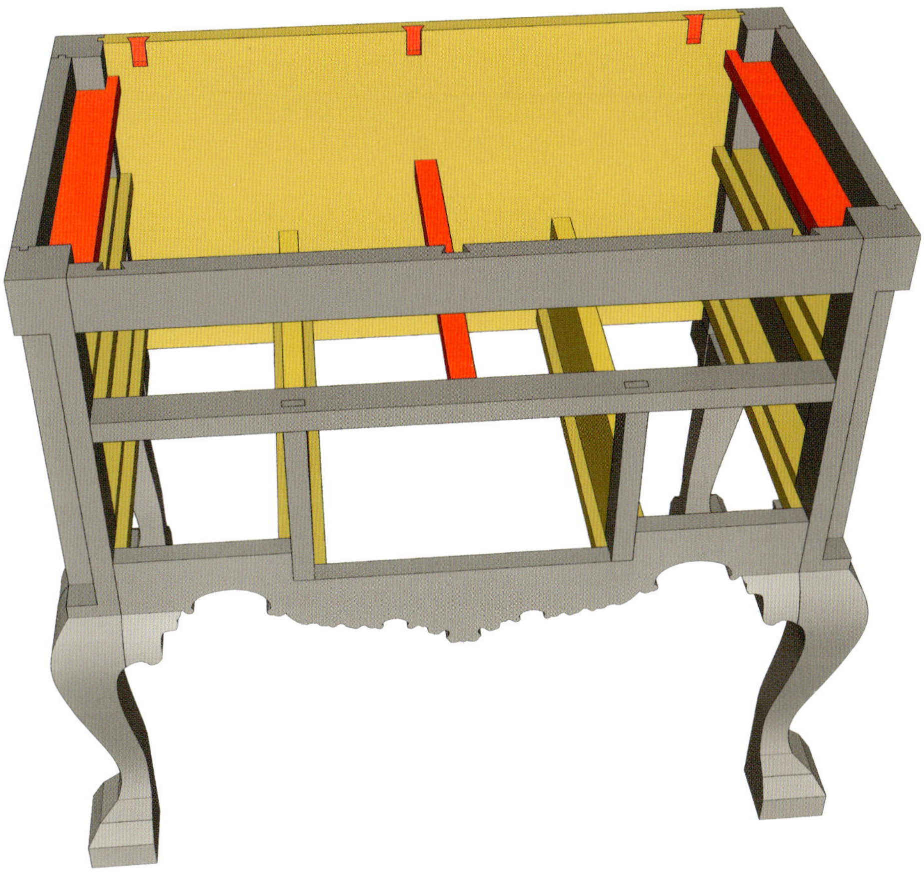

FIG. 1-12. Nail the outside drawer runners and guides. These runners and guides are built from two pieces of pine. Nail the two red top-drawer kickers. These are my addition to prevent the top drawer from tipping down when open.

FIG. 1-13. Glue the three red top attachment bars. Screws are used from the bottom of these bars and hold the top in place. These are my addition to make attaching the top easier.

Case Joinery

Back Subassembly

The last chapter gave a high-level view of the case construction. This chapter will go into detail about each of the subassemblies. My approach is to cut and fit the joints on a particular piece before I carve it. I do it this way for a few reasons. One, it is easier to cut joints when the stock is square, because the reference surfaces are intact and the stock clamps easily to the bench. Two, if any adjustments are needed, it is easier to tweak the carvings or profile than it is the joints. Three, if adjacent parts are already joined, I know that they will fit together after all the shaping and carving.

To start the case, first look at the goal of this stage. **Figure 2-1** shows the case fully joined as square blocks of wood. This is only a dry fit at this point, because seven of the twelve pieces need significant shaping and carving.

FIG. 2-1. Cut all the joints prior to any shaping and carving. Dry-fit the parts to make sure things go together.

As mentioned, the front and back are two subassemblies, and each side is a single piece of wood. Each of these can be worked independently of the others. Let's start with the back subassembly.

Figure 2-2 shows the back subassembly. It consists of a pine back board and two legs connected with haunched mortise-and-tenon joints. **Figures 2-3** and **2-4** show the dimensions for the back board and the legs, respectively. Study these figures until you understand how the back board and legs are joined. Select the stock that you will use, orient them as desired, and mark them so that orientation can be re-created later.

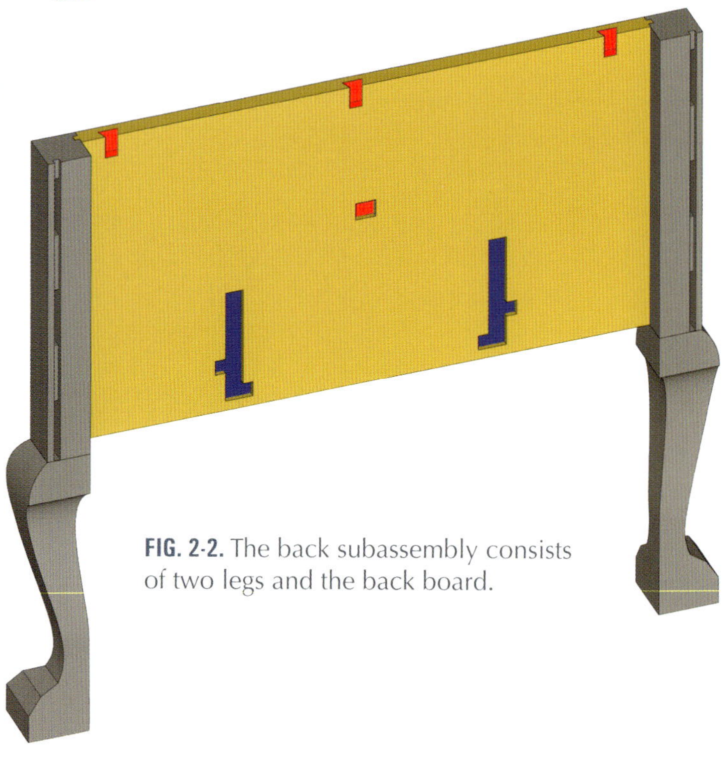

FIG. 2-2. The back subassembly consists of two legs and the back board.

To lay out the mortises on one of the legs, use a mortise gauge, with the inside face as the reference surface. Set the gauge for 5⁄16" mortise with a 1½" offset and score lines the entire length of the leg post. Also mark the mortise heights as defined in **figure 2-4. Figure 2-5** shows the technique and result.

Now cut the mortises. Don't do the ¼" haunch until later. I cut mortises by drilling out the centers with a drill press and then squaring them with a flat chisel. **Figure 2-6** shows a series of holes drilled along the length of the mortise. **Figure 2-7** shows the completed mortise after cleanup with flat chisels. Also notice how each of the faces is marked to keep the orientation correct.

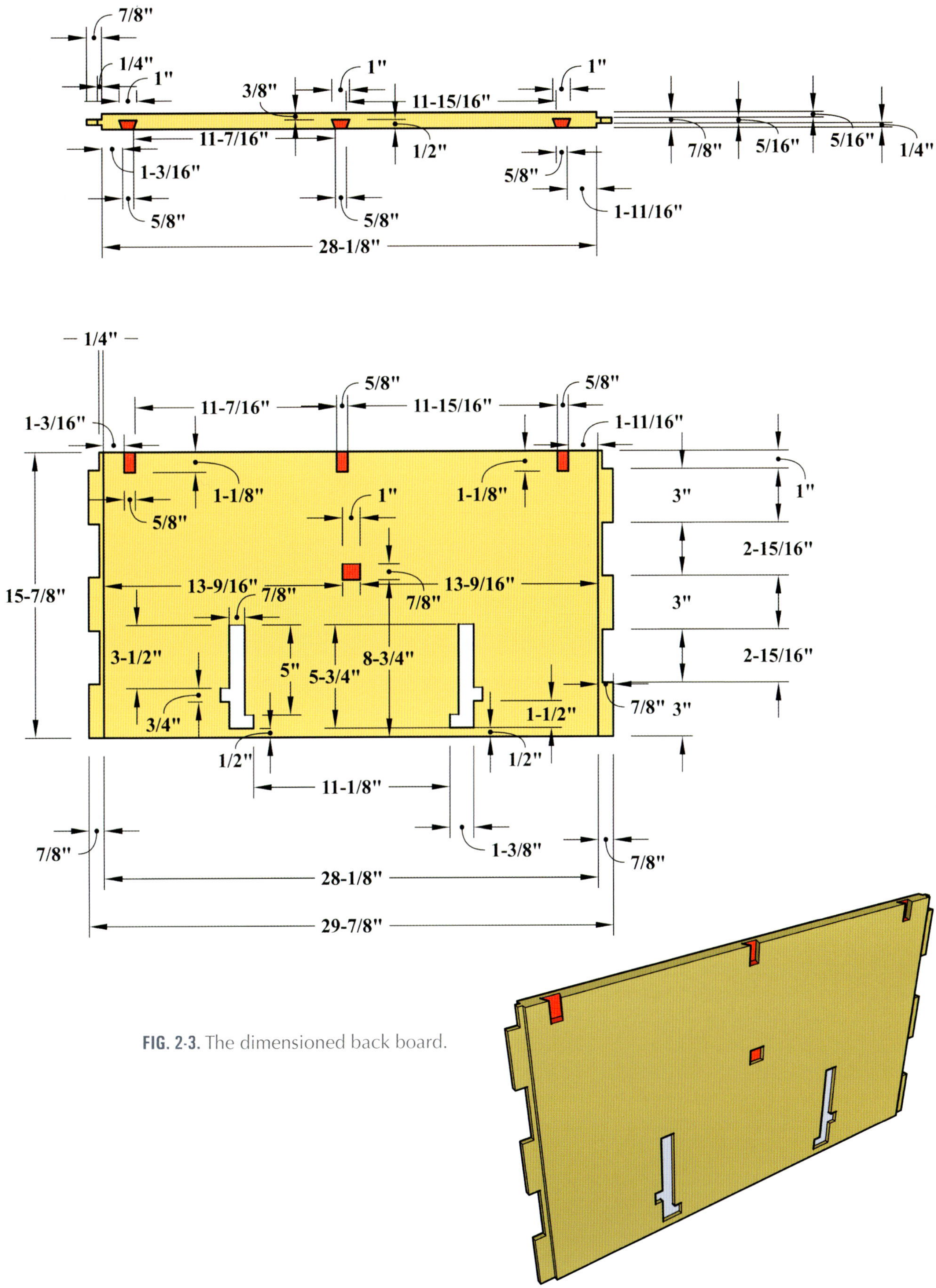

FIG. 2-3. The dimensioned back board.

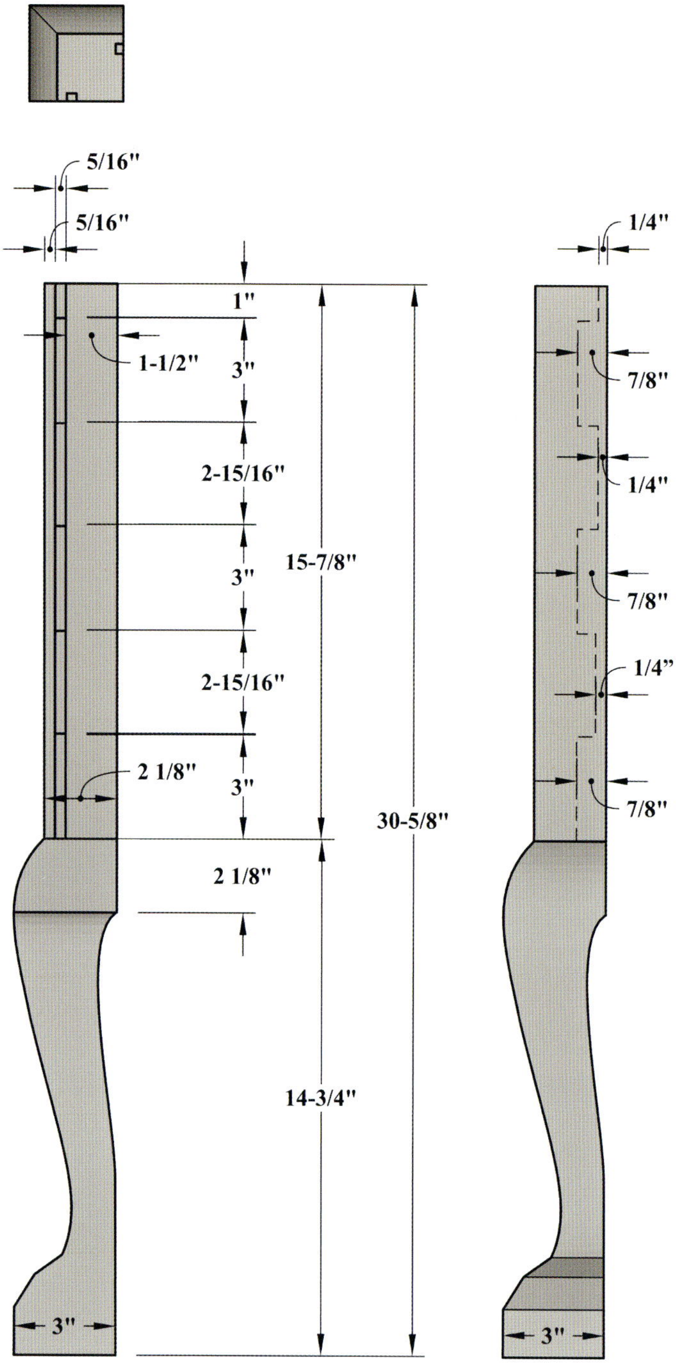

FIG. 2-4. The dimensioned back legs. Cut the mortises prior to cutting and shaping the cabriole leg.

FIG. 2-5. Use a mortising gauge and the inside leg face to place the mortises.

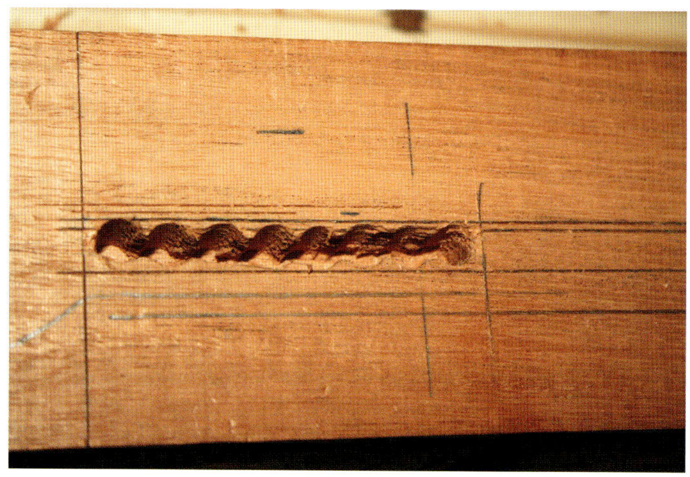

FIG. 2-6. Drill out the mortise centers with a drill press.

FIG. 2-7. Complete the mortise with flat chisels of appropriate width. The haunch area will be done later.

It is important to get the mortise hole reasonably square. Use a small square inside the mortise hole to verify that the walls are 90° to the face of the leg. I also use a small router plane to flatten the bottom of the mortise. Ideally everything would be perfectly square. Since things are seldom perfect, it is better to have the walls slightly undercut than not. In this way the tenon will not be pinched.

There are six mortises on each back leg. Lay out and cut the others now.

The back board is next. Square a piece of ⅞" thick pine to 29⅞" (length) × 15⅞" (width). Length is with the grain, and width is across the grain. Use a mortise gauge to scribe the 5⁄16" tenon lines with a 5⁄16" offset from the back face, as shown in **figure 2-8**. Note that if the back board is a little thicker or thinner, that is okay. Just make sure to reference both the mortise and tenon lines from the back faces of the legs and back board, respectively. In this way the back surfaces of the legs and back board will be in the same plane, which is what is desired. Whatever thickness remains on the back board will be on the inside of the case and thus of no consequence.

Next, use a knife and framing square to scribe the tenon depth line at ⅞", as shown in **figure 2-9**. Carry this line around to the other side and onto the edges.

Typically I would use a handsaw to cut along the tenon lines. Because this is so long, I did not feel that I would be able to do an adequate job with the saw. My alternate way was to use a chisel and shoulder plane to extract the tenon. Most of the waste is removed with the chisel in an iterative process. Chop straight down on the shoulder line and bevel into this from the edge. **Figure 2-10** shows initial progress with the chisel. **Figure 2-11** shows intermediate progress, and **figure 2-12** (*see* p. 16) shows the bevel complete down to the depth of the shoulder wall.

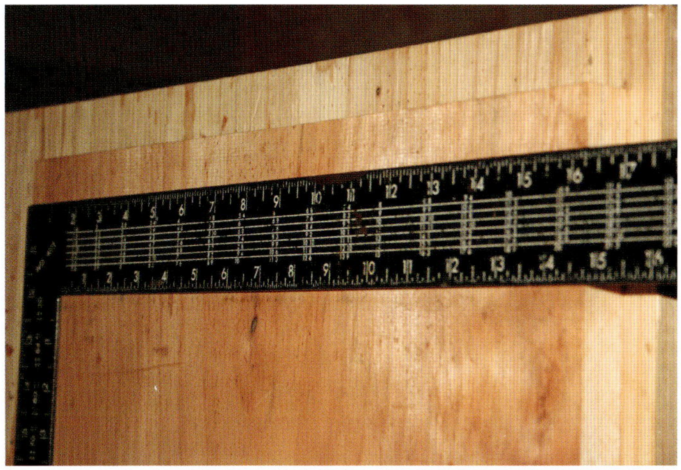

FIG. 2-9. Use a straight edge and knife to score the tenon shoulder.

FIG. 2-10. Use a large, flat chisel to cut into the shoulder line.

FIG. 2-8. Use a mortising gauge to mark the tenons on the back board.

FIG. 2-11. Deepen the shoulder cut with a flat chisel.

FIG. 2-12. Progress on one side of the tenon.

FIG. 2-13. Use a large, flat chisel to remove material quickly.

FIG. 2-14. Use a shoulder plane to remove material close to the lines. Adjust the blade so it does not undercut the vertical shoulder wall.

FIG. 2-15. One face of the tenon is complete.

FIG. 2-16. Complete the other side of the tenon.

FIG. 2-17. Align the back board to the proper back leg post. The bottom of the back board is aligned with the bottom of the lowest mortise.

Next, remove the triangular section with a chisel and shoulder plane. **Figure 2-13** shows the technique and process with the chisel, and **figure 2-14** shows the shoulder plane as it cleans up the chiseled surfaces and squares the tenon face to the wall. **Figure 2-15** shows the tenon face complete. Use the same technique on the other tenon face. **Figure 2-16** shows both complete.

The tenon blank now needs to be further cut to fit the matching leg mortises. **Figure 2-17** shows the back board and the leg to which it will be connected. Transfer the mortise locations to the tenon, as shown in **figure 2-18**. Notice the ¼" haunch line between two adjacent tenons. **Figures 2-19** and **2-20** show a technique for transferring the mortise lines to the tenon.

FIG. 2-20. Extend the end line onto the tenon face. The line parallel to the edge is the haunch.

FIG. 2-18. Mark the tenons from the mortises.

FIG. 2-21. Use a handsaw to cut the tenon lines that are parallel to the grain.

FIG. 2-19. Use a square aligned with the mortise line to mark the tenon placement.

FIG. 2-22. Use a knife to repeatedly cut along the haunch line. Do this from both sides and meet in the middle.

FIG. 2-23. Most of the material is removed. Clean up the remainder with a flat chisel.

Now remove the sections marked with an "X." Use a handsaw to cut lines along the grain, as shown in **figure 2-21**. Then use a knife to cut the lines across the grain, as shown in **figure 2-22**. With the cross-grain cuts, use the knife on both sides. The cuts will meet in the middle, as shown in **figure 2-23**. Clean up the knife cuts with a flat chisel. **Figure 2-24** shows the completed tenons.

It's now time to cut the mortise haunch. I use a #9 7 mm carving gouge to remove the center portion, as shown in **figures 2-25** and **2-26**. Then use a flat chisel to square the walls, as shown in **Figure 2-27**. This will take a couple of iterations. Finally, use a small router plane to flatten the bottom, as shown in **figures 2-28** and **2-29**.

Now fit the back board tenons to the leg mortises, as shown in **figure 2-30**. If the fit is a little tight, make any refinements needed.

FIG. 2-24. Repeat these steps to complete the other tenons.

FIG. 2-26. Get close to the ¼" depth with the gouge.

FIG. 2-25. Begin to cut the ¼" deep haunch area with a #9 7 mm gouge.

FIG. 2-27. Square the sides with a flat chisel. Use the mortise-gauge lines to reference and guide the chisel.

FIG. 2-28. Use a small router plane to flatten the bottom and clean up the corners.

FIG. 2-29. The router plane is perfect for this job.

FIG. 2-30. Dry-fit the back and leg.

Front Subassembly

As mentioned earlier, the front face frame consists of the lower front subassembly plus the upper rail and two front legs. The lower subassembly is the lower rail, middle rail, and two stiles.

Figure 2-31 shows the parts that compose the front face frame and how they fit together. The overall dimensions of the parts are shown in **figure 2-32**. The dimensions and shapes of the individual lower front face frame components are detailed in **figures 2-33** to **2-35**.

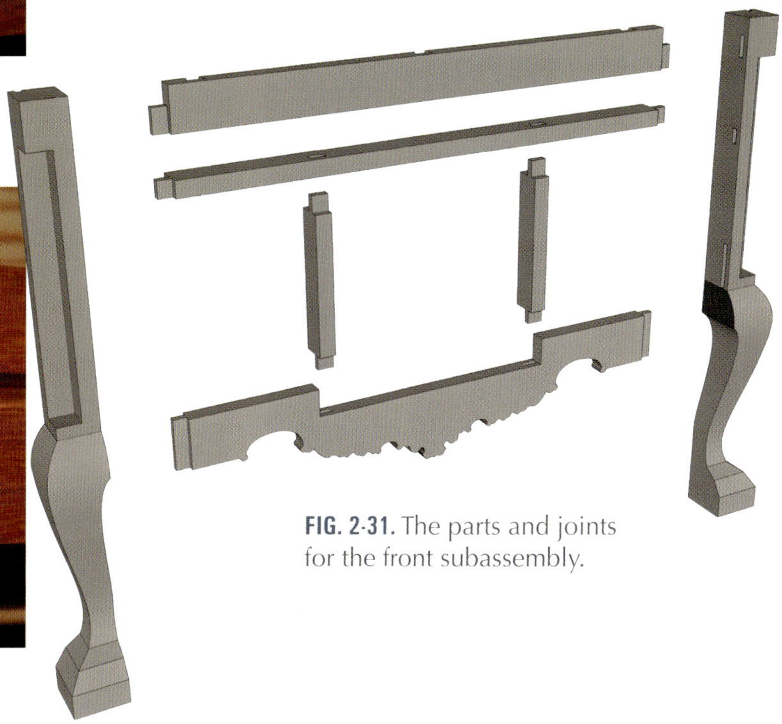

FIG. 2-31. The parts and joints for the front subassembly.

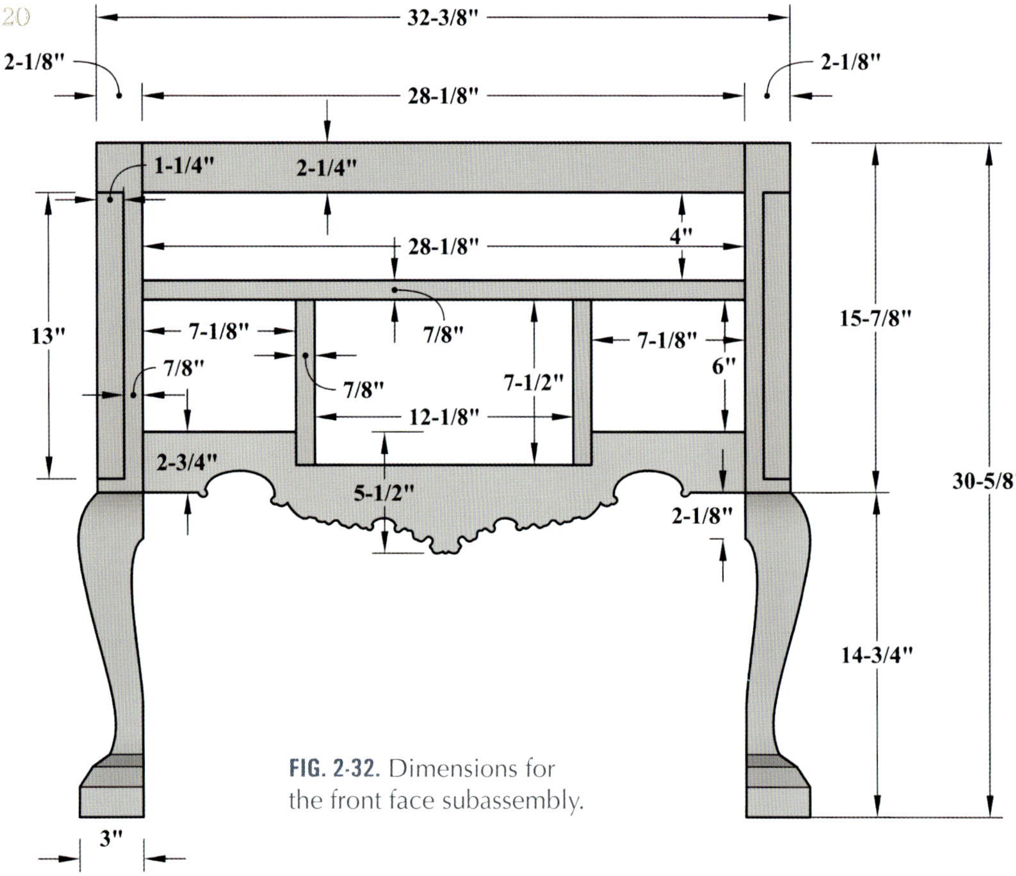

FIG. 2-32. Dimensions for the front face subassembly.

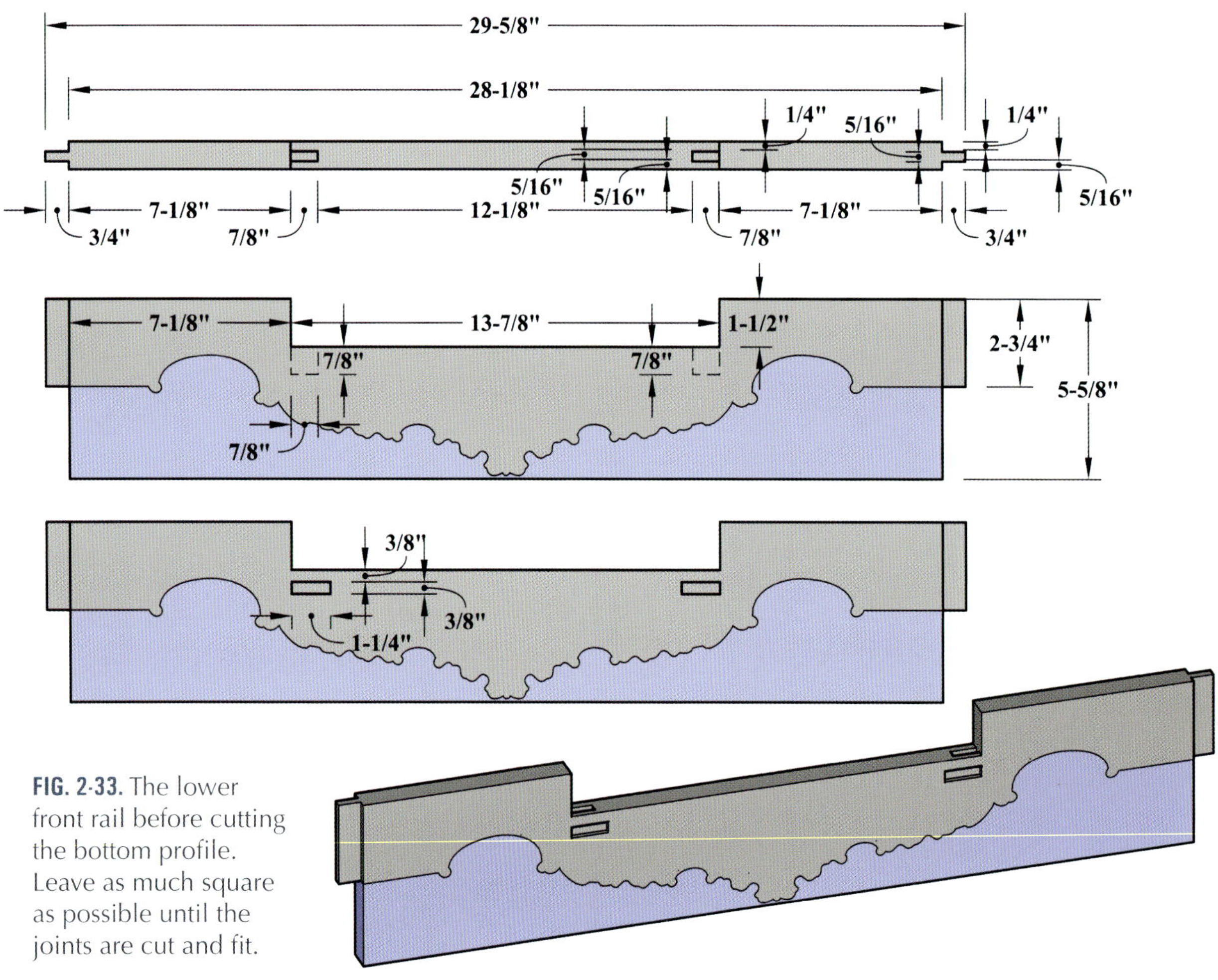

FIG. 2-33. The lower front rail before cutting the bottom profile. Leave as much square as possible until the joints are cut and fit.

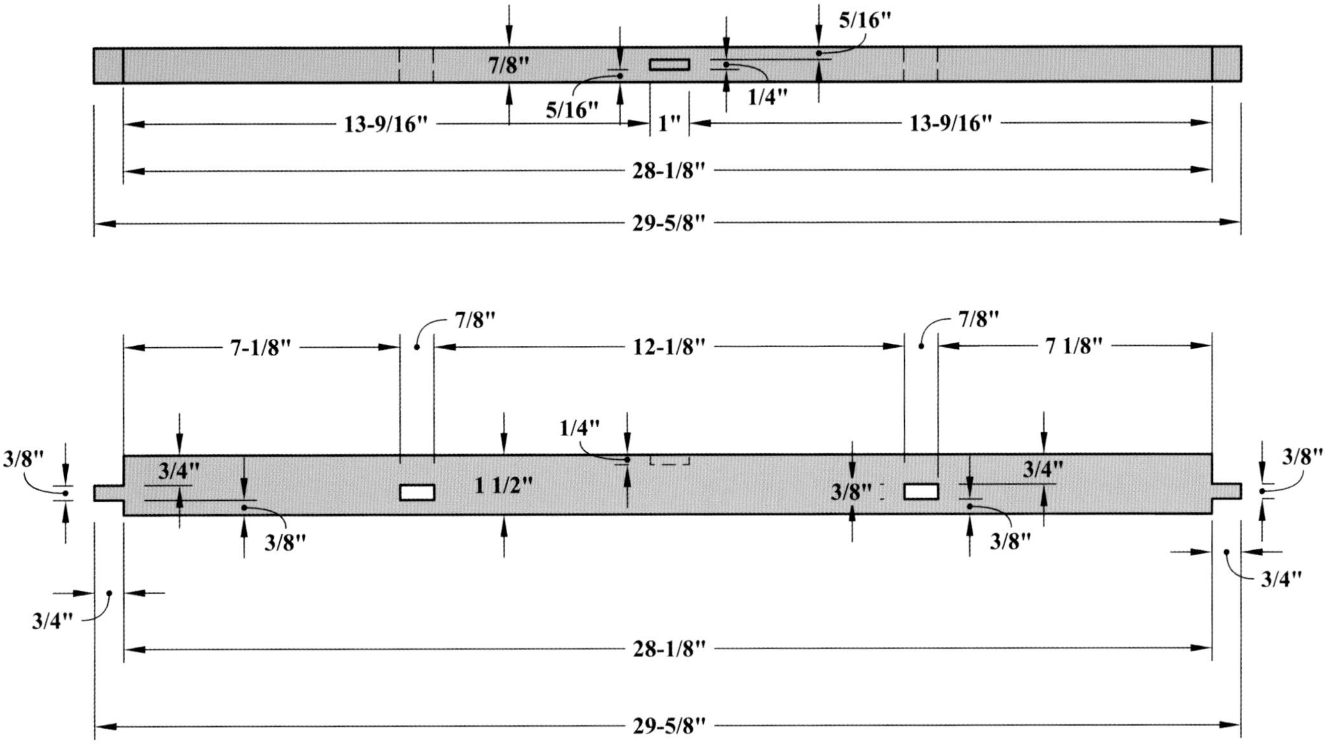

FIG. 2-34. Dimensions and joint placement for the middle front rail.

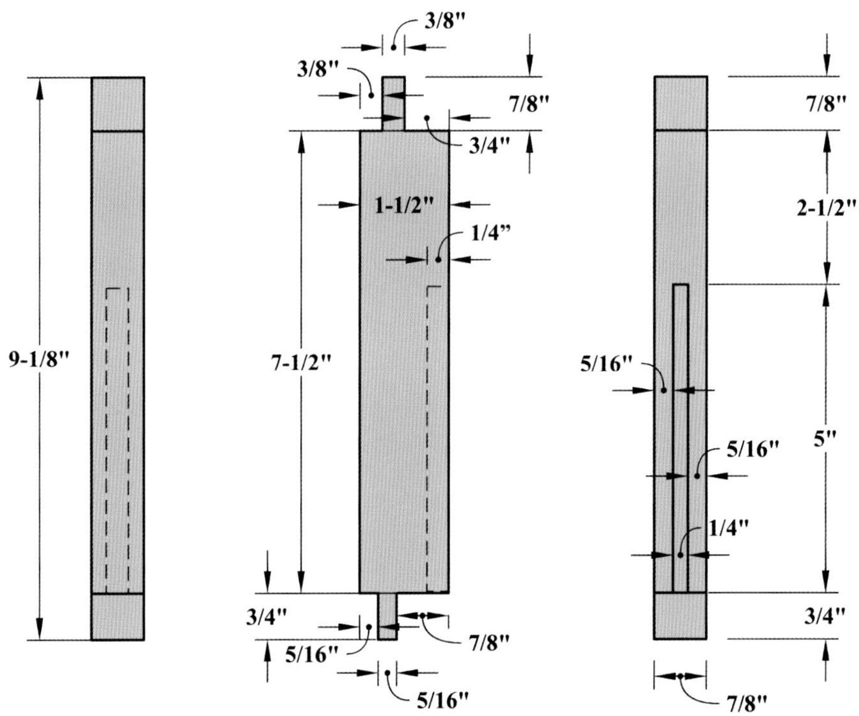

FIG. 2-35. Dimensions and joint placement for one of the stiles. The tall mortise on the back edge is for the drawer divider.

When you are comfortable with the components and how they fit together, start by marking the middle and bottom rails, using the dimensions from the diagrams. Mark the two rails together to ensure they will line up when assembled. **Figure 2-36** shows this step.

First, work on the lower rail. I will also call this the front skirt board. Use a marking gauge as shown in **figure 2-37** to score a line that will be the cutout for the middle drawer. Use a knife and a square to mark the vertical lines that meet the horizontal one. Use a handsaw to cut out this section; **figure 2-38** shows the result. It is extra important that the horizontal edge in the cutout is flat and smooth, because it will frame the drawer and be visible when completed. As shown in **figure 2-39**, use a flat chisel to pare to the marking-gauge line.

When the horizontal edge is completed, mark and cut the mortises for the stiles. The outside wall of each mortise is in line with the vertical edge of the cutout. Drill out each mortise center with a drill press (**figure 2-40**). Clean up and square the faces with a flat chisel. The result is shown in **figure 2-41**.

FIG. 2-36. Align the upper and lower front rails and mark the joint placement together. Or mark one and then transfer them to the other. In either case, make sure the two boards are aligned properly.

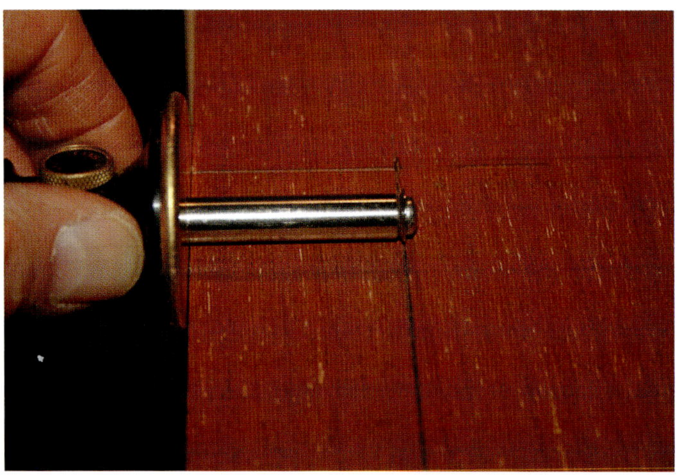

FIG. 2-37. Use a marking gauge to score the middle-drawer-opening line. Mark it both on the front and back faces. This will help when cutting out the notch.

FIG. 2-38. Remove the notch with a bandsaw.

FIG. 2-39. Pare to the marking-gauge lines with a flat chisel.

FIG. 2-40. Mark and drill the mortise for the stile.

FIG. 2-41. A top view of the lower front rail with the stile mortises cut.

FIG. 2-42. Cut a shallow mortise—about 3/16"—for the drawer support.

Next, cut the drawer support mortises in the back face of the front skirt board. These are only 3/16" deep so that they do not break into the stile mortises. As with the other mortises, drill out the middle section and clean up with a chisel. **Figure 2-42** shows one of these complete.

The leg tenons are the last portion of joinery on this piece. Set a mortise gauge to 5/16" wide with a 5/16" offset, as shown in the dimension diagram. Use the front face as the reference surface, and scribe lines along each edge left and right. Score the shoulder lines at 3/4" with a straight edge and knife. These tenons are only 3/4" so that they will not break into the quarter-column wall. Use a handsaw for the cheek and shoulder cuts, and clean up the tenons with a shoulder plane.

Because much of the front skirt is below the connection to the leg posts, only the top 2¾" of the tenon will be used. **Figure 2-43** shows these tenons complete.

FIG. 2-43. Mark and cut the leg tenons. The top of the tenon is flush with the top of the rail.

FIG. 2-44. Dry-fit the two front rails and the stiles.

FIG. 2-45. Dimensions and joint placement for the upper front rail.

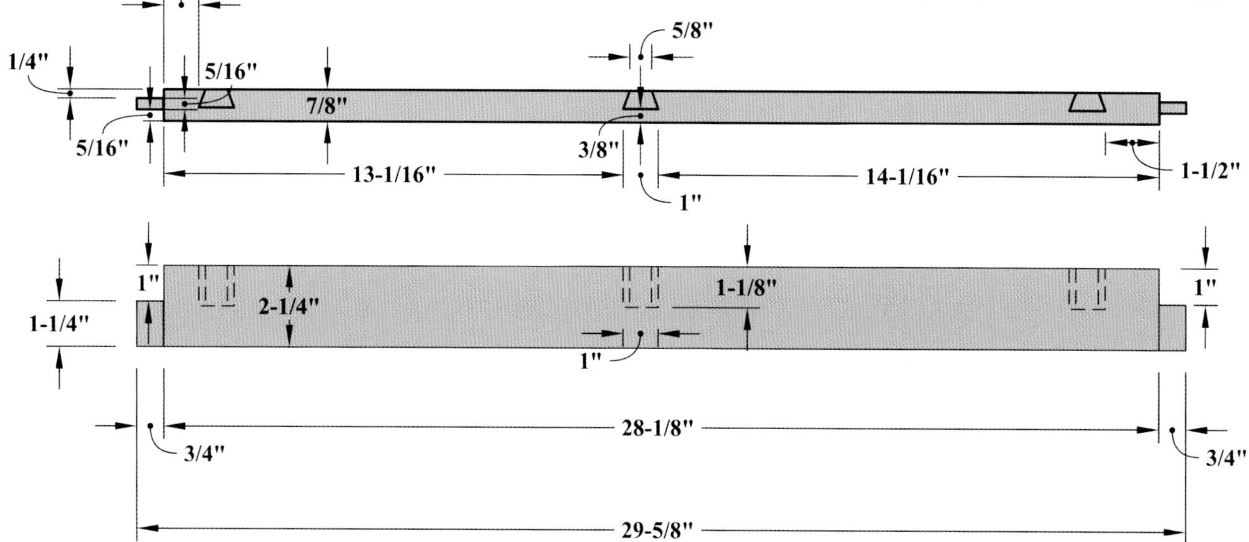

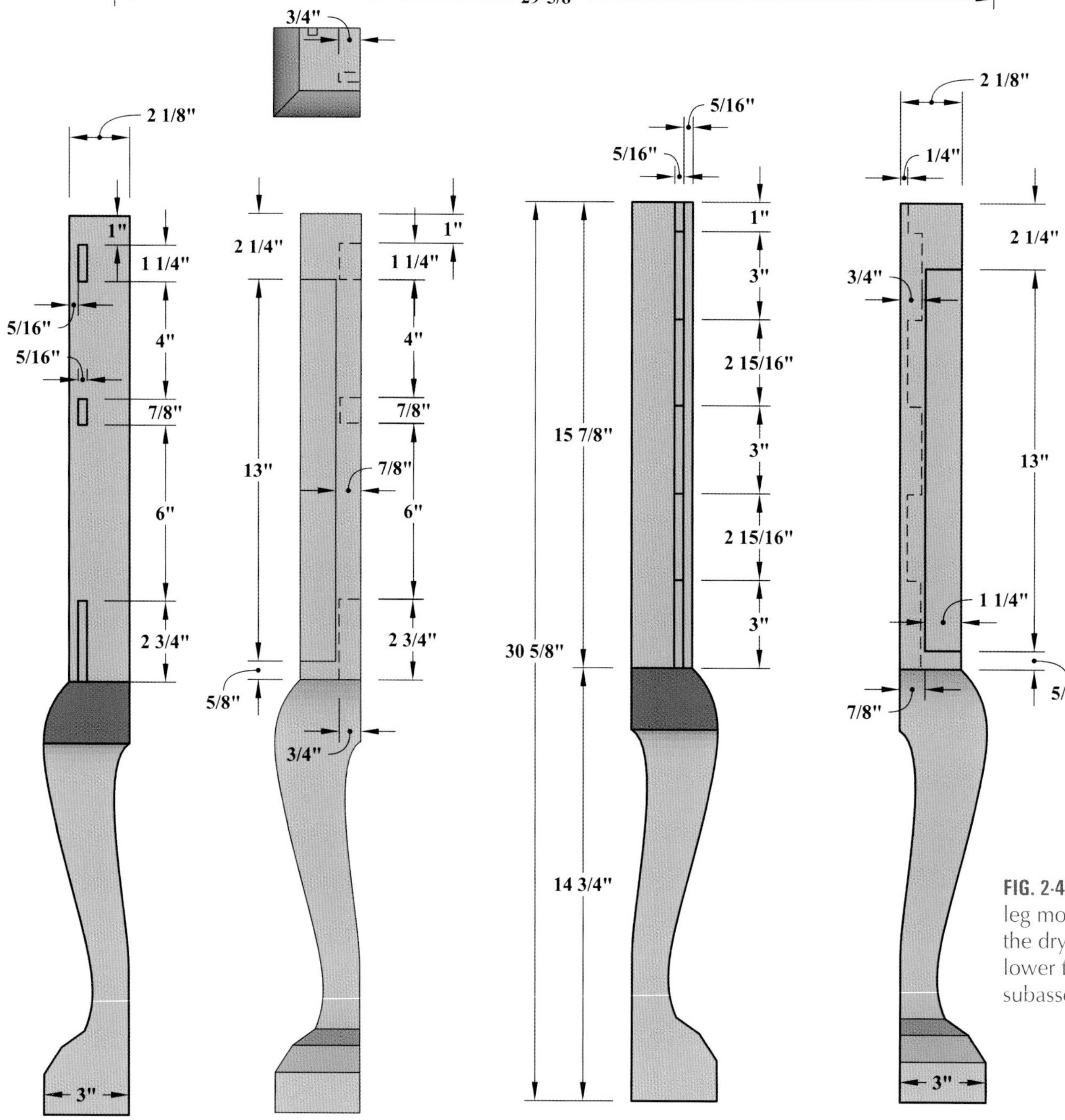

FIG. 2-46. Mark the leg mortises from the dry-fitted lower front subassembly.

Put the skirt board aside for now and work on the middle rail and stiles. The next work to do on the skirt will be the carving, which will come later.

Work on the middle front rail next. **Figure 2-34** shows all the dimensions. The mortises for the stiles are all the way through. The tenons that match with the leg mortises are full height, and the ¼" deep mortise on the back edge is for the central drawer kicker. Cut the mortises and tenons, using the same techniques as before.

Next, mark the stiles according to the dimensions in **figure 2-35**. Make the through tenons a little longer than listed so they will stick proud of the middle rail mortise. The extra will be cut flush with the rail after glue-up. The ¼" mortise on the back edge of each stile is for the central drawer guides.

A note on the central drawer guides. These do not have to be the exact size that is listed. They just need to be tall enough that the side drawer runners can attach. As a practical matter, any size greater than 3" serves this purpose. So the point of this is to make them approximately to the dimensions as shown, because they are pretty tall on the original. However, if you have a board that is a little shorter, but tall enough to accommodate the side drawer runners, just use it. Whatever height it is, match the mortise to it.

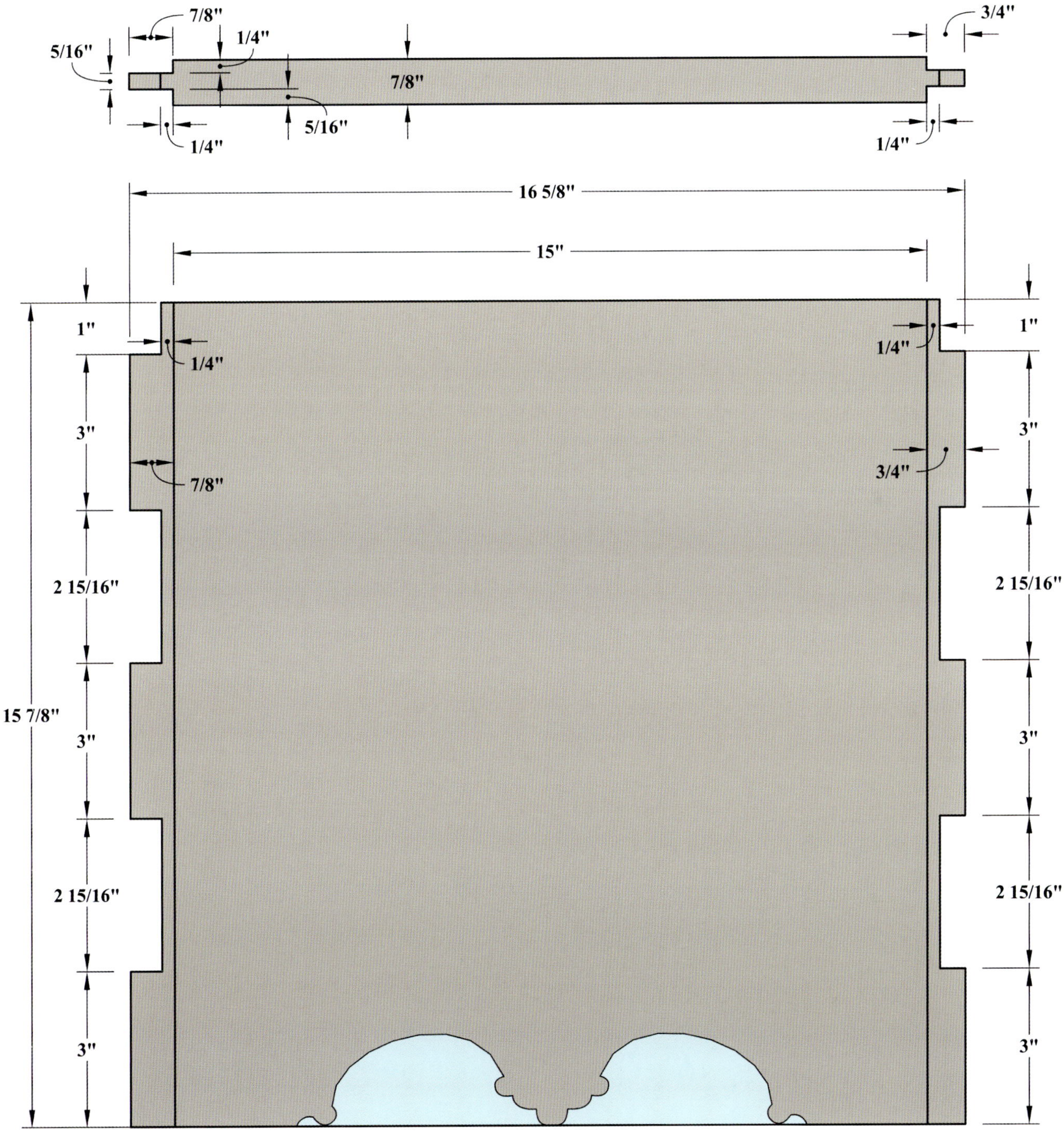

FIG. 2-47. Dimensions and joint placement for the case sides.

Figure 2-44 shows the middle and lower rails with the stiles dry-fitted together.

Mark and cut the tenons for the top front rail as indicated in **figure 2-45**.

Don't cut the top attachment bar dovetail sockets now. Wait until the case is together, so they can be coordinated with the back. If they are cut now, it is possible they will be off after the case is together. Theoretically it shouldn't make any difference. The reality is that many mistakes can be made in glue-up, and matching predefined locations that aligned earlier may not align in the end.

Next, mark and cut the mortises in the two front legs to match the tenons on the front rails. **Figure 2-46** has these details. Note that the mortises for the front rails are not haunched, and the depth is only ¾". This is so that they will not break through the quarter-column wall. Mark the quarter-column cutout, but wait to remove it until after the leg is carved. There is nothing to be gained by doing it now. There is a lot of handling that will occur as the lower leg is shaped and carved, and the edges of the cutout could get damaged. The joinery for the front subassembly is now complete.

The case sides are the last pieces that need joints; they are detailed in **figure 2-47**. Note that the only difference between the tenons on the front and back edges is that the ones on the back are ⅞" deep and those on the front are ¾". Note also that the bottom profile is not cut at this point. The drawing shows the profile, but that will be done later. Use the same techniques to cut these tenons as were used for those on the back board.

FIG. 2-49. The tenon shoulder is high in the middle. This will produce a gap when fitted to the leg.

FIG. 2-50. Cut the shoulder to at least 90°. For a tighter fit, undercut the shoulder a bit.

FIG. 2-48. The case side is fitted to the leg. The haunch mortise is not cut yet.

FIG. 2-51. The shoulder does not have a high spot.

FIG. 2-52. Use a square set to the proper depth and a knife to mark and score the haunch height.

The matching back and front leg mortises for the sides are shown in **figures 2-4** and **2-46**, respectively. Remember the ¼" depth difference between the front and back. Use the same techniques as described for cutting the leg mortises for the back board. **Figure 2-48** shows the side fitted to one of the legs before the mortise trough for the tenon haunch is cut. Next, cut this trough as previously described. Make any adjustments that are needed to get a nice snug fit.

One technique I use to help with a visually tight mortise-and-tenon fit is to make sure the tenon shoulder is slightly less than 90° to the case side. **Figure 2-49** shows a tenon shoulder that has a crown in the middle. This will show as a gap when the side is fit to the leg. Use a flat chisel (**figure 2-50**) to remove the crown. To further ensure that there is only line contact at the side face with the leg, slightly undercut the shoulder. **Figure 2-51** shows the shoulder crown removed.

Another technique concerns marking the tenon depth for the haunch. It is difficult to use a straight edge ¼" from the tenon shoulder. Use a square set to the proper depth and a knife (**figure 2-52**).

Complete all the case side tenons and leg mortises as described. The case joinery is now complete, and it should fit together as first shown in **figure 2-1**.

Lower Central Drawer Guides and Supports

Next I will describe how to construct the central drawer guides. I am putting them in this chapter because they are part of the case construction. I would recommend that they be done after the front face frame is assembled. And the front face frame should not be assembled until the front skirt is substantially carved.

Figure 2-53 shows one of the central drawer guides that are built up from three pieces of pine that are glued and nailed together: a bottom piece is one of the runners for the central drawer; a taller, central piece is a guide for the central drawer; and then the third is one of the runners for the lower side drawer. The bottom is nailed and glued to the central piece, as is the side drawer runner. The side drawer runner is placed on the central piece so that its top edge is flush with the bottom edge of the side drawer opening.

When making the bottom and side pieces, drill three holes reasonably spaced, as indicated, and sized for the nails that will be used. I use reproduction rosehead nails for this. These holes should be sized so that the nail fits through, or with minimal resistance.

The back face of the subassembly is effectively a ¼" full-height and full-width tenon that fits into a corresponding ¼" deep mortise in the back board. This profile is shown in the "Back Face" diagram of **figure 2-53**.

The bottom and central pieces are tenoned into the front skirt board and stile, respectively. Note that the tenon on the bottom piece is only 3⁄16" long. This is so the mortise in the front skirt will not cut into the stile mortise. Note also that the central piece is shorter than the other two. This is because of the extra depth of the stile.

Cut and fit the ¼" front tenon for the central piece first. Next, cut and fit the 3⁄16" front tenon for the bottom piece. Place both of these pieces in their respective mortises (**figure 2-54**). Make any adjustments that are needed so that they fit together well. When they do fit well, remove them and place glue on the bottom edge of the central piece. Put these two back in their respective mortises and clamp them together; two clamps should be sufficient. Now remove the two-piece subassembly and set it aside to dry. When this subassembly is dry, remove the clamps and pound the nails in from the bottom through the predrilled bottom piece into the central piece.

Next, put this subassembly back in the front face frame, and position the side piece to be flush with the bottom of the side drawer opening (**figure 2-55**). When it is well positioned, remove it, add some glue to the back side, and replace it. Make sure this piece is square and horizontal by checking it with a square. Clamp the side piece to the central one and set it aside to dry. When it is dry, add the nails as before. These nails will probably be shorter than the ones for the bottom, because they should not break through the central piece.

Repeat this process for the other central drawer guide. Note that these two subassemblies are mirror images; there is a left one and a right one.

Cut the mortise in the back board to accommodate the two central drawer support assemblies. From my experience, the best way to do this is to carefully measure where this mortise will be, using the inside of the legs as one reference, and the bottom edge of the back board and bottom flat edge of the front skirt board as the other reference. The bottom edges of the back board and the flat portion of the skirt board should be the same distance from the ground.

Now the central drawer supports are complete. Set them aside until the case is ready to be glued together.

The other drawer supports are not tenoned into either the back or the front; they are nailed into the leg posts, so these can be constructed and added after the case is assembled.

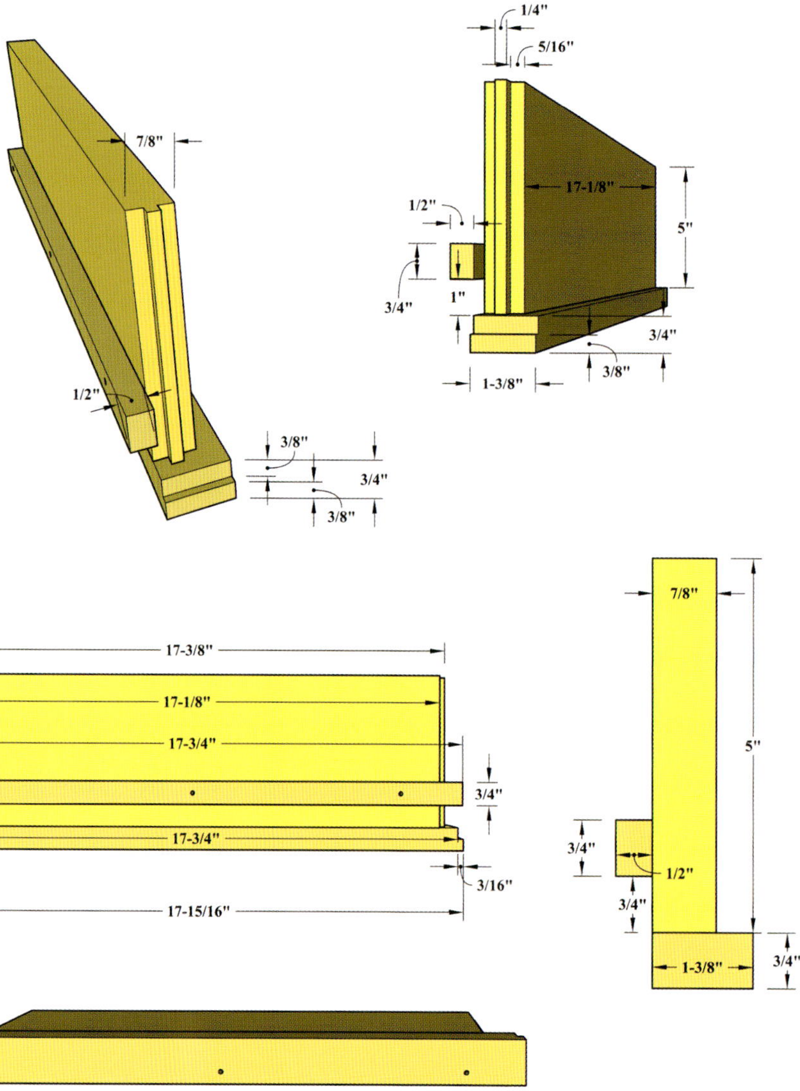

FIG. 2-53. The center-drawer support is made from three pieces. There are two supports, and they are mirror images of each other.

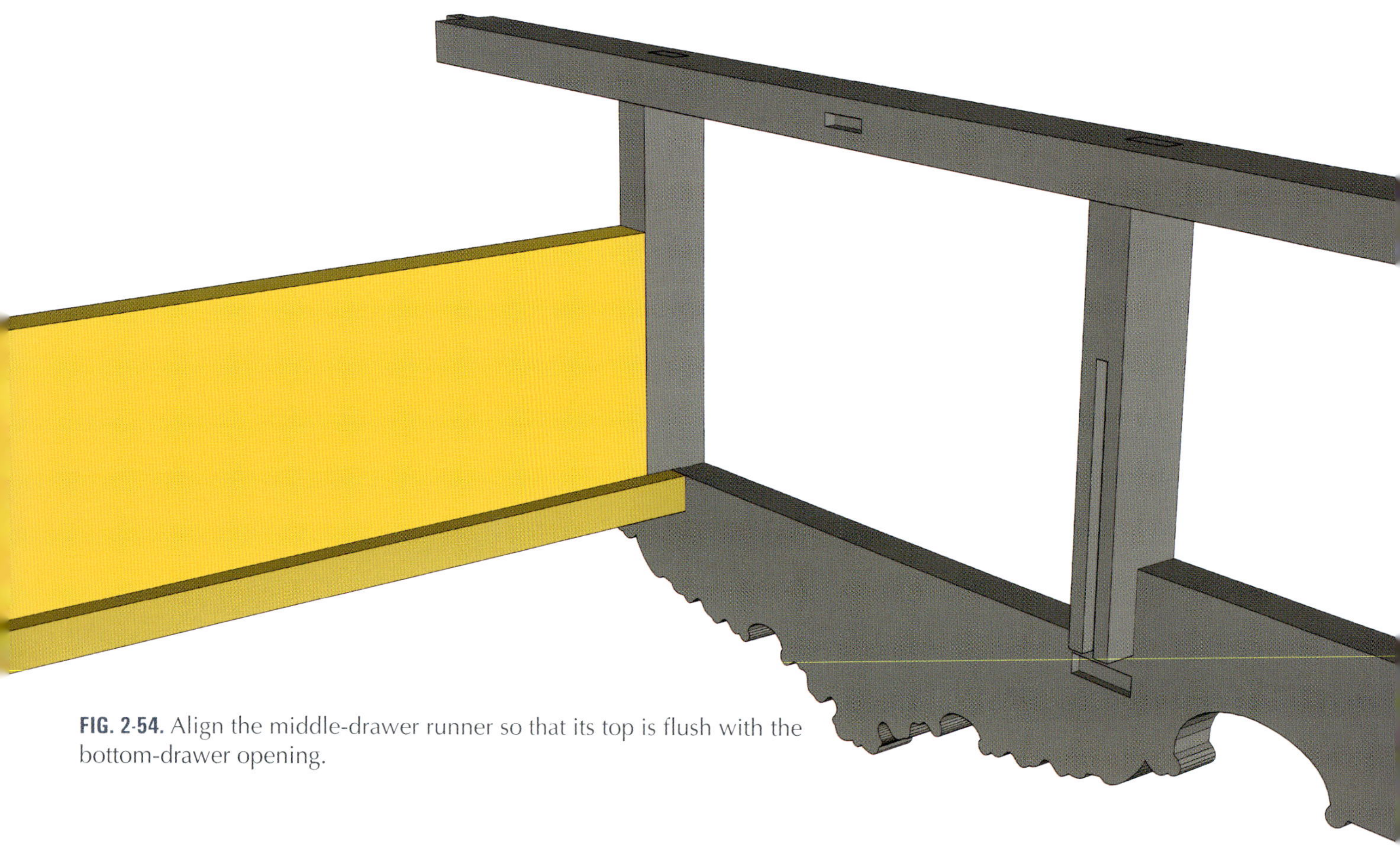

FIG. 2-54. Align the middle-drawer runner so that its top is flush with the bottom-drawer opening.

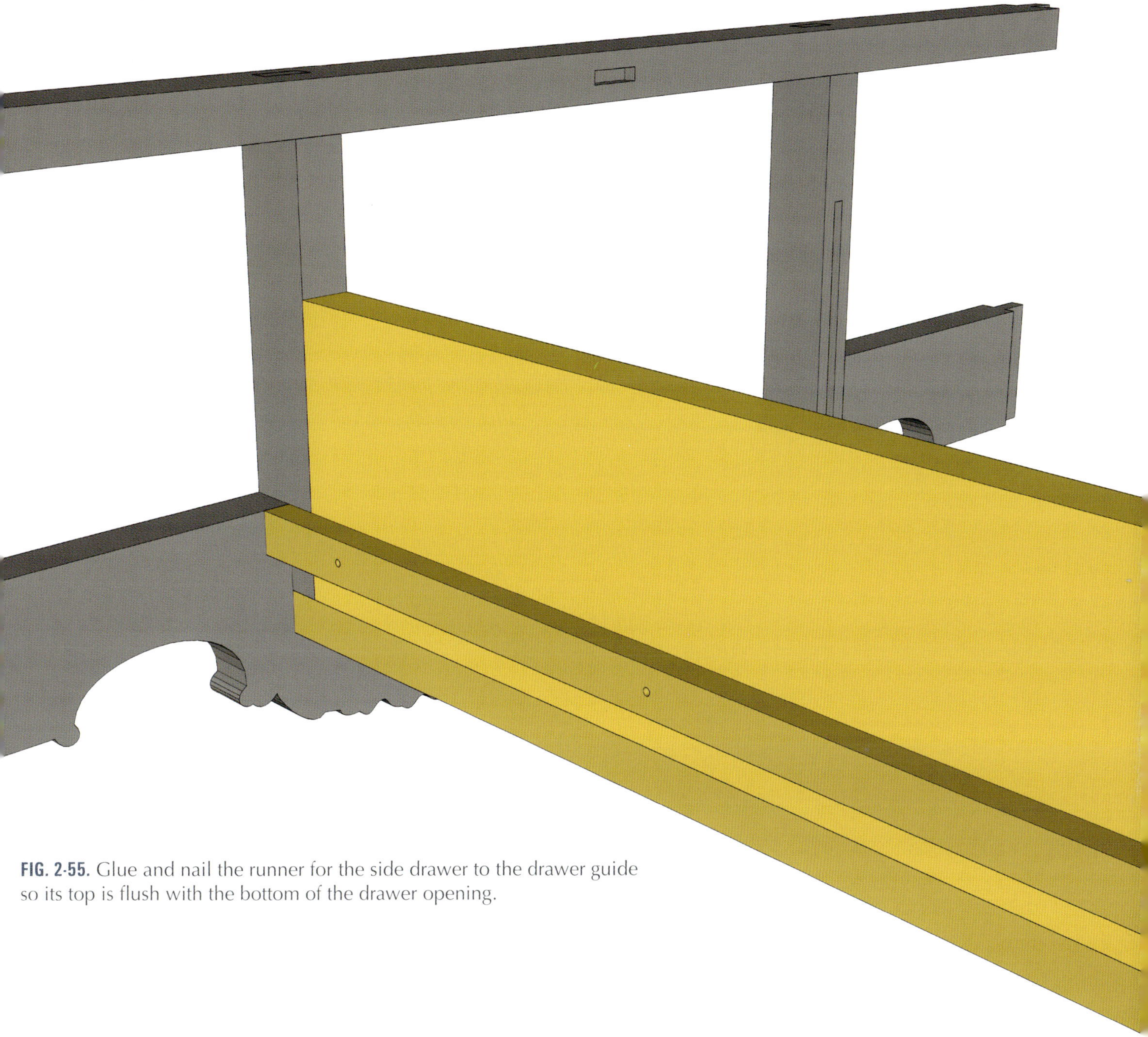

FIG. 2-55. Glue and nail the runner for the side drawer to the drawer guide so its top is flush with the bottom of the drawer opening.

Drawer Construction

All four drawers in this project are constructed in the same way, and each consists of five pieces. The two sides, the back, and the bottom are pine, and the front is mahogany. The only differences between them are the sizes. This chapter will discuss the construction techniques, using one of the side drawers as an example.

The drawer front has a 1/8" lip on three edges: two sides and the top. The bottom edge does not have a lip. The front stock is 7/8" thick, and the sides and back are 5/16". The bottom is 1/2".

The sides are joined to the back with through dovetails and to the front with half blinds. The bottom slides in from the back into a 1/4" high dado in the sides and front. It is cut flush with the back and nailed into the back from below with headless brads. **Figure 3-1** shows the assembled drawer and its parts. Note also that the drawer bottom is beveled on the two sides and the front. The angle is such that it is narrow enough to fit into the dados on the sides and front. The back is not beveled.

Start by cutting the tails on the front ends of the drawer sides. With the inside surfaces facing each other, clamp them together and cut them as one. This will save a little work, and the stock is thin enough so as not to be a problem. **Figure 3-2** shows the layout and dimensions for the sides of the side drawers.

With the two sides pinch-clamped together, use a knife to score a line 5/8" in from the front edge around the two side boards. This is the length of the tails in front. Next, lay out and mark the tails with a knife, small square, and bevel gauge set to the proper angle. The small square is for the perpendicular lines on the edge, and the bevel gauge is for the angled ones on the faces. I then use a 0.5 mm mechanical pencil to highlight the knife lines so they are easier to see.

I used the angle that drops 1/8" over the 5/8" length of the tail, and used a bevel gauge to capture it. This angle is approximately 11°.

With the two sides still clamped together, put them in a vice and make the angled cuts with a handsaw. When these cuts are done, remove the clamps and chisel away the waste on each board independently.

Next, mark the pins on the drawer front, using the side tails as a guide. Note that the depth of the pins is 7/16", and the side stock is 5/16". The extra 1/8" is for the drawer front lip. It will be removed after the drawer has been glued together. The reason I do it this way is that it is easier to mark the pins from the tails with the lip waste still in place. **Figure 3-3** shows the side and front aligned. Use a knife to mark the pins from the

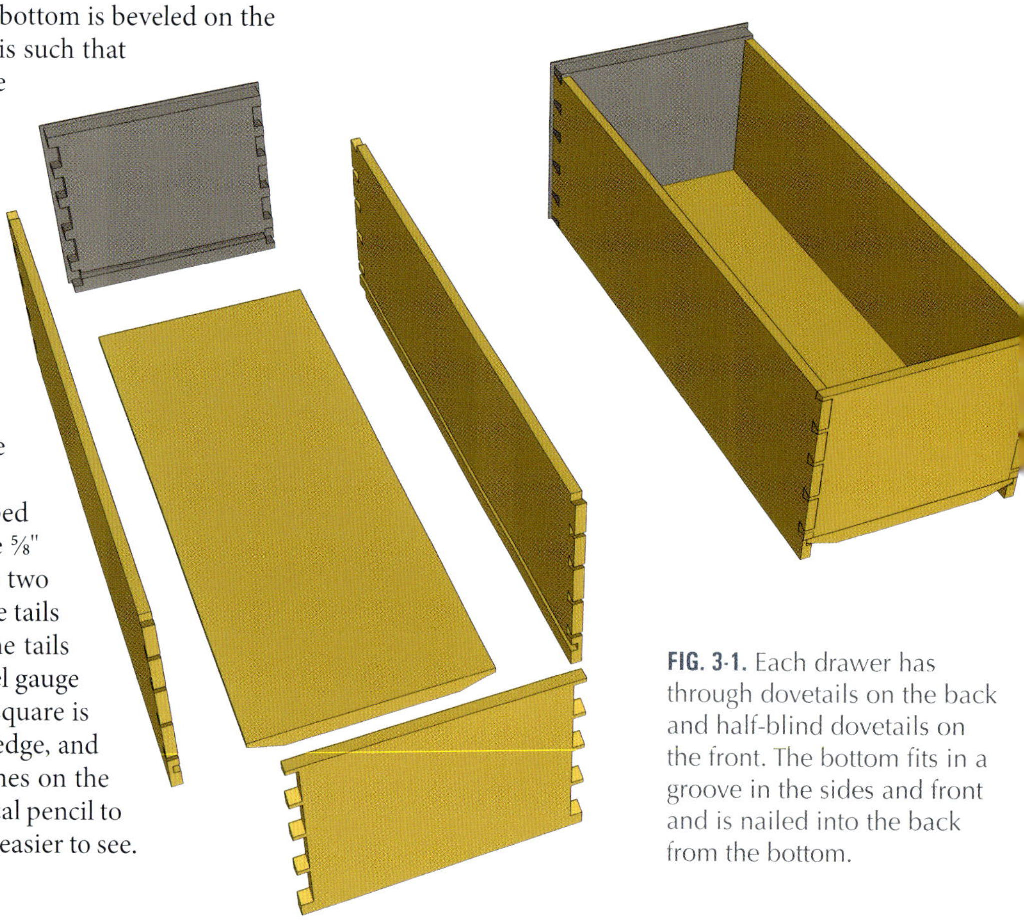

FIG. 3-1. Each drawer has through dovetails on the back and half-blind dovetails on the front. The bottom fits in a groove in the sides and front and is nailed into the back from the bottom.

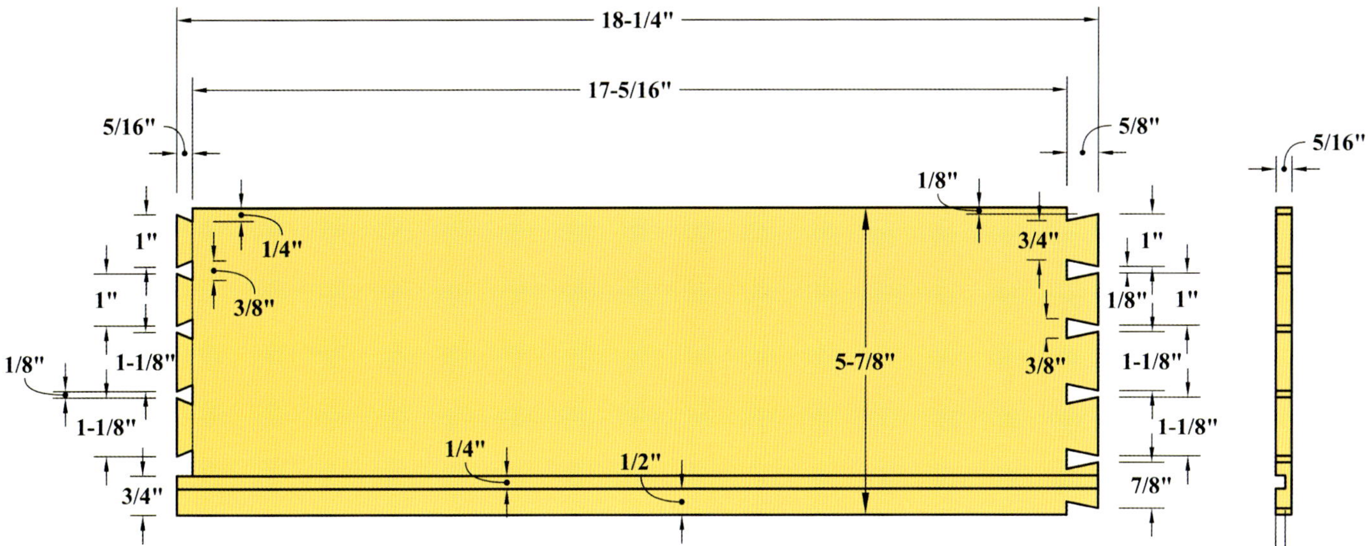

FIG. 3-2. Dimensions for a side.

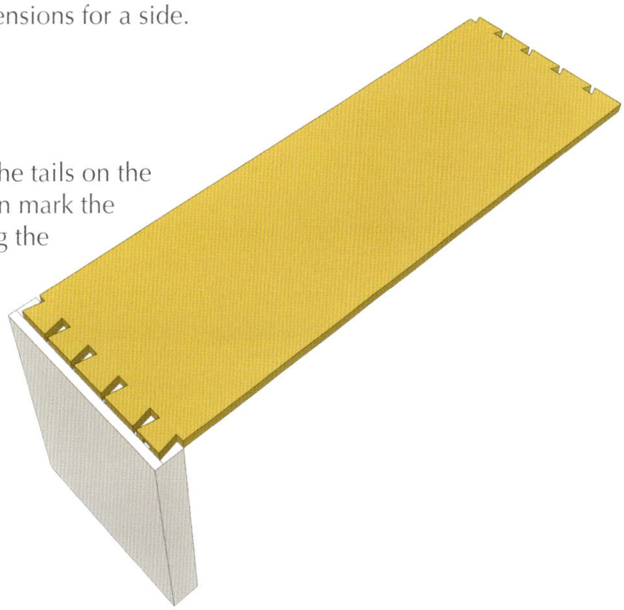

FIG. 3-3. Cut the tails on the side first, then mark the front by using the side board.

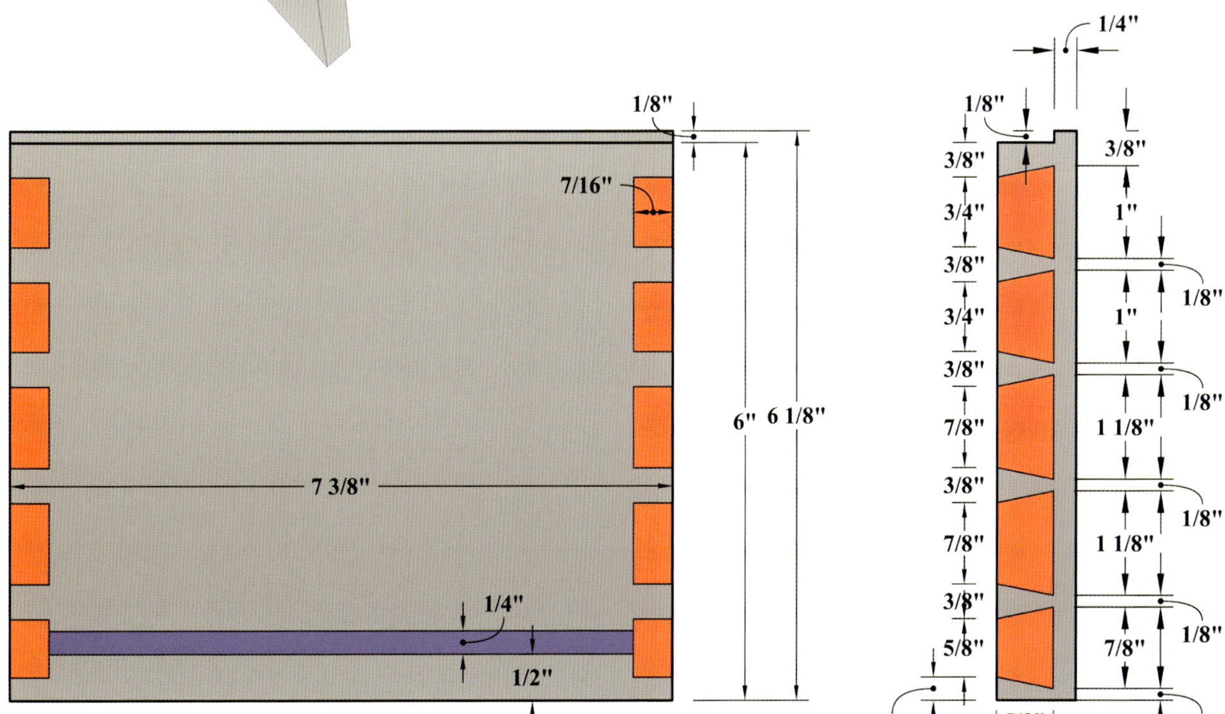

FIG. 3-4. Remove the red sections.

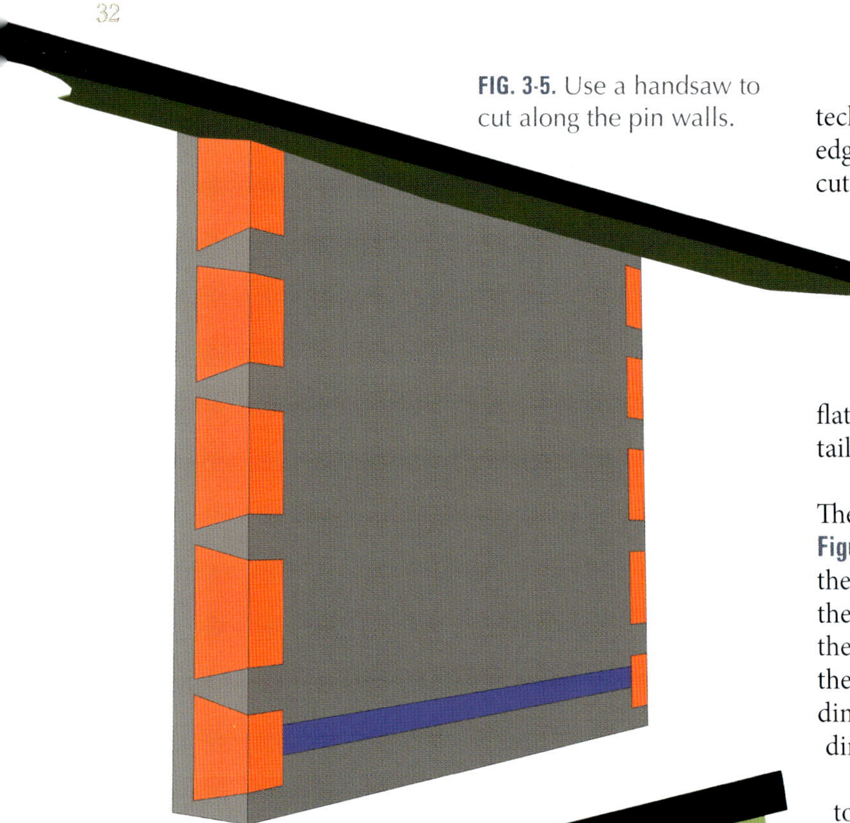

FIG. 3-5. Use a handsaw to cut along the pin walls.

FIG. 3-6. Go beyond the thickness of the tailboard. This will allow the angled cut to go sufficiently deep. This technique is evident on many eighteenth-century drawers.

tails. Sometimes it is difficult to get good markings because the openings are quite small. Mark a small section for each tail edge. Then, with the pin board alone, use a bevel gauge and the tail markings to score complete and visible lines.

Figure 3-4 shows the layout for the drawer front. Cut along the angled pin lines with a handsaw. These lines are at the tail angle of the sides on the end, and parallel to the top and bottom edges on the top surface. **Figures 3-5** and **3-6** show the technique. The angled cuts are parallel to the top and bottom edges and will extend beyond the pin depth. The length of these cuts is not exact. The reason for them is that the bottom of the cut will get closer to the pin height, which will make it easier to remove the waste with a chisel. The saw position in the drawer front in **figure 3-6** approximates the length of these cuts. This is typical of eighteenth-century Philadelphia drawer construction.

When the saw cuts are complete, clean out the waste with flat chisels of appropriate width. Finally, fit the pins to the tails. Repeat these steps for the other side.

After the front joints are complete, move to the back ones. These are a little easier because they are through dovetails. **Figure 3-7** shows the back and a side joined together. Note that the back board is ½" shorter than the side board. This will allow the bottom to slide into the dados in the sides and underneath the back. Note also that the top of the dados in the sides are in the same horizontal plane as the bottom edge of the back. The dimensions for the side board are shown in **figure 3-2**. The dimensions for the back are shown in **figure 3-8**.

As with the joints on the front, clamp the two sides together, with the inside faces touching, and cut the tails first. Use the thickness of the back board to score a line around the back end of the side board. This is the length of the tails. Use the bevel gauge with the same setting from the front tails and lay out the tails on the back end of the side boards, using a knife and a 0.5 mm pencil.

With the two sides ganged together, clamp the pair in a vice and cut along the angled lines with a handsaw. After the saw cuts are complete, unclamp the pair and remove the waste between adjacent tails. I use a knife and chisel for this. Work from both sides into the middle to prevent tear-out. Check that the bottom of the waste section is square to the face, as shown in **figure 3-9**.

When the tails are done, mark the pins on the back board from the tails on the side. Use the same technique as for the front, except that the tail goes through the back board. The depth of the pins will be the thickness of the side. Use a knife and square to mark the depth line on the two faces of the back board. Next, use a bevel square and knife to score the angled pin lines on the edge, and a small square to score them on the faces. Highlight the knife marks with a 0.5 mm pencil. The orientation of the drawer parts is fixed at this point, so be careful to maintain it when marking the pins from the tails. An orientation mistake at this point will mean a new back board will be needed.

Clamp the back in a vice, with the edge facing up. Use a handsaw to cut along the angled lines on the edge down to the pin depth line. In this case, that is 5⁄16". Cut a little to the waste side so that the pins are a touch oversized. This will give a bit of flexibility when fitting the pins and tails. When all the saw cuts are complete, remove the waste with a knife and chisel. Fit the pins and tails, then check the bottom and faces for square as was done on the tail board. Repeat these steps on the other side.

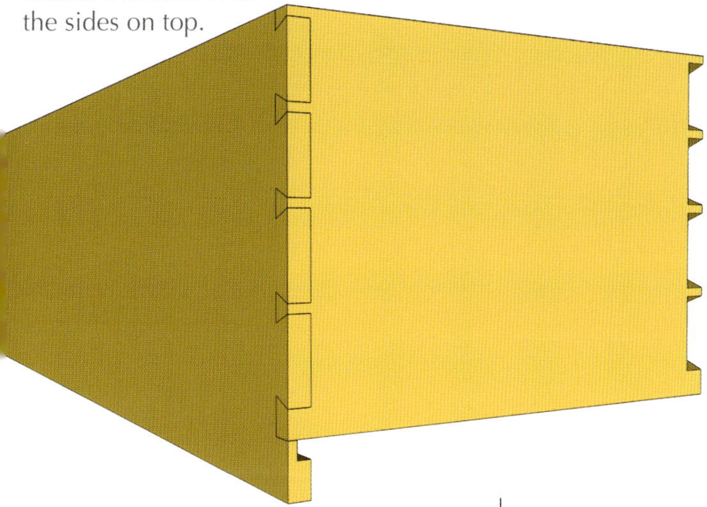

FIG. 3-7. The back board sits on top of the bottom board. It is flush with the sides on top.

Now cut the dados in the sides and front that will hold the bottom board. Use any method that you are comfortable with. I have carved these with a gouge, knife, flat chisel, and hand router plane. I have also used a table saw, taking multiple passes to get the desired width. Use a mortise gauge referenced from the bottom edge to score the lines on all three pieces.

After the dados have been cut in the sides and front, glue the two sides to the back and front. Strive to get the drawer to be as square as possible. This is not as simple as it sounds, because the clamp pressure can force the box out of square.

When the glue has dried, clean up the joints with a chisel, file, and sandpaper. The goal is for all the joint areas to be smooth and to feel and look like one surface. As part of the cleanup process, remove the extra 1/8" on the dovetail pins on the drawer front. This will leave a 1/8" lip on the drawer sides.

FIG. 3-8. Dimensions for the back.

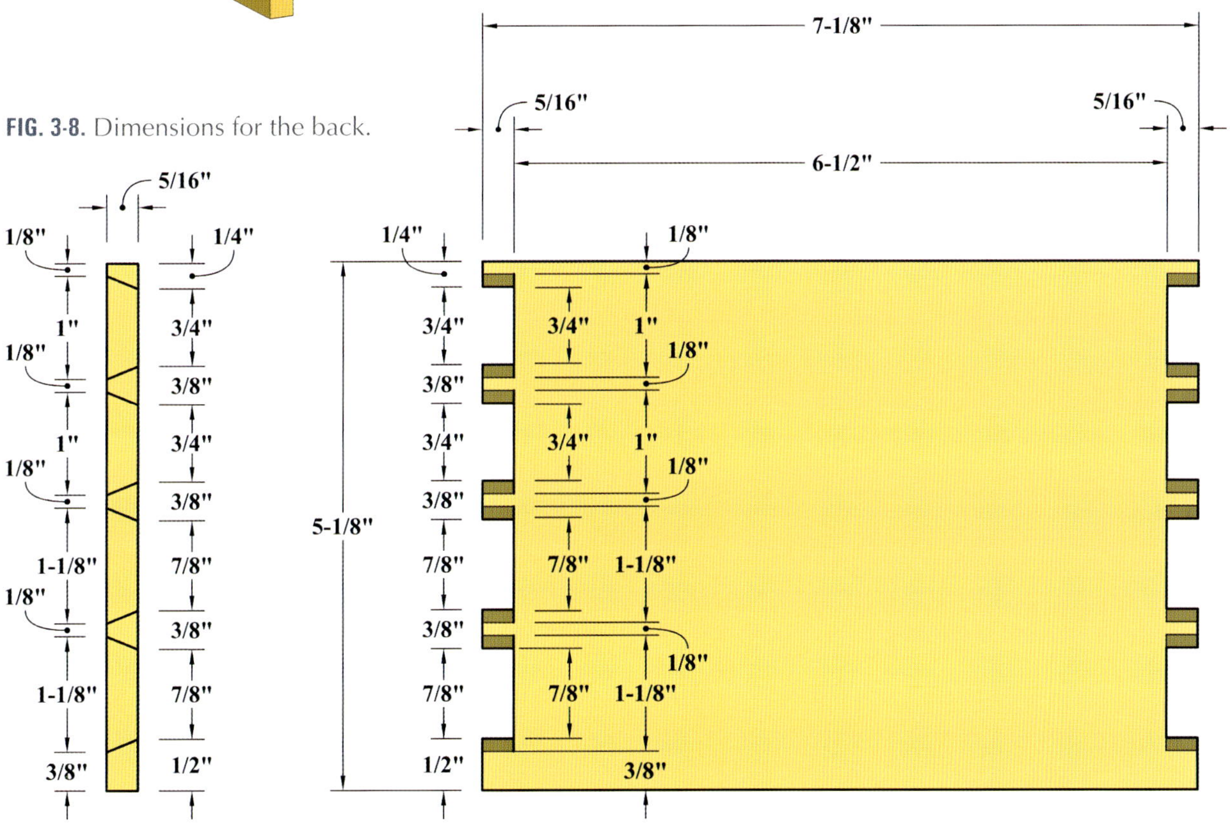

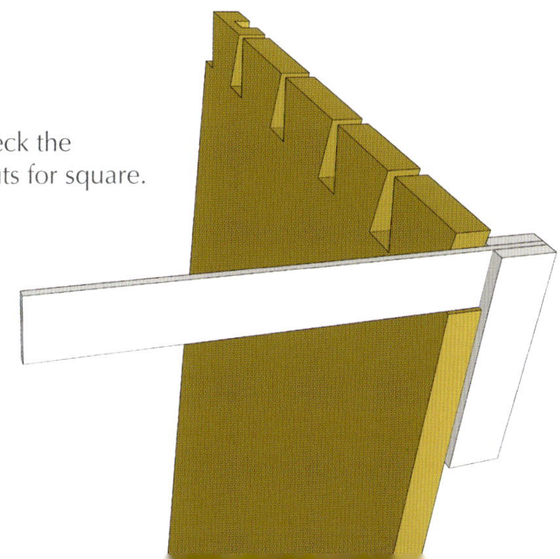

FIG. 3-9. Check the shoulder cuts for square.

Figure 3-10 shows what needs to be done. The red portion of the pins is to be removed. The two pins above the red ones show the result. Use a handsaw to remove a bigger piece, but be careful not to mar the surrounding surfaces. Flush the pins to the side with a flat chisel or a shoulder plane (or both).

Next, carve the thumbnail molding on the front face of the drawer front. Start by removing a 1/4" wide section 1/16" deep on all four edges, as shown in **figure 3-11A**. This will "raise" the drawer front panel. Score the 1/4" lines on the front face with a knife and a square. Use a marking gauge set to 1/16"

FIG. 3-10. When the drawer is glued, the red sections are intact. These are sawed and chiseled away after the glue dries. This completes the lip on the side.

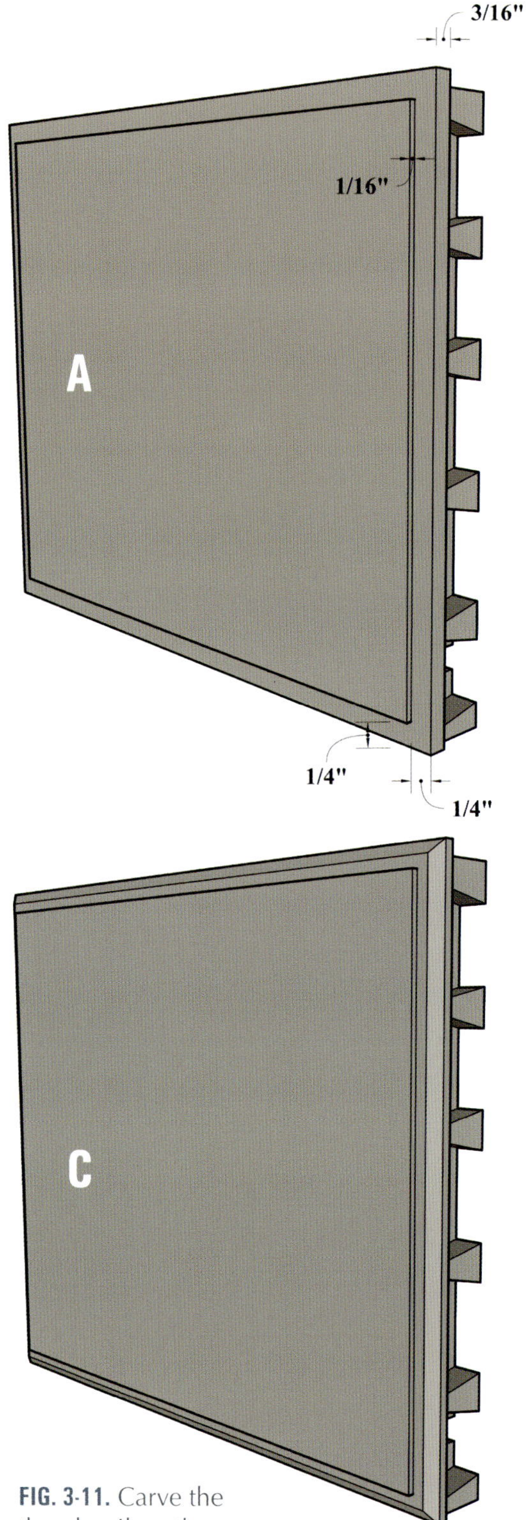

FIG. 3-11. Carve the thumbnail on the drawer front.

and referenced from the top face to draw lines on the four edges. Highlight the lines with a 0.5 mm pencil. Iteratively remove this material with a flat chisel and shoulder plane. Use a flat chisel to bevel into the vertical line at the ¼" mark. Use the shoulder plane to lower the material from the bevel to the outside edge. Repeat these steps until the entire section is removed.

The flat area below the raised panel will be rounded over from the base of the raised panel down to the lip line on the outside edge. This will be accomplished by removing the corner and then blending the remaining facets to a smooth, rounded surface.

Start by drawing the bisecting lines as shown in **figure 3-11B**. There should be four on the front face and one on each edge. These can be drawn freehand, using your finger as a guide along the outside edge. Since they are guide lines, they do not have to be perfect. Use a block or shoulder plane to bevel the corner between a line on the front face and the adjacent one on the edge. **Figure 3-11C** shows the results.

Next, blend adjacent facets with a flat chisel, file, and sandpaper. Use a flat chisel with a light touch to remove the corners created by the initial bevel. This operation will create smaller and finer facets. With each successive pass, less and less wood is removed. Use a small file to blend from the lip line on the edge toward the raised panel. The goal is to create a pleasing, smooth, rounded surface. As the rounded surface is created, use a small piece of sandpaper, with your finger as backing, to complete the rounding. Your finger will tell you how smooth the surface is. Continue with the sandpaper until you are satisfied with the results. **Figure 3-11D** shows the finished thumbnail. Strive for a nice, crisp line at the corners, where two rounded surfaces meet at 90°.

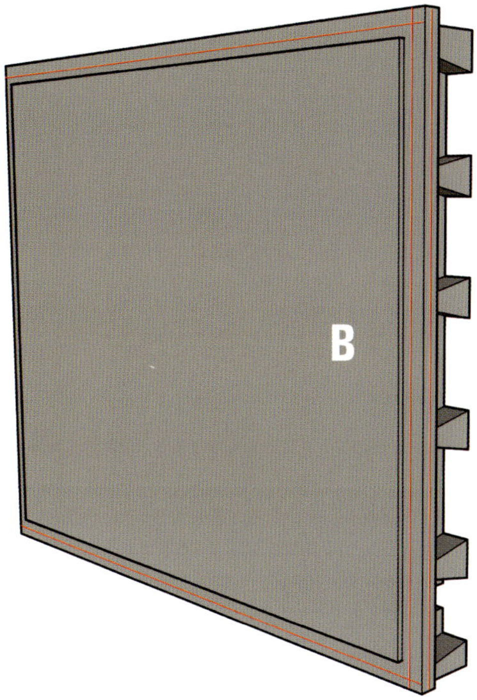

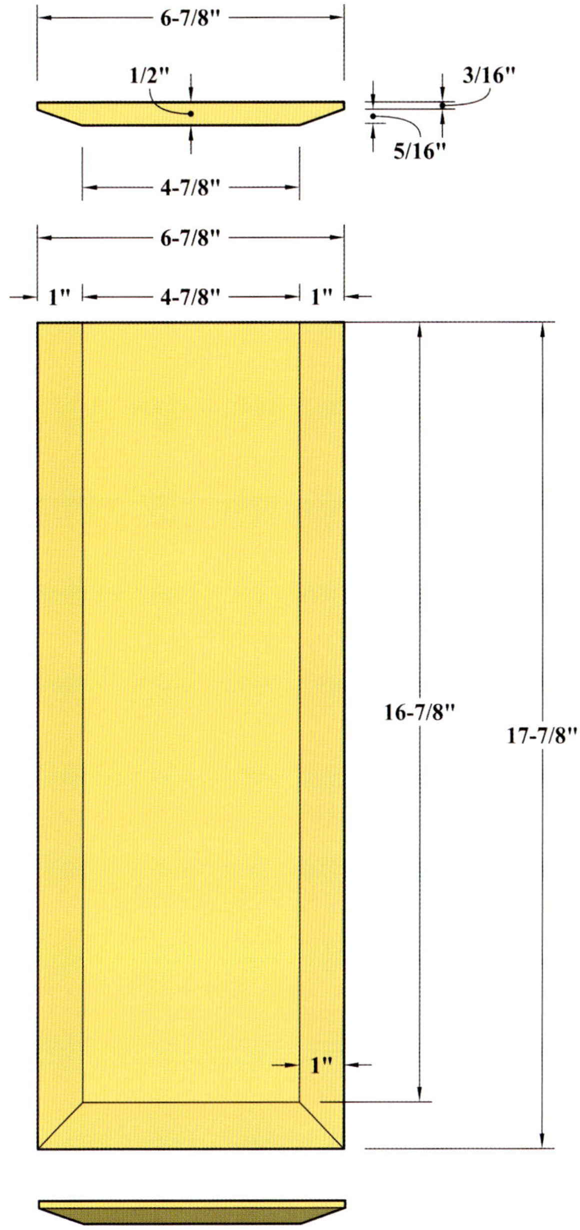

FIG. 3-12. The bottom board is beveled on the sides and front. These angled edges fit into the dados on the sides and front.

Finally, make the drawer bottom. On the side drawers the grain runs front to back, and on the other two it runs side to side. **Figure 3-12** shows the dimensions. The edges on the two sides and front are beveled on the bottom face. The back edge is not. The bottom board is flush with the back of the drawer and is nailed from the bottom into the back with headless brads.

Cut the bottom board to the proper width and a little longer than needed. The excess will be trimmed and flushed after it is installed. Use a marking gauge set to 3⁄16" and score a line from the top face along the sides and front. Draw in lines 1" from the sides and front on the bottom face. Use a hand plane to bevel the corner between the scored line on the edge and the adjacent pencil line on the bottom. Do the front one first because it is cross-grain. If there is any tear-out, it will be erased when beveling the sides, which are with the grain.

As mentioned, the bottom slides in from the back. If the bottom is tight side to side, shorten the width as needed. Try to balance any width adjustment by taking equal amounts from each side. If it is tight top to bottom, use the plane on the beveled surface to remove as much material as needed. Strive for an easy fit without being loose.

When the bottom has been fitted, slide it in to its fullest position. It should fully engage the dado in the drawer front. Use a pencil to mark the proper length on the bottom board at the back. From this line, draw one parallel 5⁄32" toward the front. This is half the thickness of the drawer back. Drill small pilot holes on this line for the brads. These holes should be slightly smaller than the brads and will help prevent the bottom board from splitting when the brads are hammered in. Use as many nails as needed, depending on the width of the drawer. For this one, two or three is enough.

Finally, after the bottom board has been nailed, flush up the back edge with the drawer back. I use the bandsaw to cut pretty close to the back. Be careful not to nick the back board. Clean up the saw cut with a rasp, file, and sandpaper.

As a final touch, I use some sandpaper to soften all the corners. I do this to all exposed corners on all parts, but especially on the drawers. I think it is a more refined feel. Without this softening, some of the edges are almost knife sharp, and one can get cut with normal use. This doesn't have to be a lot and is almost invisible.

The other drawers are made in the same manner, with the sizes varied to match the specific opening. Make the sides about 1⁄8" shorter than the opening height. This allows for a little expansion of the sides. Sometimes the backs are flush with the sides at the top, and sometimes they are a little shorter. Occasionally I have made them shorter because I have a board that is almost perfect, but it is an 1⁄8" too short. I will use it because I have seen original drawers with the back board shorter than the sides. So the takeaway here is to make reasonable decisions based on the facts in your case. After all, these are drawer internal parts and will mostly not be seen. Sweat the visible details and don't obsess about an 1⁄8" on a hidden part.

Middle-Drawer Carving

The embellishments on the lower central drawer front consist of two applied vines and a shell that is carved from the solid. The two applied vines are mirror images of each other. **Figure 4-1A** shows the original, and **figure 4-1B** shows my reproduction.

Carved Shell

Prior to carving the shell, size the drawer front blank according to the dimensions in **figure 14-11** and cut the dovetail joints for the sides and the dado for the bottom.

Make templates for the inside and outside profiles from the "Middle Drawer Carving Templates" page in the insert packet and referenced in **figure A1-2**. My versions are shown in **figures 4-2** and **4-3**, respectively. Draw the drawer front vertical centerline and the four lines ¼" from the edges, as shown in **figure 4-4**. The lines around the edge are for the thumbnail molding that will be added later. Use the templates to trace the shell perimeters, as shown in **figure 4-5**. Note that everything is symmetrical around the vertical centerline.

By hand, draw the line shown in **figure 4-6** on the inside perimeter of the inside template. This line will be the perimeter from which the "bowl" will be shaped. It keeps all the scalloped edges at full height. Note that this line comes close to but does not touch the inside perimeter. This is just a temporary approximation, so there is nothing to be gained by getting too close to the inside-perimeter line.

Set in around the central flower, as shown in **figure 4-7**. The flower will remain high for now. Note that I stayed

FIG. 4-1A. This is the original. The leaf tips on the bottom left and right vines are missing. Witness marks indicate that something was there at one point in time.

FIG. 4-1B. This is my reproduction. The missing leaf tips have been added.

FIG. 4-2. The shell inside profile.

FIG. 4-3. The shell outside profile.

FIG. 4-4. Draw lines ¼" from each edge. This will become the thumbnail molded edge. Place the vine and outside shell templates. There should be a little margin between all the templates and the thumbnail lines. Make any adjustments needed to make the templates fit between the thumbnail boundaries.

FIG. 4-5. The templates have been traced.

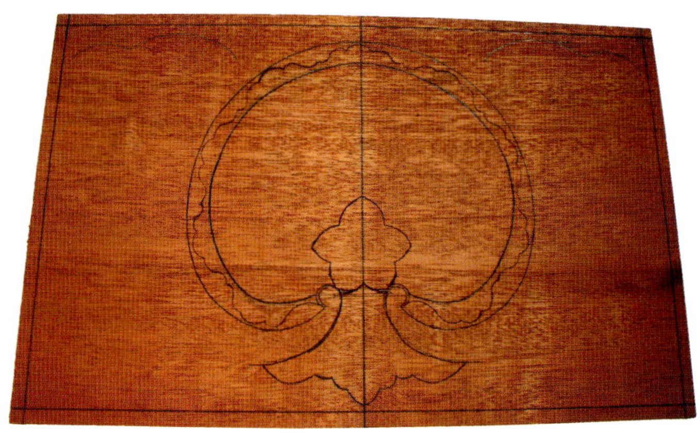

FIG. 4-6. By hand, draw a curve inside the scalloped edge. This will be the initial bowl perimeter.

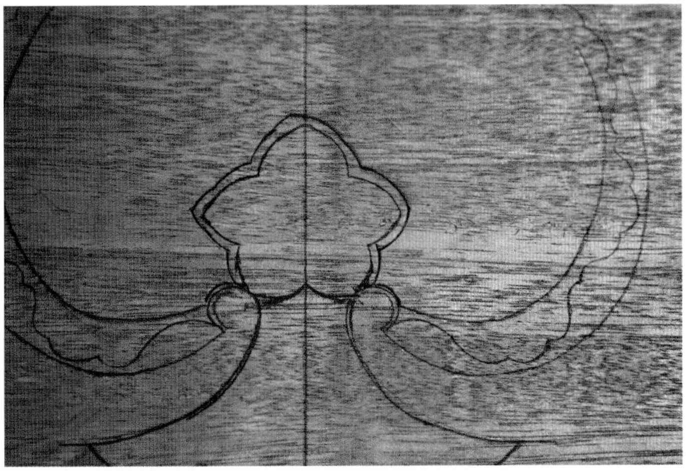

FIG. 4-7. Set in around the central flower. This is just an approximation, so stay on the outside of the lines.

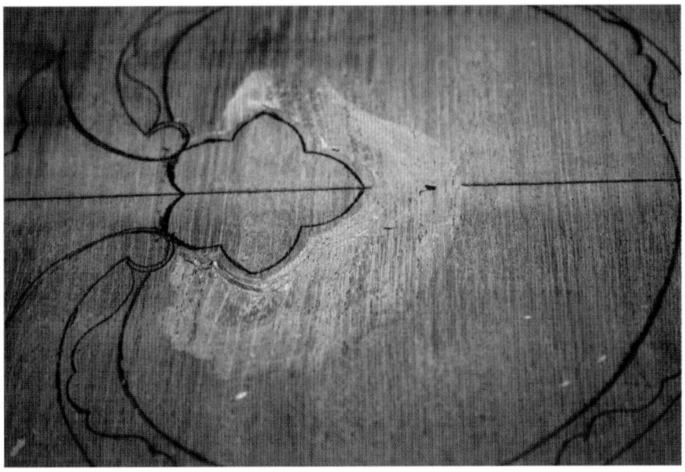

FIG. 4-8. Raise the flower by lowering the background around it. The bottom petals are flush with the top of the blank, and the inside tip is 3/8" deep.

a little proud of the flower perimeter. This will protect the flower wall from getting nicked as the "bowl" is shaped. Bevel into the bottom of the stop cut, as shown in **figure 4-8**. Continue to lower the central flower to a depth of 3/8". **Figure 4-9** shows how to use a depth gauge to determine the height of the flower.

With the depth of the flower set, connect this level to the hand-drawn line in a smooth, uniform surface. This will form a "bowl" (see **figure 4-10**). **Figure 4-11** shows the "bowl" from another angle. Use medium- and wide-width #5 and #7 gouges to rough out the "bowl." Then use a curved scraper to blend all the facets. A French curved scraper works well for this because it has many different curvatures around its perimeter.

Next, carve the scalloped edge of the inside template. Start by making stop cuts on one segment (**figure 4-12**). Using the same techniques as before, bevel into the bottom of the stop cut, using a #7 gouge of appropriate width. Create a smooth, uniform surface with the perimeter of the outside template as the edge. Note that the depth of the scalloped edge is shallower the closer it gets to the outside edge, and deeper the farther away it is (**figure 4-13**). Make the deepest

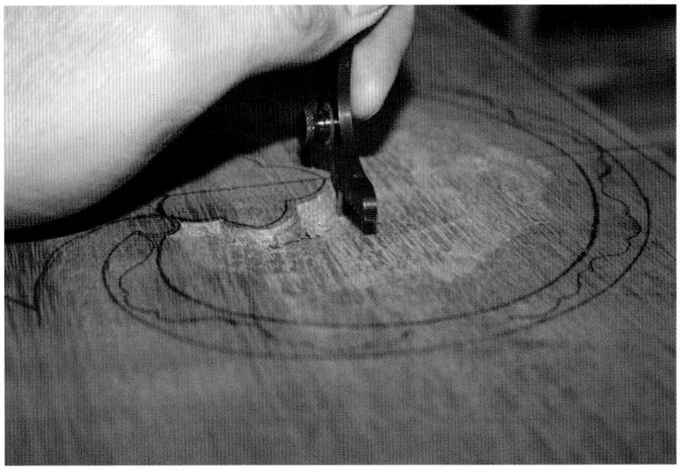

FIG. 4-9. Continue to remove material around the flower until the 3/8" depth is reached.

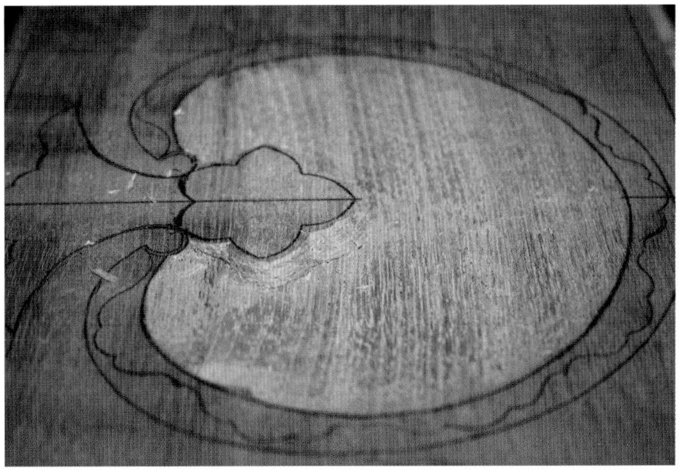

FIG. 4-10. Once the 3/8" depth is reached, sculpt a uniform and smooth surface bowl out to the hand-drawn perimeter from figure 4-6. Use gouges, scrapers, and sandpaper to create this surface.

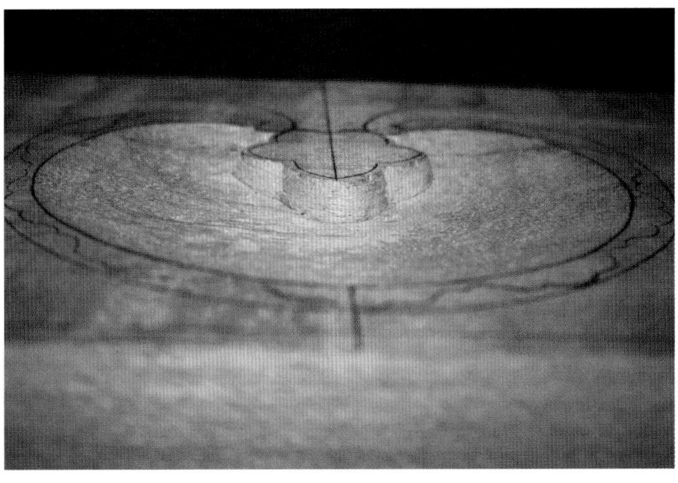

FIG. 4-11. The flower and bowl from a different angle.

FIG. 4-12. Raise the scalloped inside shell edge. Set in around the scalloped perimeter with gouges of appropriate sweep and size. Bevel into the stop cuts to establish the edge.

part at least ⅛". Within reason, deeper is better; it gives a more dramatic effect. In the same manner, complete the remainder of the perimeter. **Figure 4-14** shows the result.

Separate the lower portion of the central flower. Make stop cuts as shown in **figure 4-15**. Clean out the material, as shown in **figure 4-16**. **Figure 4-16** also shows the extra material around the flower in the "bowl" removed. Note that the walls of the flower are angled out. This is the opposite of undercut and will give a little more material to work with when the flower is detailed.

The central flower is angled back in the shell. This translates into it being slanted from bottom to top. Make a mark 3⁄16" down from the top (see **figure 4-17**). Use a flat chisel to bevel the flower surface down to this mark. Start the bevel close to the bottom, as shown in **figure 4-18**.

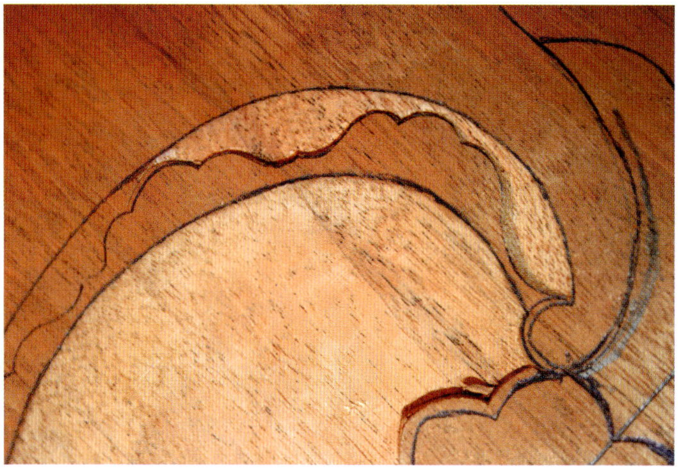

FIG. 4-13. Feather the background surface out to the outside template perimeter. The areas farther away from the outside perimeter will be deeper than those closer to it. Strive for a smooth and uniform surface.

FIG. 4-15. Raise the bottom portion of the flower between the applied vines.

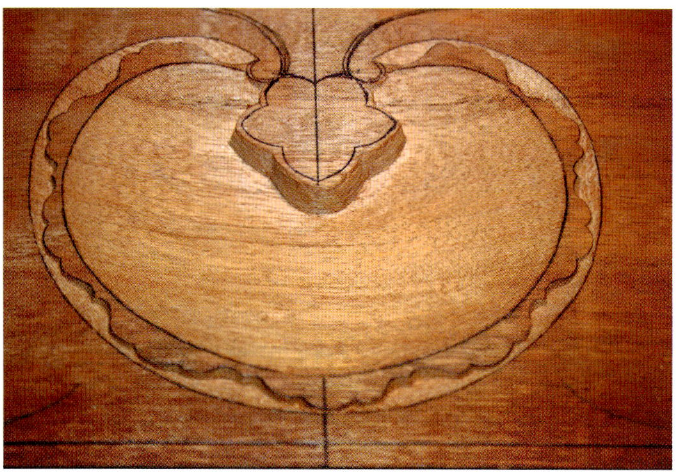

FIG. 4-14. The scalloped perimeter is complete.

FIG. 4-16. This is all that will be done for now.

FIG. 4-17. Make a mark on the flower tip 3⁄16" up from the bottom. This is half of its height.

Draw a vertical centerline and a 3⁄8" diameter circle (see **figure 4-19**). Raise the circle by setting in around its perimeter with a #5 5 mm gouge. **Figure 4-20** shows the technique. Use a #7 6 mm gouge to remove the area around the circle, as shown in **figure 4-21**.

Separate the five petals of the flower. First, draw boundary lines as shown in **figure 4-22**. Next, set in along the boundaries with a #5 5 mm gouge and round over the edges of each petal. **Figures 4-23** and **4-24** show these techniques, respectively. **Figure 4-25** shows the five petals separated and their edges rounded.

Make the perimeter around the center circle more uniform. **Figure 4-26** shows the result. Draw circular segments on each lobe and then carve to these with a #7 6 mm gouge.

FIG. 4-18. Crave a flat ramp down to the 3⁄16" mark. The flower leans back into the bowl. This is how that effect is created.

FIG. 4-20. Raise this center circle. Set in around the circular perimeter with a #5 5 mm gouge.

FIG. 4-19. Draw a 3⁄8" circle centered in the flower.

FIG. 4-21. Separate the center circle. Make it about 1⁄8" tall.

FIG. 4-22. Draw in leaf separation lines. These run radially and hit the cusp points between the leaf tips.

FIG. 4-23. Separate the leaf petals with a #5 5 mm gouge. Round over the edges of each petal.

FIG. 4-24. Each petal looks like a convex walnut half shell.

FIG. 4-25. The petals are shaped enough for now.

FIG. 4-26. Make the circular opening around the middle disk a little more uniform.

Figure 4-27 shows an additional circular segment on each lobe. The centers of these arcs will be the high points when complete. Since the high spots are on the same circle, that circle will be visible after the detail is added. This adds balance and cohesion and gives a nice visual effect.

Figure 4-27 also shows a crosshair in the center of the circle. This circular cylinder will become a dome. First, use a flat chisel to round over the corners (see **figure 4-28**). Now use a #7 6 mm gouge to round the edges to form a dome. **Figure 4-29** shows the dome mostly complete. Use a riffler to blend the facets and get a smooth, spherical surface.

Each of the petals has three segments. **Figure 4-30** shows various stages of refinement. First, separate two adjacent tips with a V-tool. One of these is labeled "A." Next, use a #7 10 mm gouge to extend the "V" and round the tips. "B" is an example. **Figure 4-31** shows the completed flower petals.

FIG. 4-29. The dome surface is smooth and complete.

FIG. 4-27. The arc on each petal will be the high point for that petal. Because all high spots are on a larger circle, this will be noticeable when complete and visually appealing.

FIG. 4-28. Round over the corners of the middle disk. This will become a dome.

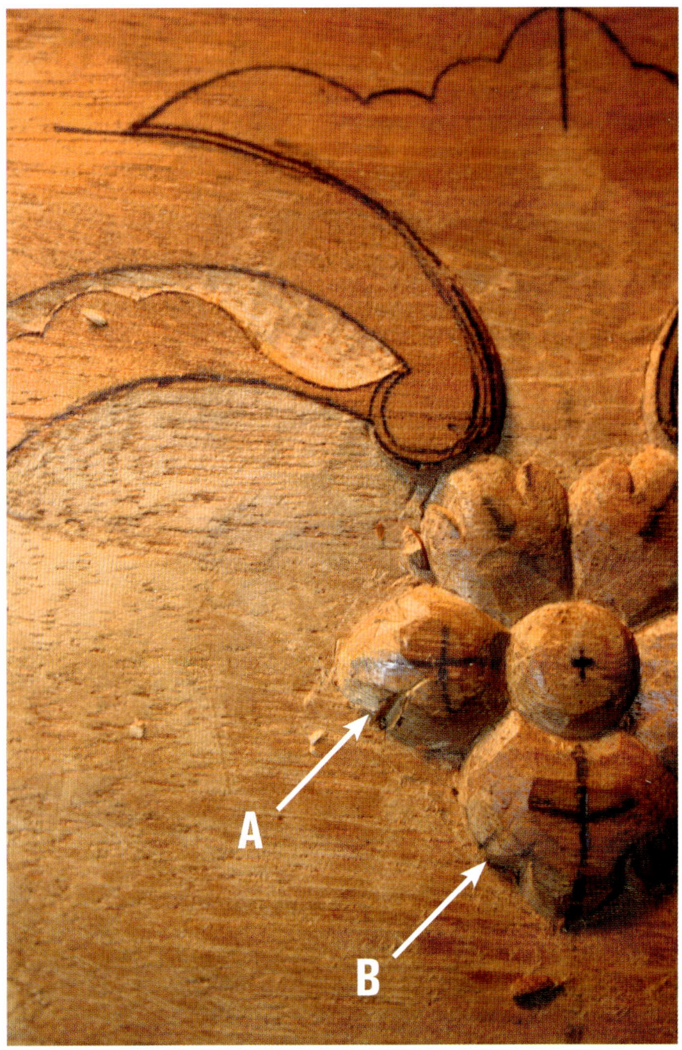

FIG. 4-30. Each petal has three tips. Use a V-tool to create the tip separation.

FIG. 4-31. The petals are fully sculpted.

Use the outer template to transfer the lines, as shown in **figure 4-32**. The shapes labeled "A" are lowered. The in-between areas labeled "B" are rounded over. Note the lines labeled "C"; these lines connect the cusps of the scalloped edge with the cusps of the lowered areas. These lines will remain high, with a deep scoop on either side.

Begin to lower the areas "A" by making stop cuts around the perimeter with gouges of appropriate width and sweep. **Figure 4-33** shows the technique. Bevel into these cuts (see **figure 4-34**). Deepen the cuts to about ⅛" or a little more. There needs to be enough height difference to get a decent rounding on the in-between areas. Note the cut "A" at the bottom of the lowered area. This is made with a #7 4 mm gouge. **Figure 4-34** also shows some of the lowered areas. **Figure 4-35** shows all the lowered areas.

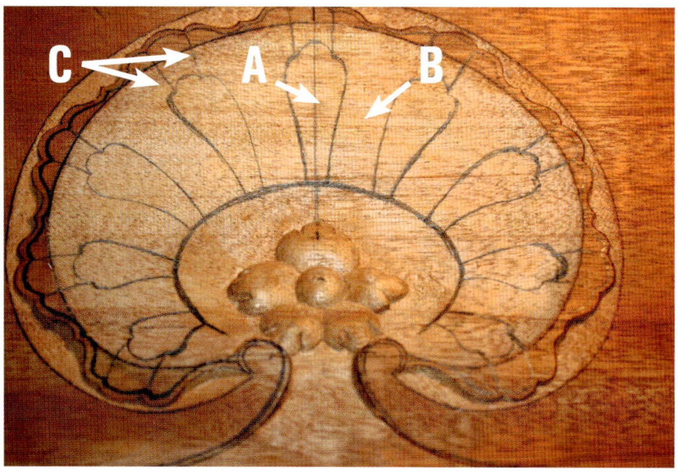

FIG. 4-32. Use the outside template to help draw the shell lobes. The "A" sections are low and the "B" sections are high. The lines "C" connect cusps of different elements.

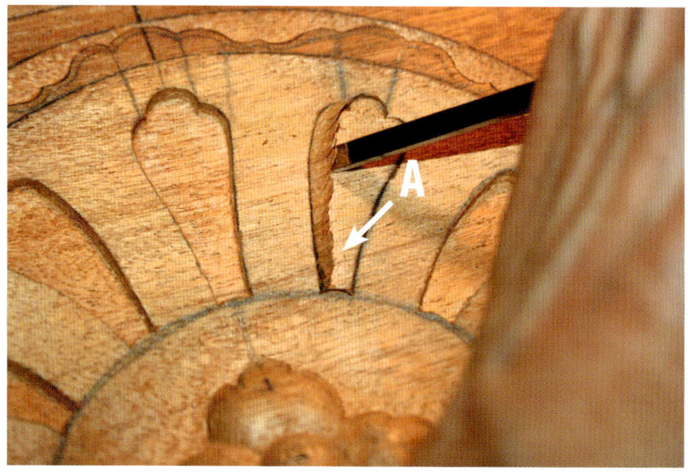

FIG. 4-34. Bevel into the stop cuts from the "A" side, because these are low.

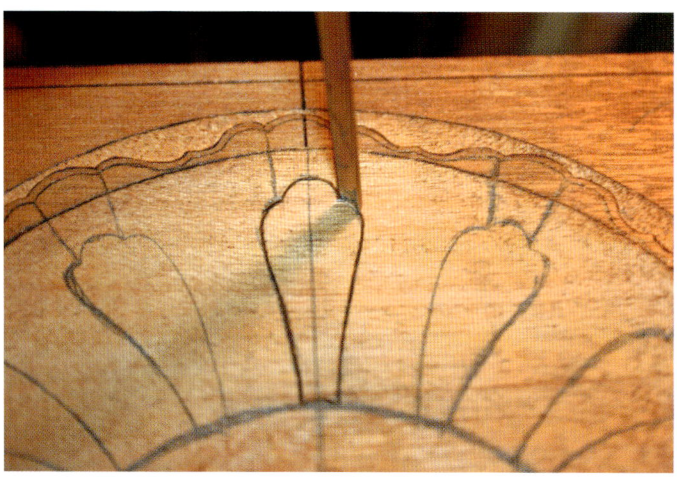

FIG. 4-33. Make stop cuts along the "A" lines.

FIG. 4-35. Excavate all the "A" sections.

Use a #9 10 mm gouge to make the cuts labeled "A" in **figure 4-36**. Make these troughs in multiple cuts. Be careful not to break the cusp lines between two adjacent troughs, especially where they enter the lowered area. The area "B" is made with a #9 5 mm gouge. Note how the gouge cut at "C" also removes the initial edge of the in-between area. Use a flat chisel to round over the in-between areas. "D" shows one of the in-between areas rounded. Repeat these steps on all the other areas. **Figures 4-37** and **4-38** show the completed troughs and rounded lobes.

Use a #11 1 mm veiner gouge to make detail cuts on the flower petals, as shown in **figure 4-39**. The middle cut on each petal is longer than the other two. Make the small holes in the middle cut with an awl. Also note the hole in the center of the central dome element.

FIG. 4-38. A different angle of the modeled shell. Detail marks still need to be done.

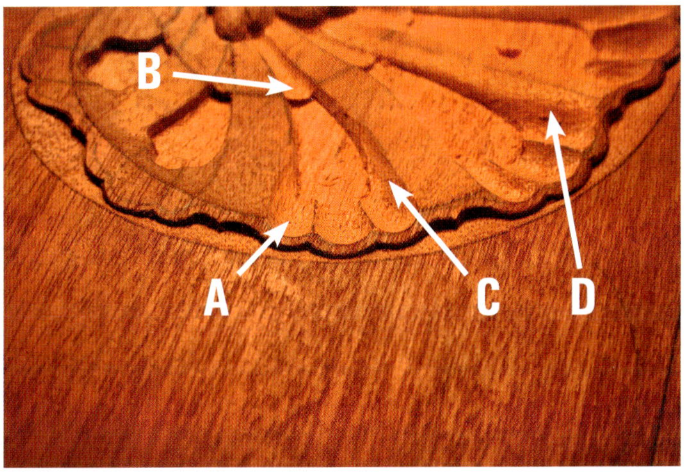

FIG. 4-36. There are three "A" cuts on the outside perimeter of each low section. The ones next to a convex lobe will blend into that lobe, as shown by "C." The "B" cuts are a tapered scoop at the bottom of each low area. "D" is a more rounded version of "C."

FIG. 4-39. Use a #11 1 mm gouge to make the detail cuts. The middle one is longer than the other two. Use an awl to make the holes.

FIG. 4-37. Round all the convex lobes and blend them into the adjacent troughs.

FIG. 4-40. Make stop cuts around the perimeter of the lower leaves.

Make stop cuts around the perimeter of the bottom leaves (see **figure 4-40**). Bevel into these cuts with a narrow, shallow gouge. **Figure 4-41** shows early progress. Stay away from the areas labeled "A." If more is needed here, it will be done when the vine is applied. Also be careful of the area labeled "B." Do not cut through the fillet, because this will break up the straight line at the bottom, and it will not be visually appealing.

Figure 4-42 shows the completed drawer front. The detail lines "A," "B," and "C" all are made with a #11 1 mm gouge. Use an awl to make the holes "D." Blend the background "E," below the lower leaves, into the surrounding area so that it is smooth and flat. This enhances the illusion that the leaves are sitting on top. Leave a small flat area "F" for the brass knob handle. Finally, stipple the areas "G."

I used a flat nailhead to make a small stippling tool. I got this idea from Al Breed. Use a V-shaped file to cut a perpendicular, crosshatched pattern on the nailhead. Strive to get the crosshatch lines close enough so that the "V" cuts leave points. The sharper the points, the nicer the stippling pattern. **Figure 4-43** shows my version.

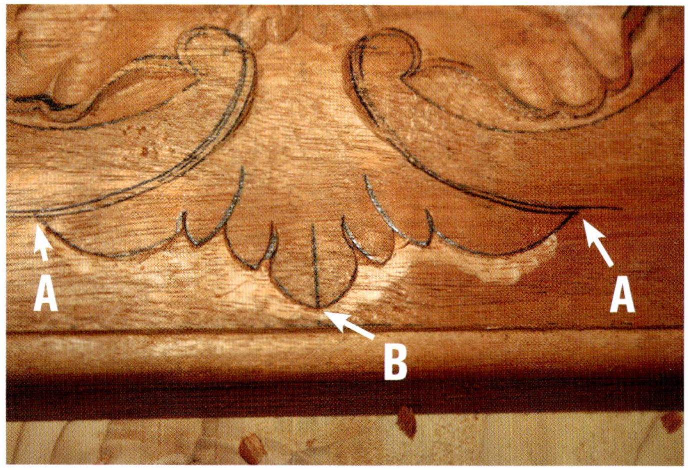

FIG. 4-41. Stay away from the area "A" for now. Be careful not to cut through the fillet line near "B."

FIG. 4-42. Many nuanced details are shown. Pay attention to these. They make the difference between an okay piece and a really good one.

FIG. 4-43. Shop-made stippling tool from a common nail.

Carving the Applied Vine

Make a template for the applied vine from **figure A1-2. Figure 4-44** shows this template. The vines are made from ¼" stock. If it is a little thicker, that is okay, but ⅜" is too much. If it is too thick, more material needs to be removed or it will look thick and bulky. Within reason, thin is better because it will look lighter and delicate, which is a more pleasing look. To minimize the stock needed, interleave the two vines as shown in **figure 4-45**. Note the left and right orientations. This section will use the right-side orientation. The left needs to be the mirror image.

Make the interior cut with a scroll or jigsaw. Drill a hole in the interior waste big enough to feed a saw blade through. Use a bandsaw for the exterior cuts. **Figure 4-46** shows one of the vines cut out and ready for carving. Note the extra material that remains around the leaf tips. This will give greater flexibility to position the leaf tips when carving.

Attach the vine blank to a backer board with double-stick tape. Put small pieces of tape in a variety of heftier spots and squeeze the blank and backer board in a vice. This will sufficiently adhere the carving blank to the backer board. When removing the carved element later, be careful when prying it from the backer board. It is quite delicate and could break.

If it does break, that is an easily solved problem. Glue it back together, touch up the glued area when it's dry, and move on. If the joint is noticeable, embrace it as patina.

FIG. 4-45. Nest the two vines to conserve wood. A right and left version are needed.

FIG. 4-46. Make the interior cut with a scroll or saber saw. Use a bandsaw for the exterior cuts. Leave extra material around the leaf tips for flexibility when carving.

FIG. 4-44. Applied vine template.

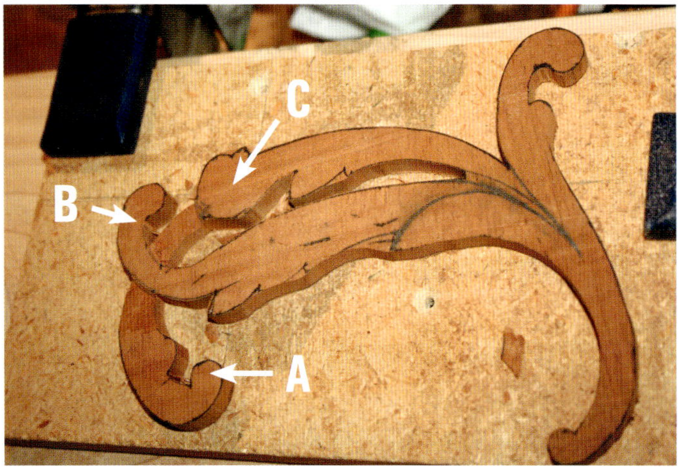

FIG. 4-47. "A," "B," and "C" are high. The "A" element is underneath "B," so it is lower.

There is no correct place to start. I usually look for an area that is a bit easier, or one that I think I understand better. If there is a particularly difficult section, I will leave that for later. As you progress, don't focus on one area to completion, especially if it depends on other elements. Try to bring the entire vine to the same level of completion before moving to the next level of refinement.

The first step to carving this vine is to sculpt the shape on which the details will be added. To sculpt the surface, one needs to understand the various levels and how they relate to each other. To that end, study the original in **figure 4-1A** and my reproduction in **figure 4-1B**.

The upper leaf cluster "A" from **figure 4-47** flows underneath "B" and disappears below the leaf cluster "C." So make stop cuts along the "B" and "C" lines, and bevel into them from the "A" surface. The stop cuts can be made with a shallow gouge on the larger-radius curve and a tighter one on the smaller-radius one.

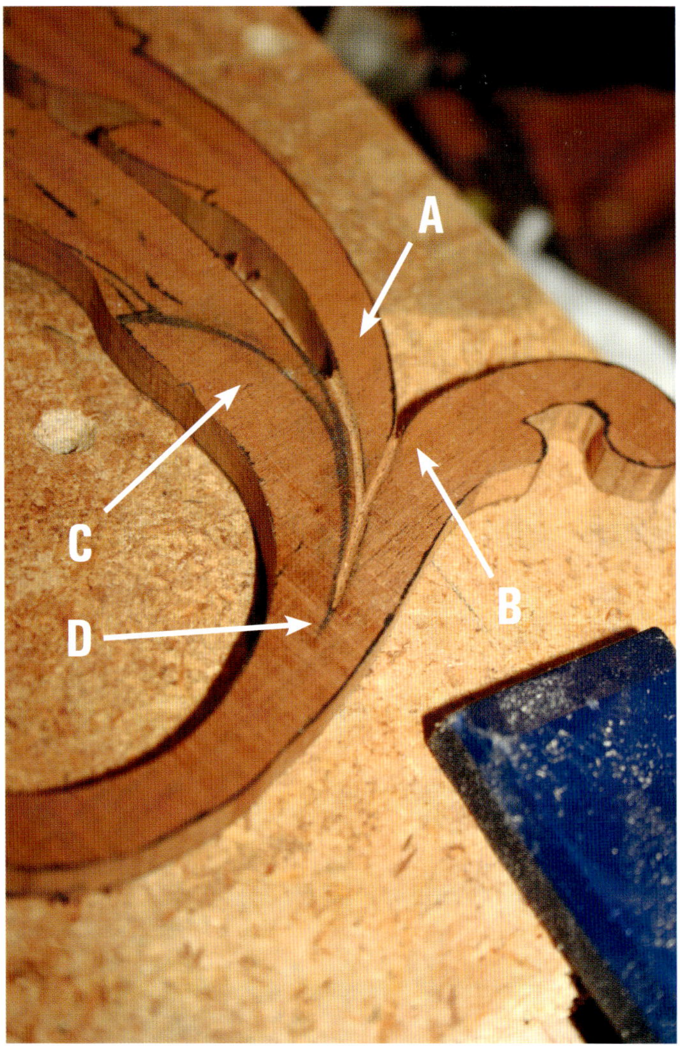

FIG. 4-48. "A," "B," and "C" all have a common root somewhere to the left of "D."

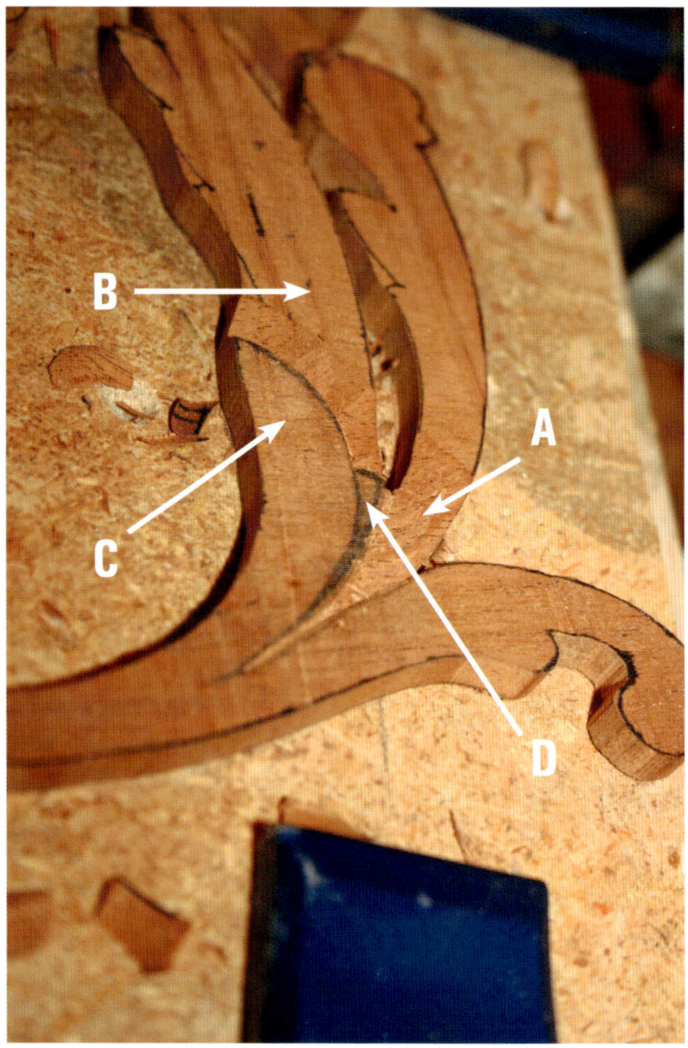

FIG. 4-49. Since "A" is below the others, lower it and create a ramp from the low point to top of the blank.

Figure 4-48 shows three other elements that start out at a common point but separate and flow in different directions. The stem "A" emanates somewhere under "B" and "C." "B" and "C" have a common root somewhere before the start of the separation point "D." Use a V-tool, starting at "D," and cut along the outside of elements "B" and "C." This is a way to have elements start from a common point and flow nicely in different directions.

Begin to transition the surface "A" in **figure 4-49** by creating a ramp from the top surface of the blank into the intersection area. Deepen the intersection area and blend that depth to the top of element "A." This will probably take two to three iterations. The final height of "A" at the intersection area is about ⅛". Strive for measurable variation in heights. Within reason, more is better. Among other things, the height differences create greater shadows, which translates to a more dramatic-looking carved element.

The stem "B" flows under "C." Separate these two by creating a similar ramped surface to the one for "A." Note the secondary leaf "D" that is part of the "C" stem.

Figure 4-50 shows good transition ramps and decent height differences between adjacent elements.

The leaf cluster shown in **figure 4-51** is isolated so it can be refined further. Draw in the leaf boundaries as shown. Because leaf "A" tucks under the "B" cluster, make stop cuts along the "B" boundaries, and bevel into them from the "A" side. **Figure 4-52** shows the result of this operation.

Draw in the separation lines as shown in **figure 4-53**. Round over the backside of the element, as shown in **figure 4-54**. This surface should smoothly connect the tip of the element at "A" all the way to point "B." Eventually the vertical wall "C" will be blended so that the backside surface is smooth and uniform all the way to the bottom.

FIG. 4-50. Progress with establishing the levels.

FIG. 4-52. The levels and separation are set.

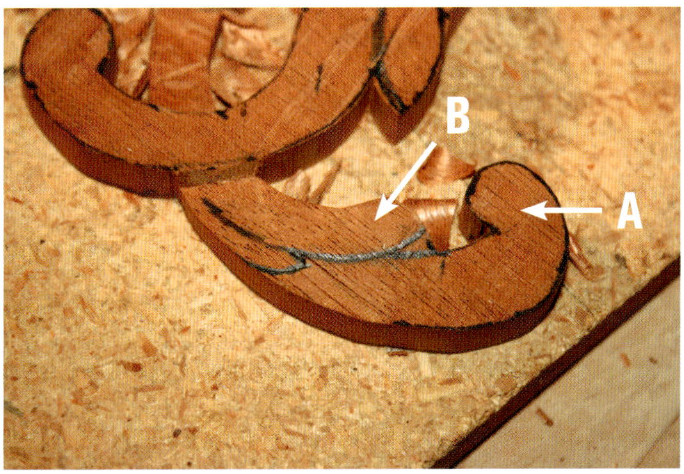

FIG. 4-51. "A" tucks underneath "B." Set in around "B" and bevel in from "A."

FIG. 4-53. Draw the ridgeline.

FIG. 4-54. Round over the back side. Eventually this back side surface will go to the ground.

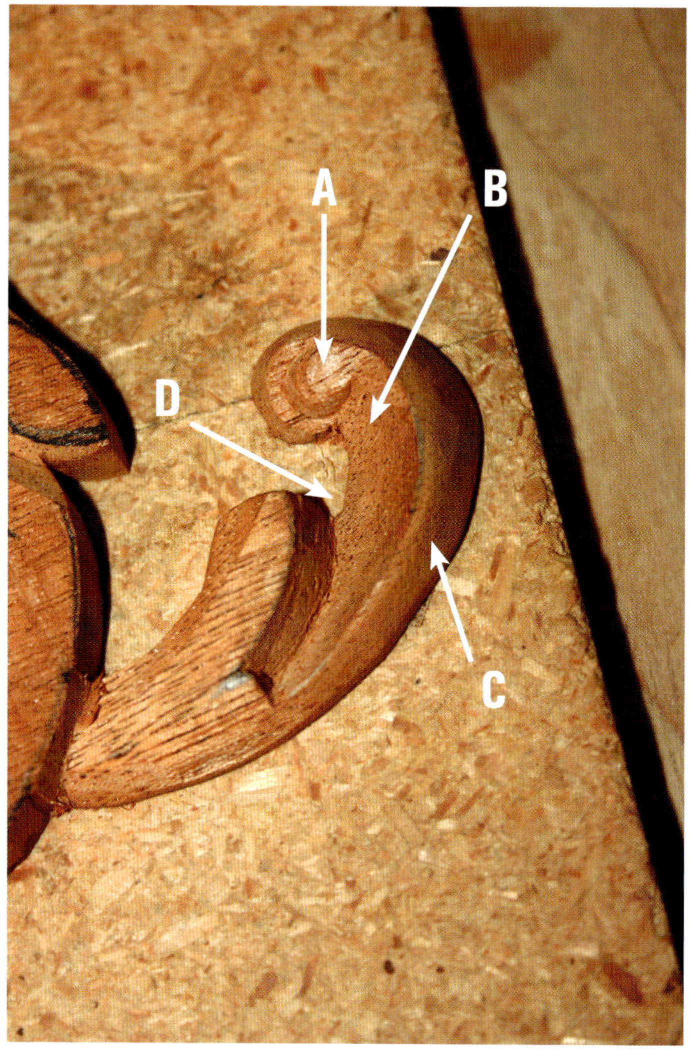

FIG. 4-55. "B" is a concave surface. Its intersection with the "C" surface forms the ridgeline.

Figure 4-55 shows further refinement. The secondary element "A" is tucked into the surrounding area. The surface "B" is scooped with a #9 10 mm gouge. Strive for a crisp and smooth line of intersection between surfaces "B" and "C." Note also that the back side surface "C" is closer to the ground. There is a bit more to do, but that will be blended after the vine is removed from the backing board. The height of the stock at point "D" is about $\frac{1}{16}$". It gets quite thin, but that is part of the goal.

Use a #9 10 mm gouge (see **figure 4-56**) to scoop the inside surface. The thickness of the material at the base is $\frac{1}{16}$" or less.

Figure 4-57 shows a small secondary leaf "A." Use a #7 4 mm gouge to shape this leaf tip. This section is almost complete and is refined enough for now.

Use a V-tool to separate leaf "A," as shown in **figure 4-58.** The separation line is such that its curve flows into the leaf tip boundary as it leaves the blank at "B." This line will also split and define shaping for leaf "C."

FIG. 4-56. Use a #9 10 mm gouge to create the concave surface.

Sculpt the leaf "A" in **figure 4-59** by creating a gentle ramp from the high point at "B" down to the tip of "A." Angle the ramp a bit so the surface slants down toward the left side of the image. This ramp is part of the continually up-and-down movement of the surface. It is this movement that gives life to the carving. **Figure 4-60** shows the same elements from a higher view.

Also shown in **figures 4-59** and **4-60** is the rounded backside of leaf "A." The high ridgeline is in pencil. The surfaces will fall off on either side of this line, so when complete the line will be the intersection of two surfaces.

Figure 4-61 shows further refinement of this area. The back side labeled "A" has been extended closer to the ground. The tip "B" is a rounded dome. Use a #7 4 mm gouge to extend the circle of the blank perimeter at "B." Then use a #9 7 mm gouge to scoop the surface "C." Note how the surfaces "A" and "C" form the ridgeline that was penciled in earlier. Also note the area "D." The surface "A" lies on top of the stem below. When shaping these surfaces, keep this relationship in mind.

Sculpt leaf "A" in **figure 4-62**. Use a flat chisel to create a dynamic, turning ramp from point "B" to point "C" and angled toward the left side of the image. Starting from point "B," turn the chisel as it is pushed along its path toward "C." Note that point "C" is almost at the ground.

Figure 4-63 shows this same ramp from a different angle. Note how close to the ground the leaf tip "C" is. Also note how the surface appears to roll over as it falls down to the left. This shape will make the leaf look like it is rolling over on itself, which is the intent. Draw in the leaf definitions, as shown, after the surface is shaped.

Figure 4-64 shows the same area from the other side. The leaf "A" is part of this cluster and is at a steep angle. Point "B" needs to have the line straightened out and be blended better between "C" and "D."

Figure 4-65 shows this section complete. Note how the ridgeline "A" starts on the left side and becomes the separation for different leaves in the cluster. The surface to the left of "A" is concave, and the surface on the right is convex. To make the concave cut, use a #7 16 mm gouge and start the cut at "B." Continually roll the chisel as the cut progresses and follows the line "A." This is a sophisticated cut that is difficult to execute and will take practice. To start, do small sections at a time. Overlap them to help with the continuity of the surface. When you have carved as much as you can, clean the surface with scrapers.

Also shown in **figure 4-65** is the lower cluster that flows to the right and down. The far right of this element is the portion that was missing on the original. There is a level difference at "C." Set in around it and bevel into the stop cut from the right. The high point of the far-right section is at "D," so the surface rises from "C," crests at "D," and falls off a little at the end.

FIG. 4-57. Use a #7 4 mm gouge to create a secondary leaf tip.

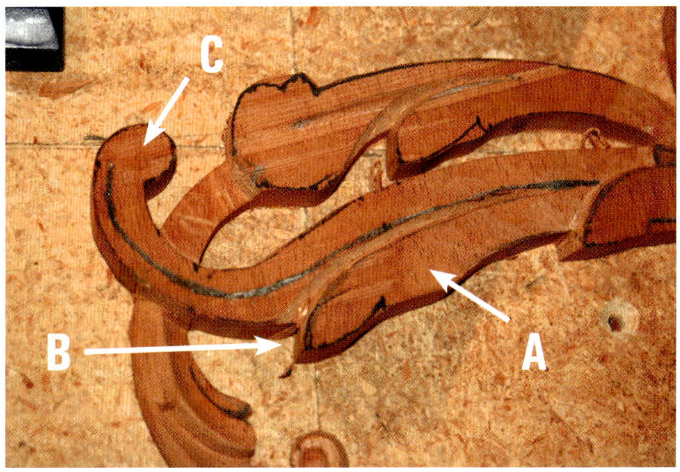

FIG. 4-58. Establish leaf "A" by using a V-tool and flowing into the tip at "B."

FIG. 4-59. Form a ramp from the high point "B" to the end at "A." The ramp also angles down toward the top of the image.

FIG. 4-60. Round over the back side, keeping the pencil line high.

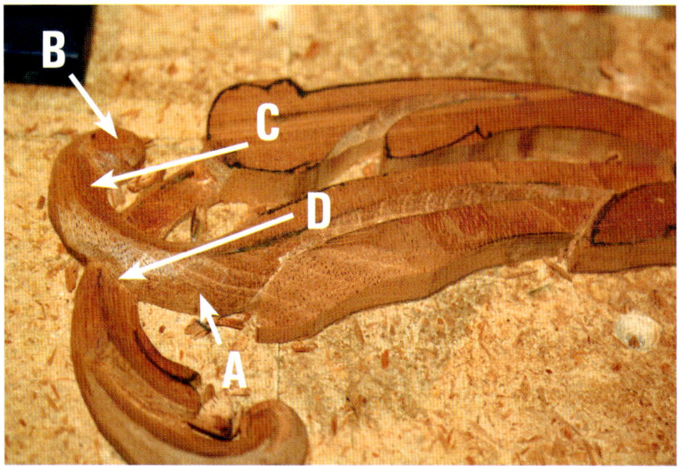

FIG. 4-61. More refinement of this area.

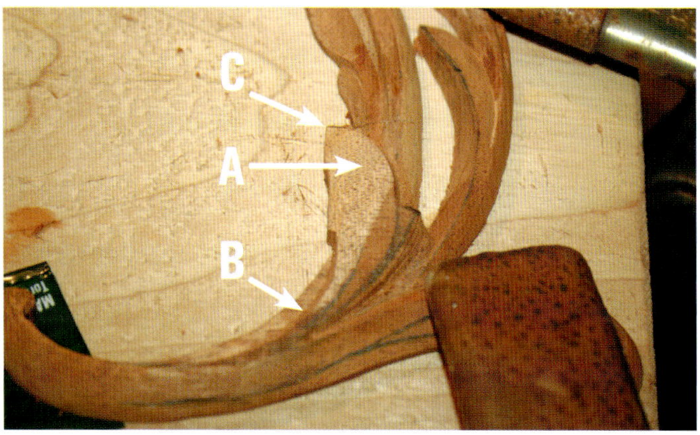

FIG. 4-62. Create an angled ramp from "B" to "C."

FIG. 4-63. Draw in the leaf tips after the surface is shaped. Note that the tip at "C" is almost to the ground.

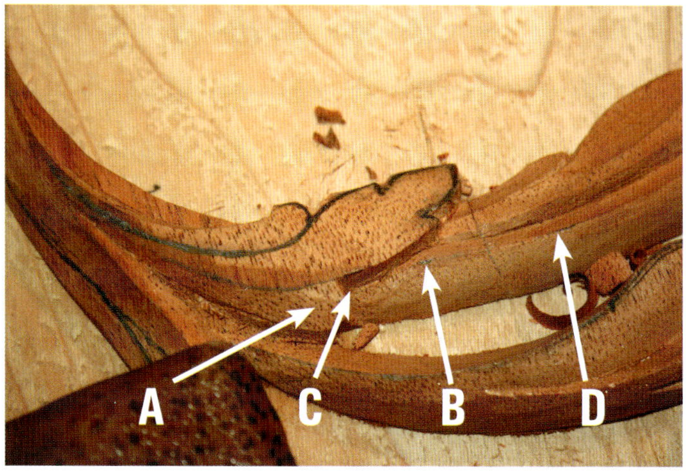

FIG. 4-64. The small leaf "A" is at a steep angle. This means that it drapes over the stem "D."

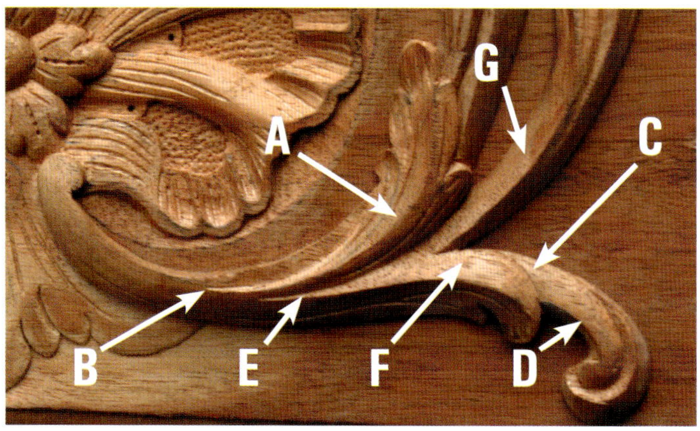

FIG. 4-65. The lower portion of the completed right vine.

Continuing with **Figure 4-65**, note how the surface "E" starts out flat to slightly concave at the left and splits and flows into a convex surface at "F" and into a concave one at "G." Strive for smooth and gentle transitions. This will look much better. Also work to get crisp and continuous surface intersection lines.

Figure 4-66 shows the completed upper portion. Element "A" is essentially a dome, with the high spot more or less centered top to bottom and left to right. It falls off in all directions from the high spot, and the surface flows to the ground wherever possible. The surface "B" is underneath "A" and connects to "C."

The three leaves "D," "E," and "F" all emanate from a common source. They are on one surface that angles down to the left, and part of each leaf is very near the ground. Once the common surface is shaped and oriented, the individual leaves are articulated with #7 gouge cuts. The intersection of these gouge cuts form ridges that are the leaf boundaries. The crisper these intersection lines are, the nicer the leaves will look. Vary the width of the gouge depending on the portion of the leaf.

The ridgeline "G" meanders the entire length of the element. It is the intersection of two surfaces at any point, but the surfaces change concavity along the length. Smooth transitions from concave to convex will give more life to the elements.

Note how surface "H" visually connects to surface "I" on both sides of the ridgeline. This convinces your eye that this is one stem and that it is underneath another.

I have mentioned a few times that many of the surfaces go all the way to the ground. This is difficult to do well when the blank is clamped on a flat surface. When the carved piece is removed from its backing board, use a small file and blend from the bottom into the surface (the technique is shown in **figure 4-67**). As you do this final blending, look for irregularities in the lines of the bottom profile and correct them with the same technique.

This vine is a complicated and delicate piece of carving. Study the pictures carefully with a critical eye, and try to understand the way that lines and surfaces flow and interact with each other. Several stems will start from a common source and flow and split into different shapes and go in different directions. Smooth and gentle transitions will bring the carving to life.

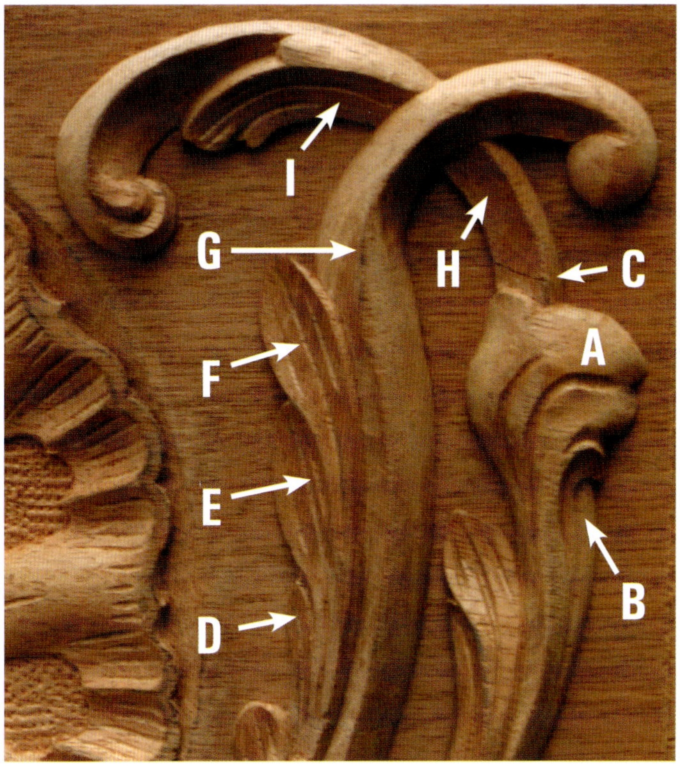

FIG. 4-66. The upper portion of the completed right vine.

FIG. 4-67. Final surface blending to the bottom of the blank, using a file. Smooth any irregularities in the bottom profile.

Attaching the Vine to the Drawer Front

After the vines are carved, they need to be attached to the drawer front. Attach them with some glue and small brads. I like to use an air nailer with 23-gauge pins. These are very thin and act as clamps until the glue dries. I like them because the force needed to drive them is very concentrated, so there is little to no chance of damaging the surrounding area. The same cannot be said of hammering a nail, no matter how careful. I know this is not an eighteenth-century tool, but the advantages outweigh the negatives.

Use as little glue as needed to minimize squeeze-out and cleanup, but use enough to get sufficient adhesion. Also make sure to get some glue on all the extended portions. Because they are extended, they will not get much holding power from an adhesion point some distance away. These points are labeled "A" and "B" in **figure 4-68**.

For brad placement, I look for areas that are more substantial and where they can be more hidden. Thin areas are more susceptible to splitting, so avoid these. "C," "D," "E," and "F" are good places to put a nail. I use as few nails as needed, so it is a judgment call as to how many. I would probably put them in "C," "E," and "F." "D"' might be a little dicey, so if I got good glue adhesion on the extended tip, I probably wouldn't.

Use several pinch clamps to hold the vine in place. Put one on each extended element if possible. To aid in clamping, install the drawer bottom after the vine is applied.

When the glue has dried, clean up any squeeze-out with small scrapers. I find that narrow, flat chisels work well.

Finally, there is a little integration carving to do. The part of the drawer front below the button "G" should be flushed with the cylinder of the button to be an extension of it. The same idea pertains to the area "H." This is the carved portion of the drawer front before blending the background into the leaf tips.

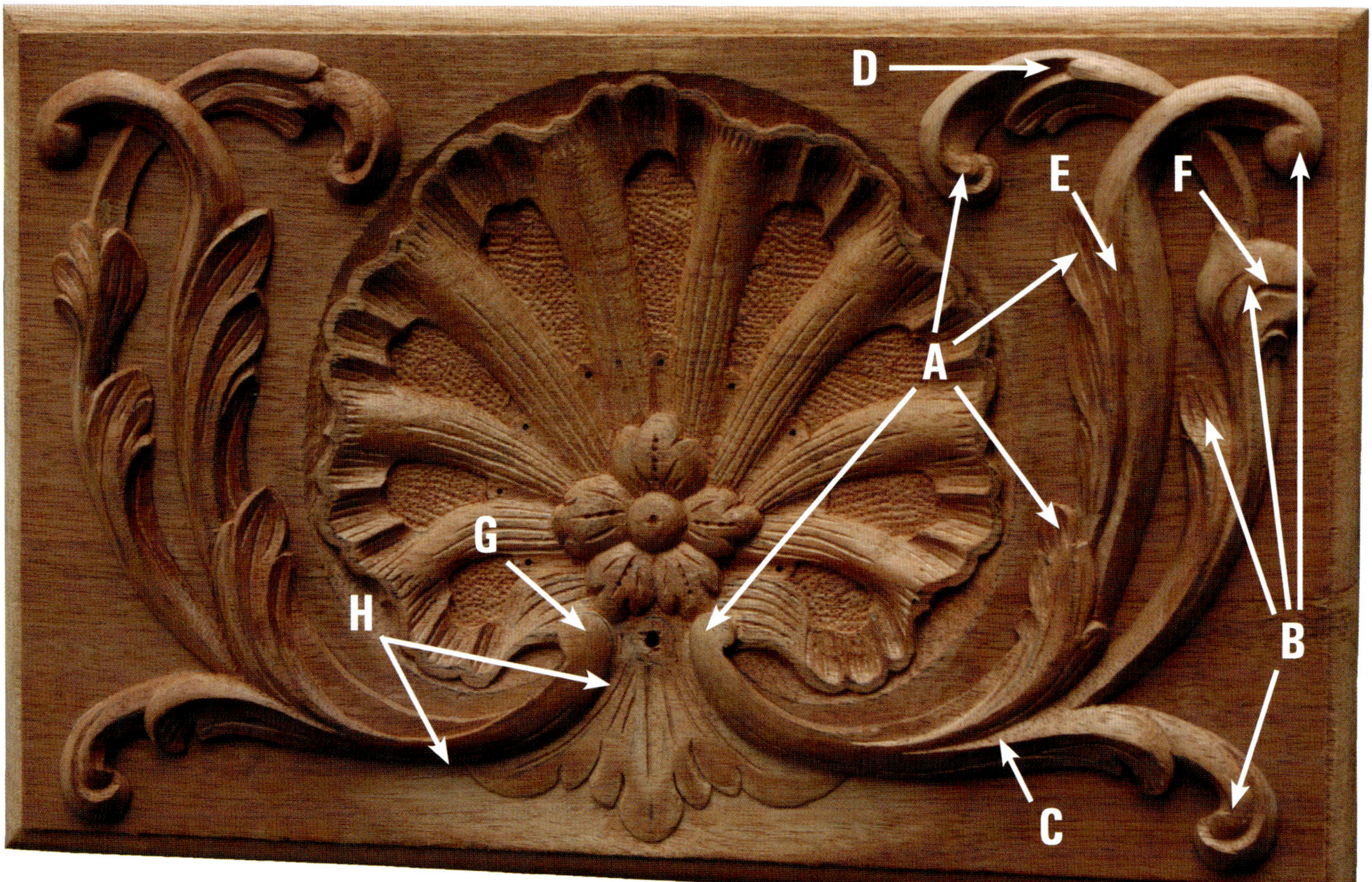

FIG. 4-68. "A" through "F" are glue and nail attachment points. "G" and "H" are areas that need carving after the vine is applied.

Cabriole Leg

This chapter will describe how to shape a cabriole leg. The mortises should be cut in the leg blanks prior to shaping them.

Make a leg template from the full scale drawing in the insert pages. **Figure A1-5** shows a reduced size version of this drawing. Both versions only show part of the post; I did this to fit it on the page. Transfer the leg template to two adjacent faces, as shown in **figure 5-1**. If possible, orient the grain so that the center of the rings is in the inside back corner. Note the soft transition between the post and leg. This will leave a little extra material for the ruffle that is carved on the leg post.

Use a bandsaw to cut along the lines, as shown in **figure 5-2**. Start each cut on the outside of the blank and stop as shown. When these cuts are done on one face, turn the blank 90° and make similar ones, but these can be completed. **Figure 5-3** shows the blank with completed cuts on one face and what remains from the cuts on the first face. Now cut through the remaining small sections. The completed bandsawn leg is shown in **figure 5-4**.

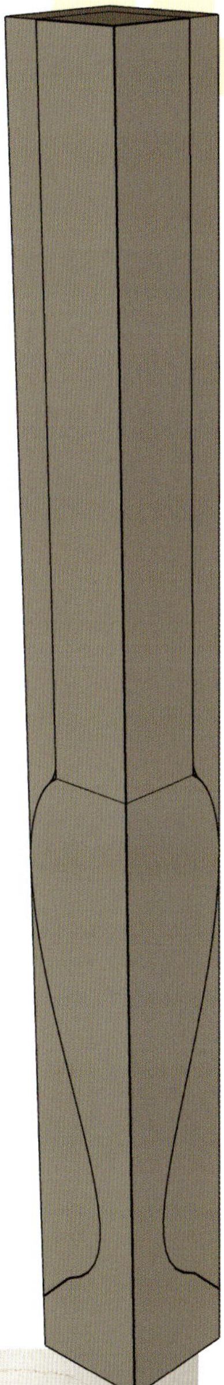

FIG. 5-1. Draw the template on two adjacent faces. This is a view from the back, and this corner needs to be square.

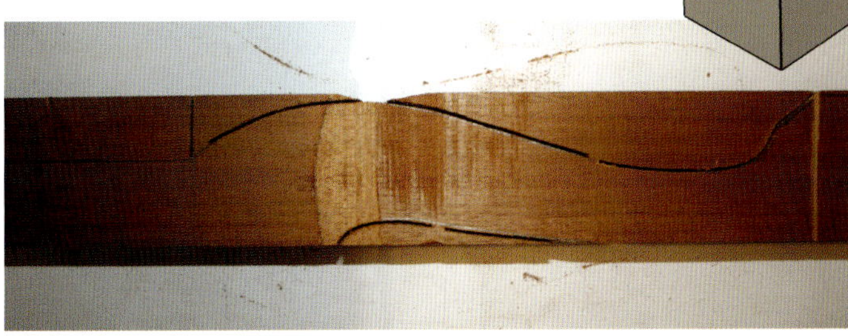

FIG. 5-2. Use a bandsaw to make the cuts shown. Leave the "bridges" so the patterns on the 90° faces are not lost.

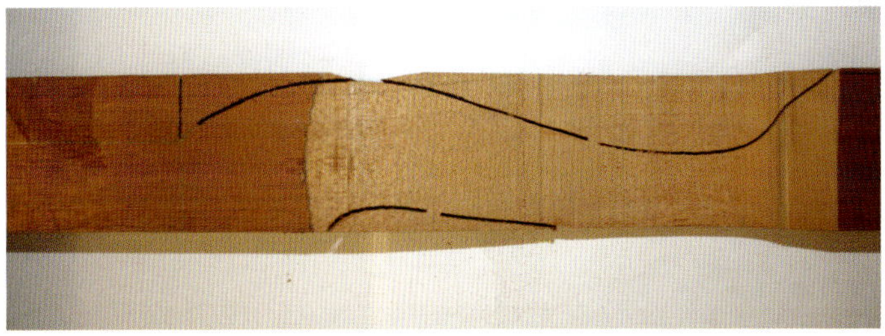

FIG. 5-3. Do not leave "bridges" on the second face. Cut the "bridges," and the rough leg is complete.

FIG. 5-4. The roughed-out cabriole leg after the bandsaw cuts.

The leg now has the familiar cabriole shape. What remains is to round the edges. A few guide lines are needed to round the edges in a visually balanced way. There will be four lines on each of the four faces. The two inside ones on each face will start at the center of the ankle and follow the outside of the leg. Start by finding the center of the leg ankle (see **figure 5-5**). Holding a pencil between your thumb and index finger, and with your other fingers as a guide, draw a line up toward the knee. **Figure 5-6** shows this line. Now start at the same point as the first line, but use the back of the leg as the guide and draw a similar line. This second line is parallel to the back edge and half the ankle thickness inward. **Figure 5-7** shows the result. Now find a point halfway between one of the edges and its closest line, and, in a similar manner as before, draw another line parallel to that edge. Repeat for the other edge. This one face should now have four lines that are more or less parallel to their respective edges. **Figure 5-8** shows the four lines. Repeat this process for the other three faces.

FIG. 5-5. Start at the center of the ankle.

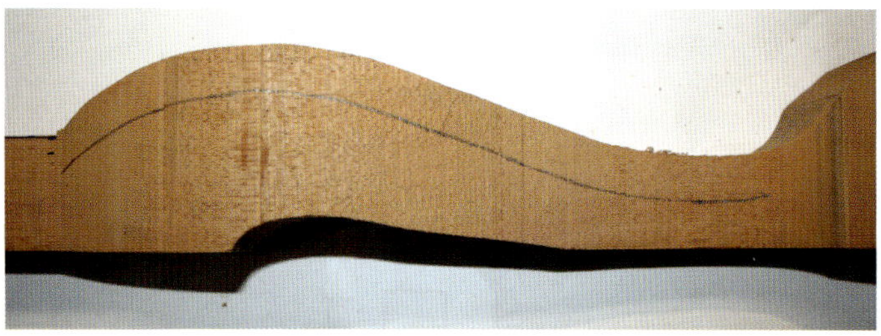

FIG. 5-6. Use your finger as a fence against the front surface of the leg blank to draw the line shown.

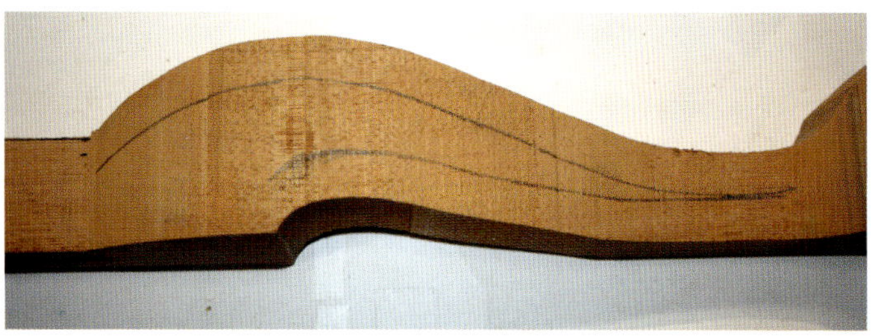

FIG. 5-7. Starting at the same ankle point, follow the back surface of the leg blank and draw the line shown.

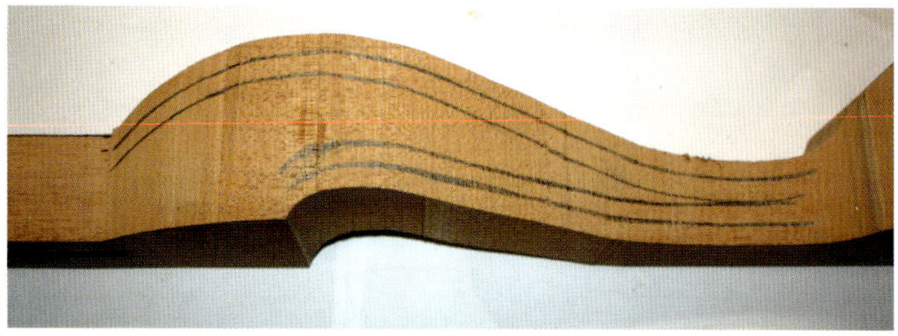

FIG. 5-8. Divide the outside segments in half. Start at the ankle and draw as before.

FIG. 5-9. Use a #49 rasp to bevel between adjacent lines on adjacent faces.

Now secure the leg in a clamp to begin the refinement process. At this point, any cross section of the leg is approximately square. After the next step, any cross section will be an eight-sided figure. To achieve this, bevel each of the four corners from the knee to the ankle. Use a #49 patternmaker's rasp to flatten the section between the two lines closest to a given edge (**figure 5-9** shows early progress). Use the flat side of the #49 for the knee and wider portions, and the curved side for the ankle. Take care when beveling on the knee not to hit the post. Also note that because the foot has not yet been carved, the ankle cannot be completely finished at this time. **Figure 5-10** shows the first bevel cut complete.

When doing the side edges, stay a little ways away from the corner. The leg will eventually have a knee block attached, and this point and edge line will be blended into it. If too much wood is removed too early, these two pieces cannot be blended well. **Figure 5-11** shows the point and line in question.

The back edge is a little different than the others in the way it terminates at the top. The goal here is to blend the two surfaces so that they start at the lower post corner and continuously flow together. As part of this step, clean up the surface right up to the back of the post. **Figure 5-12** shows the area and treatment in question.

With these details in mind, bevel the remaining three edges. **Figure 5-13** shows the leg after all four edges have been beveled.

A similar series of cuts will now connect the innermost layout line with a line approximately centered in the beveled surface. Use the #49 for this also. **Figure 5-14** shows early progress, and **figure 5-15** shows later progress. Keep in mind that the idea here is to get a smooth, round surface the entire length of the leg. This is achieved by continually adjusting the angle of the rasp as it is run from knee to ankle. In addition, vary the pressure on the rasp, depending on the surface. If the surface

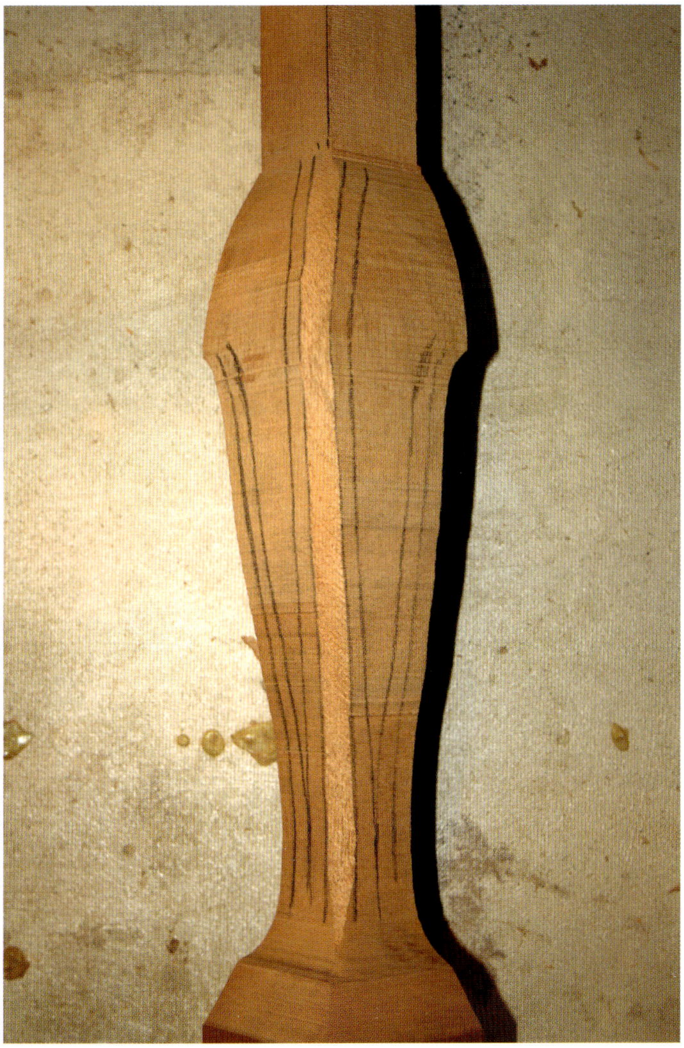

FIG. 5-10. The first front bevel is complete.

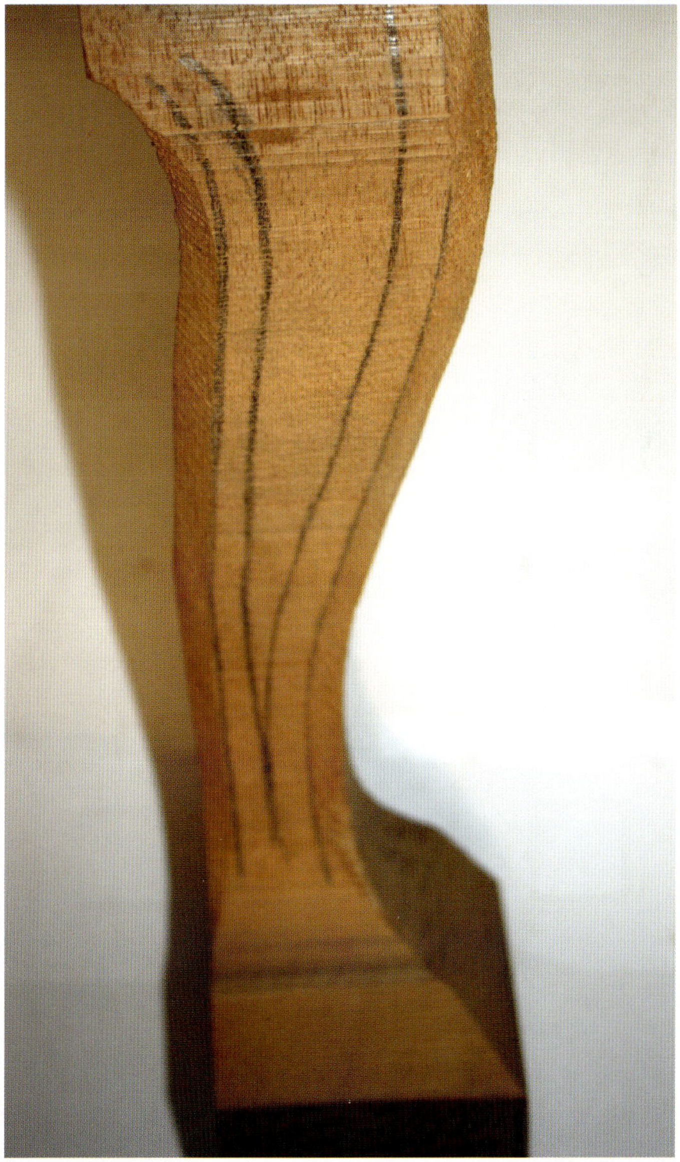

FIG. 5-11. The side bevel is done.

FIG. 5-12. The back bevel is done.

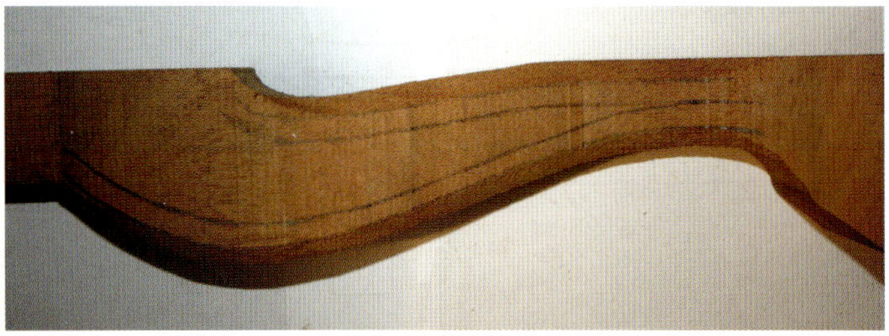

FIG. 5-13. Use the #49 rasp to blend from the next guide line to the middle of the beveled surface.

FIG. 5-14. The second rasp cut blends from the inner guide line.

FIG. 5-15. Continue blending the newly created facets until the surface is smooth all the way around the leg and from the knee to the ankle.

is relatively level—that is, no divots or irregularities—use light pressure. If the surface is more uneven, use heavier pressure in those areas, lightening up as the pass completes.

At this point the surface should be uniform, round, and even, but rough. From now on, the shape of the leg will not change much, but the roughness will be smoothed. I use a bastard-cut half-round file for this operation. It is difficult to describe the smoothing operation in a series of steps. Run the file up and down the leg, removing all the facets while continually changing the angle and pressure used. The surface should be continuous to the touch, and your hand should not feel any hills or valleys when moving in any and all directions. After the file has removed the rasp marks, you can use a smooth-cut file or sandpaper, or both. It depends on how smooth you want the surface. I have used both, and I usually end up with 120-grit sandpaper. **Figure 5-16** shows progress after filing, and **figure 5-17** shows the completed shaped and smoothed cabriole leg.

The next operation will be to carve the ball-and-claw foot.

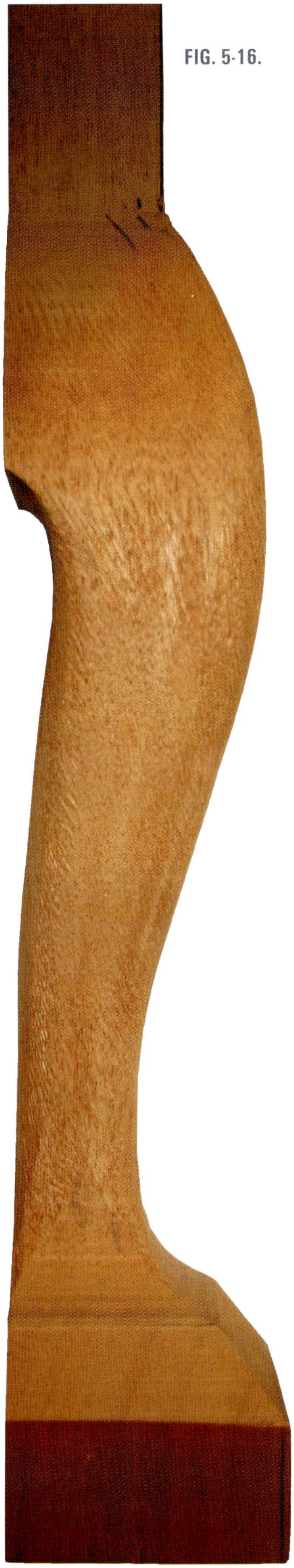

FIG. 5-16.

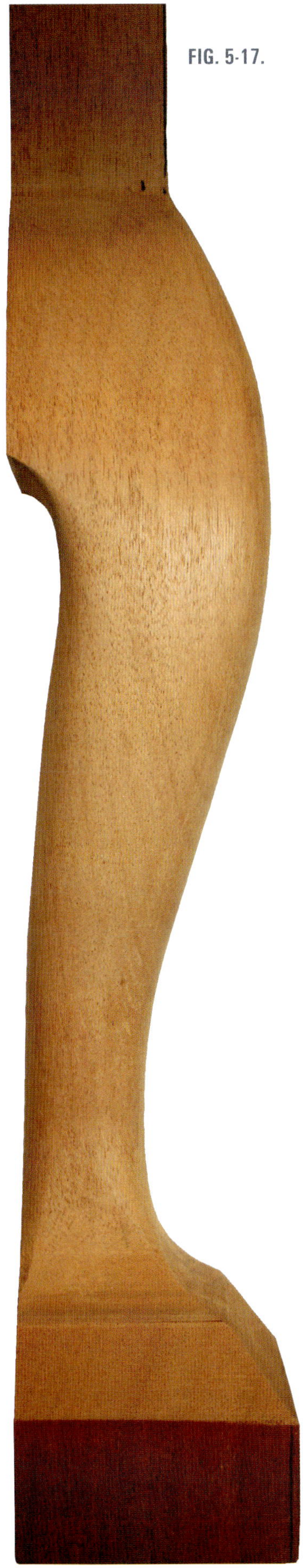

FIG. 5-17.

Ball-and-Claw Foot

This chapter will describe how to carve the ball-and-claw foot. The leg blank should have the mortises cut and the cabriole leg shaped prior to carving the foot. However, the quarter-column opening should not be cut yet. The quarter-column opening will be the last step on the leg after the mortises, foot, and knee carving.

The goal will be to get the largest possible ball out of the blank. If your blank is square, this should be relatively easy. If your blank is slightly rectangular, this may require some minor adjustments to the stated description. A slightly rectangular blank is not a problem; just use the blank faces as if everything was square. Any furniture of this style requires constant adjustments and judgment calls. The more comfortable you become with making good judgments, the better your outcomes will be.

My method for carving a ball-and-claw foot is deterministic and reproducible. It is a series of steps done in a specific order, on the basis of referenced measurements. In fact, the foot is completely determined by these measurements. The foot begins with using these measurements to draw lines and circles on the foot blank that define the limits of the ball and its separation from the toes.

The way to think about and visualize the ball-and-claw foot is as four sections of a slightly flattened sphere that are separated by four toes. The sections of the sphere need to visually connect across a toe, and they need to appear to meet at the "North Pole," which is not visible and is buried inside the top of the foot. The procedure for shaping the ball will be to turn the square cylinder that is the foot blank into a circular cylinder in four segments that is defined by the *break point* diameter. Then, each circular cylindrical section is converted to a spherical one. Keep this in mind as you lay out and then carve the foot.

The foot begins with some layout. It is important not only to get the layout lines on the blank correct, but to understand why they are there. As you better understand what the lines represent, you will become more comfortable and confident with cutting and carving to them.

The measurements that define the feet on this dressing table and their placement are shown in **figure 6-1**. The defining measurements are also listed in the table titled "Ball & Claw Layout," shown in **figure A1-5**.

FIG. 6-2. Use a divider to draw the two circles, and highlight the lines with a 0.5 mm mechanical pencil.

FIG. 6-3. Draw lines parallel to the diagonals ¼" on each side. These determine the placement and size of the toes.

Ball and Claw Foot Layout Diagrams

Ball & Claw Layout (Inches)	
Diameter at Floor:	2 11/16
Diameter at Break Point:	3
Break Point Height:	7/8
Ball Height in Back:	1 11/16
Ball Depth in Back:	5/16
Ball Height in Front:	2 1/16
Ball Depth in Front:	15/16
1st Knuckle Height Front:	1 1/8
1st Knuckle Height Side:	1 7/16
1st to 2nd Knuckle Front:	1 1/8
1st to 2nd Knuckle Side:	1
1st Knuckle Back:	1 3/8
Toe Width:	1/2
Claw Height:	3/8

Definition of Terms	
A	Break point diameter
B	Diameter at the floor
C	Ball/toe intersection line
D	Toe edge line
E	Ball longitudinal center line
F	Diagonal line
G	Height of ball at back
H	Break point (equator) height
I	Bevel back to this point.

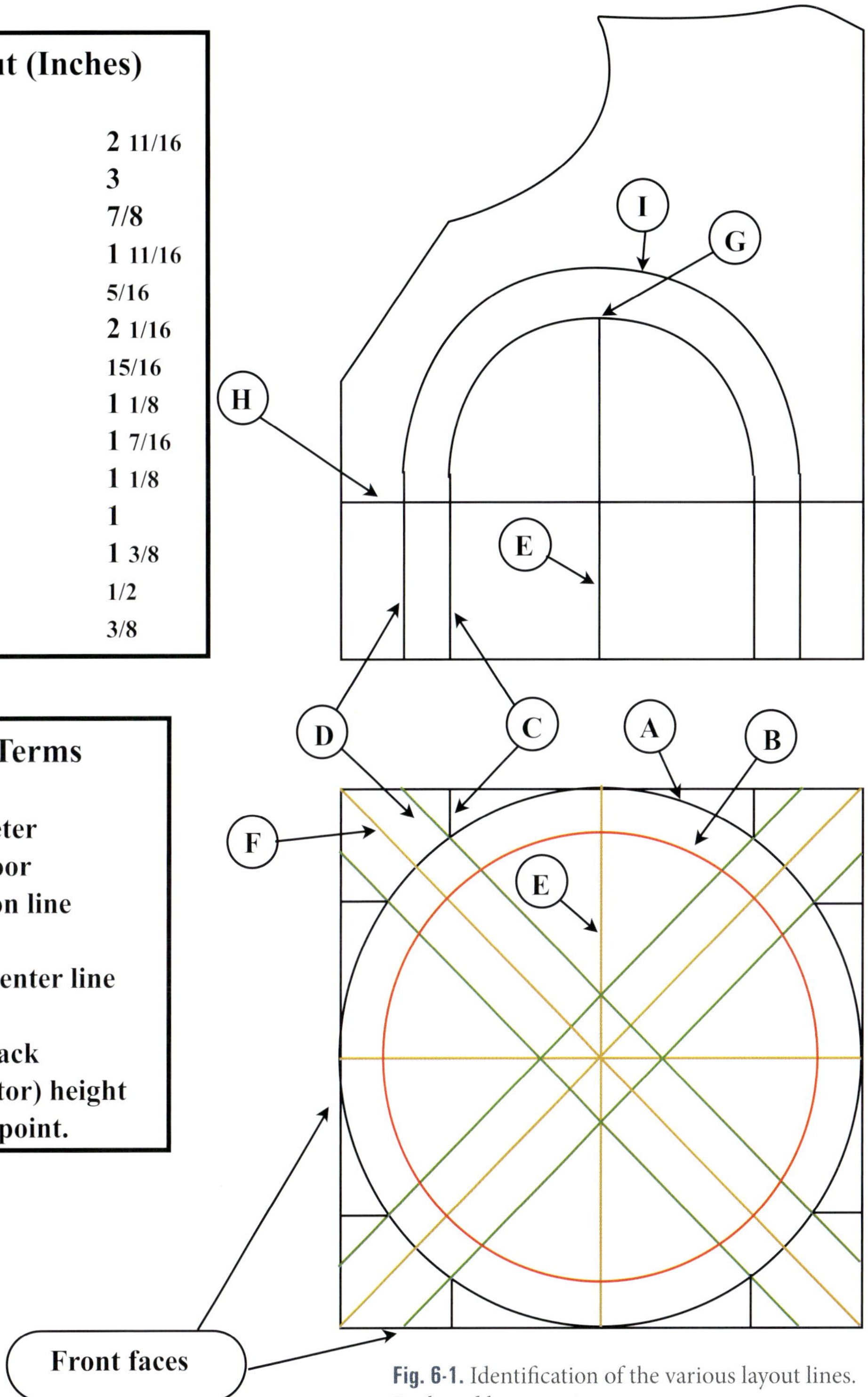

Fig. 6-1. Identification of the various layout lines. Back and bottom views.

The layout starts on the bottom of the blank. Draw in the two diagonal lines connecting opposite corners, and locate the center of the blank. With this center, use a divider to scribe two concentric circles: one with the break point dimension as the diameter and the other with the "diameter at floor" dimension. Use a 0.5 mm mechanical pencil to highlight these circles. This makes them easier to see. I use a divider instead of a compass because I want a line cut into the wood. This will give a much-crisper termination line when I carve to it. **Figure 6-2** shows these lines.

Next, draw two lines parallel to each of the diagonal lines, ¼" on either side of the diagonals (see **figure 6-3**). These lines will place and define the width of the claws and talons. Use a square to draw a line perpendicular to each of the four faces of the blank through the center. These lines will be extended up the faces of the block and will locate the longitudinal center of the four sides of the ball. Now use a square to draw the lines labeled "C" in **figure 6-1**. These lines will be transferred onto the two back faces and are the left and right limits of the ball segment on that face. The layout on the bottom is now complete and is shown in **figure 6-4**. The next step is to transfer some of the lines from the bottom onto the faces of the blank and add a few others.

Use a square to transfer each of the lines from the bottom to the faces of each of the four sides (see **figure 6-5**). Now draw a line parallel to the bottom, ⅞" up from the bottom, on each of the four faces, as shown in **figure 6-6**. This is the horizontal centerline of the ball, which I will call the break point or, in geographical terms, the equator.

On the two back faces, locate the point "G" from **figure 6-1**. This is the height of the ball at the rear. With a compass, draw in a semicircle that goes through point "G" and is tangent to the two limit lines at the break point, as illustrated in **figure 6-1**. **Figure 6-7** shows this on the leg blank. Using the same technique, connect the two outer lines labeled "D" with a semicircle labeled "I," as shown in **figure 6-1**. After these steps are repeated on the other back face, the layout for the back will be complete.

Next, locate the height and depth of the ball along the centerline on a front face. This point is the intersection of three orthogonal planes and is buried in the blank. The object of this discussion is to understand how to locate this point so that you can carve to reveal it. When the foot is carved, this will be the top of the ball in the front, located along the vertical centerline of the ball, and it will be the "ball depth in front" distance back from the front face. This is the most difficult and obscure concept of all the ball-and-claw defining dimensions. You will need to think about this for a while before you fully appreciate how to visualize and locate it.

FIG. 6-4. More layout lines. These will be used to carry the locations up the faces of the foot blank.

FIG. 6-5. Use a small square to carry and draw the lines shown.

FIG. 6-6. The break point lines on a front and back face.

FIG. 6-7. Use a compass to draw the arc as shown. This will determine the size of a rear ball segment.

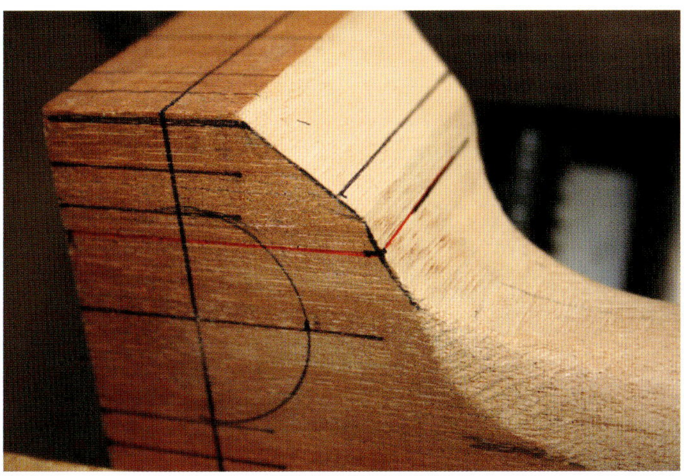

FIG. 6-8. The red line is the "ball depth in front." It is measured from the front foot face.

FIG. 6-9. Capture the distance to the center. This will be used to carry the centerline farther up the leg.

To locate this point, we need to use the square portion of the base and bottom of the foot as references. Using one of the front faces as a reference, draw a vertical line on the adjacent back face the distance that is specified by the "ball depth in front." Use a square referenced from the bottom to draw this line the entire height of the back face. Then use the square to extend this line on the top surface. These are the red lines shown in **figure 6-8**. Next, find the intersection of the red line on top with the extension of the centerline on that face. Use a ruler, depth gauge, or small square to locate this point. **Figure 6-9** shows how to retrieve the centerline distance from one of the back faces, and point "B" in **figure 6-10** shows the distance transferred to the top line.

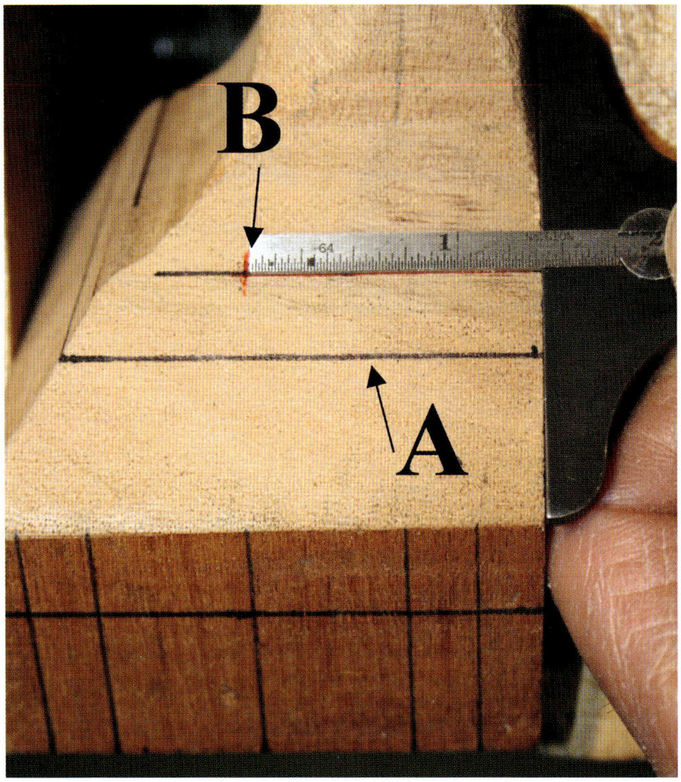

FIG. 6-10. Locate point "B" with the centerline distance measurement.

FIG. 6-11. Use a handsaw to fully separate the side and front toes.

Use similar techniques to draw the line labeled "A" in **figure 6-10**. This will be the height of the ball as seen from the front. Measure from the bottom the distance that is the "ball height in front," and make a mark at this height on a back face. Now use a square to carry this line to the front angled surface. This is the line labeled "A." Repeat this process to locate an analogous point and line on the other front face. As I said earlier, the top of the ball is hidden within the blank at this stage. This hidden point is directly below the point "B" on the horizontal plane denoted by line "A." This completes the layout of the foot. It's now time to extract the ball-and-claw foot from the blank.

This starts with making a few saw cuts that will establish the toes. The front toe and the two side toes are sawed their entire height down to the depth of the break point diameter. Only the bottom half of the back toe can be sawed on each side; otherwise, the back webbing would be impacted. Secure the leg in a clap and use a handsaw to cut on each side of one of the side toes. **Figure 6-11** shows these cuts. The two cuts should be parallel so as not to undercut the toe. Rotate the blank and cut the front and other side toes in the same manner. **Figure 6-12** shows how to saw the back toes. Note that the cut is at an angle and stops at the outer circle on the bottom and the break point line on the face. This sawing operation is beneficial for two reasons. First, it will make the carving easier because the wood will break away as one carves into the cuts, and second, it is much less likely to damage the toe.

The strategy for carving the foot is to first separate the ball from the toes, then shape the ball, then refine the toes, and finally establish the claws. The ball is formed by four separate segments that the eye connects to give the illusion of a continuous spherical surface. First, work on one of these four segments and then go to the other three in turn. Start with a back one, although it doesn't matter whether you start with the front or the back.

As mentioned, each segment of the ball is part of a sphere that starts as part of a cylinder. The cylinder will be formed first. Since the top of the ball at the back is completely hidden, the first thing to do is establish this top surface. With a #5 12 mm gouge, make a stop cut straight down, following the semicircular arc that was drawn on the back face. This is the arc labeled "G" in **figure 6-1**. **Figure 6-13** shows how to start. With the same #5, bevel back into this stop cut along the entire length of the arc. Using **figure 6-1** as a guide, look at the line formed by the arc "I" and the straight line "D." Also look at the line formed by the arc "G" and the straight line "C." The "G" line represents the stop cut line, and the "I" line represents the line where the bevel cut into the "G" will start. This is the end result of this step, and it will not be made in one big cut, but rather a series of small ones. Iteratively deepen the stop cut and bevel back until the depth reaches that given by the dimension "ball depth in back." I use a depth gauge to measure progress for this, as shown in **figure 6-14**. **Figure 6-15** shows intermediate progress, and **figure 6-16** shows this step complete.

FIG. 6-12. Cut the back at an angle. The cut stops at the outer circle on the bottom and at the break point line on the back faces.

FIG. 6-13. Establish the top of the ball on a back face.

FIG. 6-14. Continue deepening the cut until the "ball depth in back" is reached.

FIG. 6-15. Bevel the back as needed to achieve the desired depth.

FIG. 6-16. The cuts are now deep enough.

The top of the cylinder is done. Now form the circular portion between the toes by rounding over this segment to match the outermost circle on the bottom of the foot. In **figure 6-17**, the red area is to be removed. Feather the bevel cuts made at the top of the arc into the saw cuts made on the sides of the toes. It is important not to cut into the toe surface defined by the saw cut, but rather to blend that surface into the angled one behind the arc. Note that the vertical centerline of this segment will remain high. **Figures 6-18** through **6-22** show this process. Use a flat chisel, as shown, and a gouge to blend the bevel cuts into the toes' sides. I used a ¾" flat bench chisel for this operation. The size is not particularly important, but I feel more comfortable with a slightly bigger one. I also find that I have more control with a flat chisel than I would with a gouge.

FIG. 6-19. Use a flat chisel to create the curved surface defined by the outside circle on the bottom.

FIG. 6-17. Remove the red sections. This will create a section of a right circular cylinder.

FIG. 6-20. Blend the arc from the ball top into the toe delineation line.

FIG. 6-18. Do not impact the saw cut that defines the back toe.

FIG. 6-21. Half of the curved surface is complete.

FIG. 6-22. Complete the other half in a similar manner.

The break point line has been mostly removed. Redraw this line by hand, or with a ruler, as shown in **figure 6-23**. At this point there is a rounded, cylindrical surface with a rounded top. Form the top of the ball by rounding over the top edge down to the depth previously established. I use a ½" flat bench chisel and a #3 20 mm gouge for this operation. The break point line will remain high, and the surface will fall off smoothly toward the top. **Figure 6-24** shows the beginning of this process, **figure 6-25** shows intermediate progress, and **figure 6-26** shows the top half of the ball complete.

FIG. 6-23. Redraw the horizontal centerline.

FIG. 6-24. Round over the top portion of the cylinder down to the depth line.

FIG. 6-25. The top of the ball is approximated.

FIG. 6-26. Smooth the surface with a small file by blending the facets created by the chisel cuts.

FIG. 6-27. Extend the toe surface at the bottom by resting the flat chisel back on the toe side surface.

Now work on the bottom half of the ball. Because this portion of the cylinder is still connected to the toes, I will have to separate them as I go. Start with a flat chisel resting on the saw cut surface of one of the adjacent toes, and make a cut into the cylinder parallel to the toe side surface. It is important that the chisel back be flat against the toe side. This will ensure that the cut is going in the correct direction. It is easy to accidentally cut into the toe surface that will translate into undercut toes, which is undesirable. **Figure 6-27** shows registering the back of the flat chisel against the toe side and the direction of the cut. Note that this cut will follow the line "D" on the bottom (see **figure 6-1**). After making the flat chisel cut, carve off the bottom edge into this cut. **Figure 6-28** shows this technique and early progress. Repeat these cuts down to the inner circle, as viewed from the bottom. Analogous to the top half, keep the break point line high, and round down continually to the inner circle along the entire arc length between the two toes. Use the technique described above to separate the ball from the second toe. **Figure 6-29** shows intermediate progress, and **figure 6-30** shows this step complete. This is the point where using the divider to score the inner circle on the bottom makes a difference. It is easier and more exact to get a nice, crisp line when carving to a scored line than to a pencil line. At this point, one-quarter of the ball has been formed. It is probably a little rough, with many facets left from using the flat chisel. These will be removed with a file and sandpaper.

FIG. 6-28. Carve down to the inside circle.

FIG. 6-29. The bottom of the ball is approximated.

FIG. 6-30. Smooth the bottom portion with a small file. Note that the surface falls off above and below the break point line.

FIG. 6-31. Continue to blend the top and bottom sections with a small file.

FIG. 6-32. Use sandpaper to further smooth the surface.

FIG. 6-33. One back section of the ball is complete.

Now that the first segment of the ball has been carved, clean up the surface with a small half-round file. The goal here is to smooth this segment to be part of a sphere. With the flat portion of the file, smooth the surface of the ball in all directions while continually altering the angle of the file. Vary the pressure depending on the surface texture and contour. As a final smoothing operation, take a small bit of 120-grit sandpaper and, with your finger as support, move over the entire surface of the ball until it is smooth, continuous, and uniform. **Figures 6-31**, **6-32**, and **6-33** show how to perform these steps. Repeat these operations on the other back face. **Figure 6-34** shows both of the back faces of the ball complete.

Now work on one of the front sections of the ball. The front sections are a little less work because the top of the ball is more exposed and the toes were completely separated from the ball with the saw cuts. Start by rounding the section between the toes to conform to the outer circle as drawn on the bottom of the foot. **Figure 6-35** shows early progress, and **figure 6-36** shows this complete. As with the back surfaces, I use a ½" flat chisel.

The next step is to uncover the hidden point that I mentioned earlier. This is the top of the ball, some distance into the blank. If the "ball height in front" horizontal line has been carved away, redraw it. Also sketch in a curved line that connects the inside surfaces of the toes and passes through the depth point. In addition, redraw the break point line if needed. **Figure 6-37** shows these lines.

FIG. 6-34. Complete the other back section, using the same techniques.

FIG. 6-35. Begin to define a front ball section, using a flat chisel. This is easier because the top is open.

FIG. 6-36. A front cylindrical section is complete.

FIG. 6-37. Redraw the break point line on the front cylindrical section.

FIG. 6-38. Use a flat chisel to create a horizontal surface that will establish the top of the ball.

FIG. 6-39. Use a #9 15 mm gouge to carve to the lines above the horizontal top surface.

Use a flat chisel to set in parallel to the bottom surface along the ball height line. Be careful that the corners of the chisel do not dig into the toe side surfaces. If they do, the marks they make can be difficult, if not impossible, to remove. You can get pretty aggressive in the middle of the ball, though. **Figure 6-38** shows what I mean. Now use a #9 15 mm gouge and remove material between the toes down to the ball height line. **Figure 6-39** shows the first couple of cuts. The goal is to carve to the curved line sketched in earlier, and connect it to the inside surfaces of the toes down to the ball height line. A #7 16 mm gouge gives a good transition curve when blending into the toe side surfaces. **Figure 6-40** shows intermediate progress, and **figure 6-41** shows the operation complete. At this point there should be a smooth, continuous surface connecting the inside faces of the toes and a flat horizontal ledge in between.

FIG. 6-40. Use a #7 16 mm gouge to extend the #9 surface just created.

FIG. 6-41. The horizontal plane that is on top of the ball is complete.

FIG. 6-42. Use a flat chisel to connect the side wall of the toe with the curved surface.

FIG. 6-43. By connecting the toe surfaces, the ball becomes isolated and established and the toes become more fully defined.

FIG. 6-44. Round over the top, keeping the the break point line. Form a spherical section between the two toe walls and the connecting curved wall.

This is now a section of a circular cylinder with an angled corner. Now covert this modified cylinder into a spherical section. Use a flat chisel, as shown in **figure 6-42**, to establish more of the toe side surfaces. The direction of the chisel should be such that its flat back connects the curved section just completed with the toe sides from the saw cuts. Now use the same flat chisel to remove the material on the ball side immediately next to the toe. This will start to form the top of the ball while also creating the sides of the toes. **Figure 6-43** shows early progress. Iteratively repeat these steps to increase the toe height and round the top of the ball, using the ball height and toe sides as constraints. **Figure 6-44** shows late progress. The goal is to create a smooth, uniform, spherical section between the toe walls. Use a flat chisel and a #3 20 mm gouge to form the spherical surface. **Figure 6-45** shows the top section complete. Shape the bottom half of the ball, using the same techniques as on the back section. Clean up the remaining facets with a small file and sandpaper as before. **Figure 6-46** shows the completed section. Repeat this process for the other front face. **Figure 6-47** shows the front two sections complete.

FIG. 6-45. Smooth the facets with a small file and sandpaper.

FIG. 6-46. Carve and smooth the bottom portion of the ball segment.

FIG. 6-47. Carve the other front ball section. Your eye should see one spherical surface with the toes sitting on top.

On a typical Philadelphia ball-and-claw foot, the ball is slightly higher in front than in back. If things have gone well, your eye should be able to sense a continuous spherical surface when sighting two sections across a toe. **Figure 6-48** shows this continuous surface.

It is now time to work on the toes. The front and back toes are pretty straightforward, and there is one extra step to the side toes. Work on the back toe first. The webbing between the back toe and the adjacent side toes needs to be excavated and blended. This will further define each toe so that detail can be added. Using a #7 16 mm or a #5 12 mm gouge, gently blend the ankle into the top of the ball. The depth at the ball should not be increased, so feather the cuts such that no material is removed right at the top of the ball. As you feather the web up the ankle, also extend the blending to include the side surfaces of the toes. It is somewhat of a judgment call as to how far up the ankle to take this, but a generous 2" or so is typical. **Figure 6-49** shows intermediate progress, and **figure 6-50** shows the result of this operation. Complete this step on both sides of the back toe before detailing it. **Figure 6-51** shows both sides of the back toe complete.

FIG. 6-48. The spherical surface looks connected across the toe.

FIG. 6-49. On one of the back faces, use a #5 12 mm gouge to connect the side and back toes.

FIG. 6-50. The surface connecting the side and back toe starts a few inches up in the ankle. Note how this surface connects to the ball perimeter.

FIG. 6-51. Repeat the same operation on the other side of the back toe. Note how the back toe blank is extended up the ankle.

FIG. 6-52. Remove the triangle above the red line as the first step in refining the toe.

FIG. 6-53. Use a #49 rasp to remove the triangle.

FIG. 6-54. The triangle is removed and the toe blank is ready for more refinement.

FIG. 6-55. Round over the top of the toe blank.

Notice that each toe is in one corner of the original square. Thus, there is a sharp corner running down its center. This needs to be removed. When viewed from the bottom, visualize the triangle formed by the corner. Remove this triangle by using the #49 rasp. **Figure 6-52** shows the triangle. **Figure 6-53** shows intermediate progress, and **figure 6-54** shows it removed. What remains is a rectangular tube; this needs to be turned into a semicircular tube. I use a ½" flat chisel for most of this and clean up the facets with a file. **Figure 6-55** shows a partially formed tube, and **figure 6-56** shows it complete.

FIG. 6-56. Use a file to smooth the toe surface and strive for a symmetrical shape.

FIG. 6-57. The back toe blank is sufficiently rounded. Note how it flows into the surrounding surfaces.

FIG. 6-58. The claw height is ⅜". Establish this height with a flat chisel.

Make a mark ⅜" up from the foot bottom on the back circular tube. This is the "claw height" dimension. Carry this line around the perimeter of the tube, as shown in **figure 6-57**. With a flat chisel and the bevel side facing the bottom of the foot, score along the perimeter line just drawn. **Figure 6-58** shows this cut. From the bottom side of this stop cut, pare away the tube into it along the entire length of the cut. A couple of light passes should give a suitable depth. **Figure 6-59** shows this step. This lower segment will become the claw.

The claw will be a rounded, narrow, convex, curved ramp from the top of the tube down to the inner circle on the bottom of the foot. It will be narrower away from the ball and gradually get wider at the ball surface. **Figure 6-60** shows the completed claw from two different angles on different toes. The point here is to visualize the completed claw.

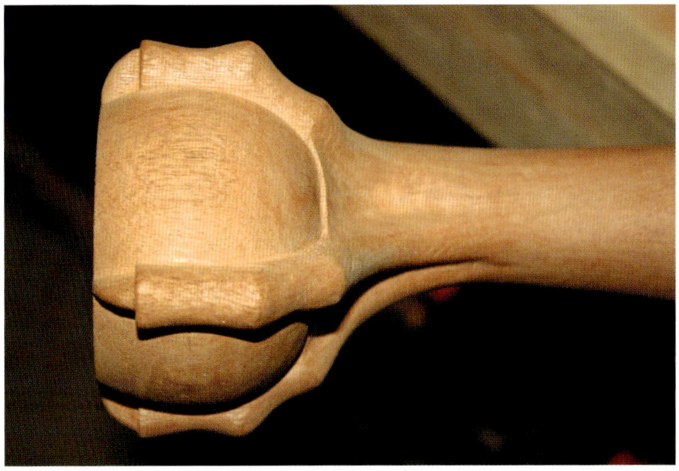

FIG. 6-60. A completed foot. Note the claw shape; it is curved from top to bottom and narrow.

FIG. 6-59. Lower the claw segment from the toe segment above it. Bevel into the cut made by the flat chisel.

FIG. 6-61. Use a flat chisel to approximate a convex ramp from the top of the claw down to the ball.

Use a ½" flat chisel to create a faceted, convex ramp. Draw a centerline on the ramp to help remove material equally from each side. With the same flat chisel, taper the corners as shown in **figure 6-61**. The goal is to create a faceted surface that is narrower away from the ball and wider at the claw/toe boundary while coming to a point at the ball surface at the bottom face. **Figure 6-62** shows late progress. Slightly round over the spine of the claw, using the chisel as a scraper. Blend the rounded spine into the sides with a file, sandpaper, or both. **Figure 6-63** shows a profile view of the completed claw.

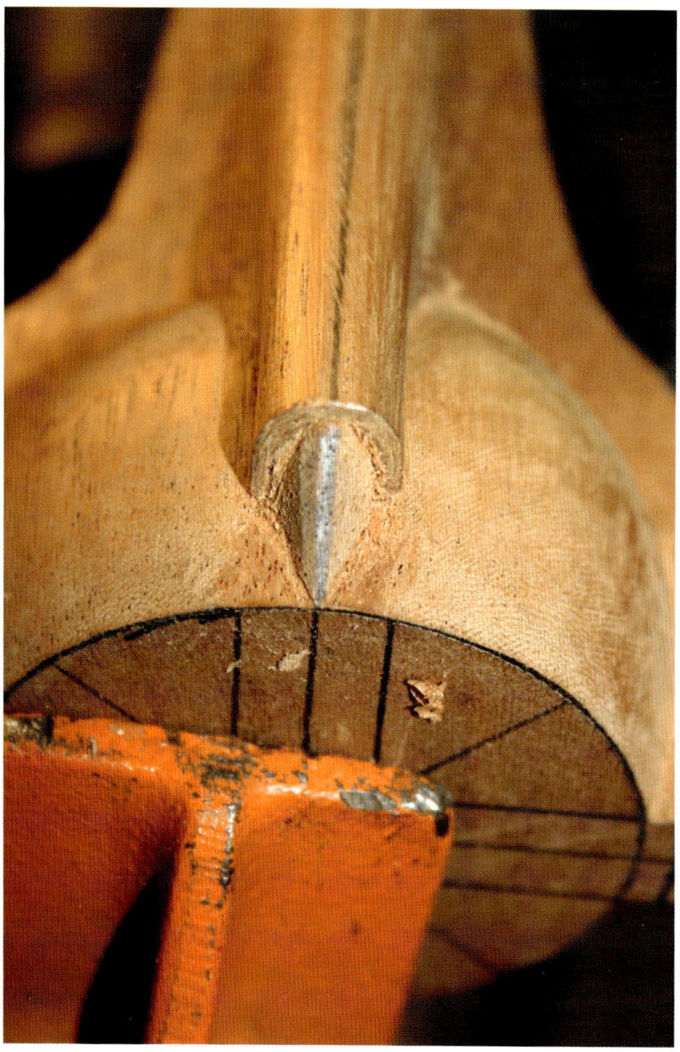

FIG. 6-62. Narrow the claw. The base is wider than the top.

FIG. 6-63. The convex, narrow claw is complete.

FIG. 6-64. Use a #49 rasp to isolate the single back toe segment.

Now make a mark on the back tube, using the dimension "height of knuckle in back." This is measured from the top of the claw. With the round side of the #49 rasp, create a semicircular depression centered just above the mark just made. Go to a depth of about ⅛" to start. **Figure 6-64** shows this cut. With a #5 12 mm gouge, narrow the tube on each side, centered on the rasp cut. This is going to thin out the ankle and give it some tension. **Figure 6-65** shows the technique, and **figure 6-66** shows the results. Using a small file, round over the ridges and blend and smooth all the facets together. These don't have to be perfect at this point because they will get touched up later (see **figure 6-67** for progress).

FIG. 6-67. Use a small file to round over the ridges and blend the toe surfaces into the surrounding ones.

FIG. 6-65. Use a #5 12 mm gouge to narrow the portion above the toe segment. Narrow it symmetrically along the vertical centerline.

FIG. 6-68. Refine the toe segment immediately above the claw in a similar manner.

FIG. 6-66. The portion above the toe segment is narrowed and ready for more refinement.

FIG. 6-69. Both sides of the toe segment have been narrowed.

The toe segment just above the claw will be shaped in a similar manner. With a #49 rasp, make a slight depression along the spine of the toe, as shown in **figure 6-68**. Don't make this too deep or the segment won't look right. Narrow the sides with the #5 12 mm gouge as before. **Figure 6-69** shows this step. File and sand the ridges to form a uniform and smooth surface. **Figure 6-70** shows the finished toe segment.

Before work can begin on the remaining toes, form the web between them. The web between the front toe and one of the side toes will be formed by scooping out between them and leaving a slight step down to the ball. This step is on the order of 1/16" but is measured by eye. Draw guide lines (see **figure 6-71**) to define the web. Use a #9 13 mm gouge to scoop out the material between the toes. Taper the cut to feather out at the top of the guide line. **Figure 6-72** shows the technique. The goal is to form steep ridgelines that will establish and extend the toes up into the ankle. **Figure 6-73** shows significant progress in forming the web. As the web is nearing completion, use a smaller #9 to form a vertical wall between the toe and the web. This will give a nice definition to each toe and show tension when complete. **Figure 6-74** shows the technique, and **figure 6-75** shows the web complete. I want the web to be a smooth surface between the toes, so use flatter gouges to smooth the ridges left by the #9s. When the carving is done, there are many little facets on the surface. I clean these up with radiused scrapers of varying widths. Complete the web on the other side before moving to the front toe.

FIG. 6-70. Use a file to round the ridges and then use sandpaper with your finger as backing to further smooth each segment of the toe.

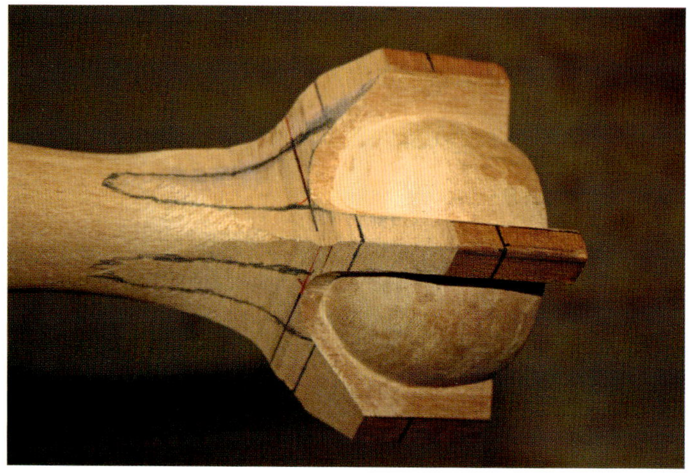

FIG. 6-71. Draw the lines as shown. These lines delineate and connect the side toes to the front one. These will be connected with a web.

FIG. 6-72. Start to establish the web. Use a #9 13 mm gouge as shown. Leave 1/16" above the ball surface.

FIG. 6-73. The connecting web surface is roughed out.

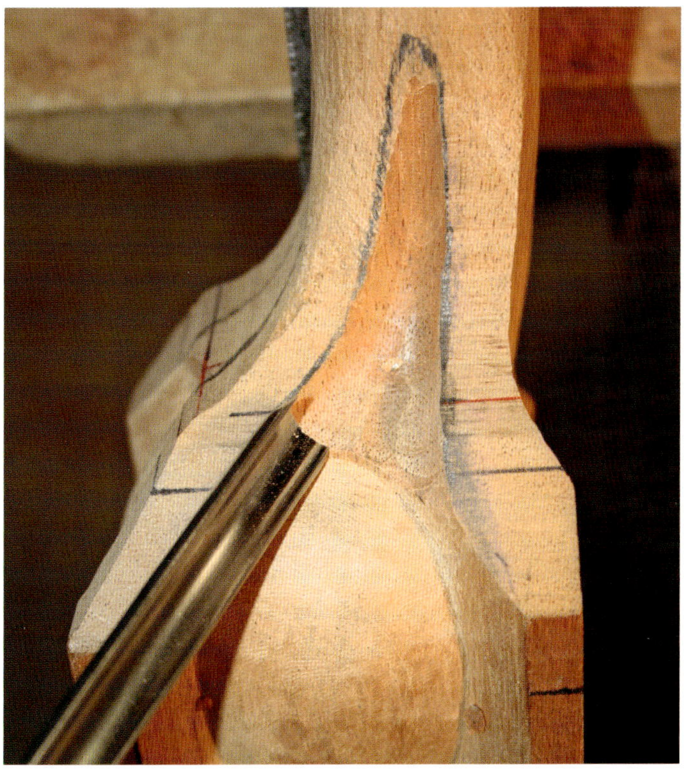

FIG. 6-74. The web surface nearest the middle toe should have a vertical wall toward the top of the toe. Use a #9 7 mm gouge to get a tighter transition between the toe wall and the bottom.

FIG. 6-75. The toe wall is vertical for a bit and then connects to the bottom of the web with a tight, curved surface.

Now that the webs are complete, it is time to work on the front toe. The same techniques are used to form the front toe as were used to form the back one, with the exception that there are more segments. However, each segment is shaped and refined the same way. Remove the triangular ridge shown in **figure 6-76**, using the #49 rasp, to form the rectangular tube shown in **figure 6-77**. Round over the edges to form a semicircular tube, as seen in **figure 6-78**. Form the claw in the same manner as in the back. **Figure 6-79** shows this complete. Mark the "first knuckle height" and the "second knuckle height" around the perimeter of the tube. These numbers will probably not align with the angles from the bandsaw. **Figure 6-80** shows this situation. Place the lines as described, and then, with a flat chisel, connect the knuckle lines with a straight segment. **Figure 6-81** shows this operation. Round over the edges to reestablish the semicircular tube. **Figure 6-82** shows the front toe reshaped with the proper knuckle heights and rounded as needed.

Starting from the bottom, work on one segment at a time. With the round face of a #49 rasp, make a slight concave depression centered in the toe segment, as shown in **figure 6-83**. With the #5 12 mm gouge, thin out both sides of the segment as was done on the back toe. **Figure 6-84** shows the results. Using the small half-round file, round over the ridges, smooth, and blend the surfaces as before. See **figure 6-85** for results. Repeat this process on the next segment up the toe. Pay particular attention to the ridgeline between two segments. Strive for a crisp and straight line. This is a sign of attention to detail and fine craftsmanship. **Figure 6-86** shows two segments complete. Finally, there is the transition segment into the ankle. This is just rounded and does not have the depression or the thinning cuts. **Figure 6-87** shows the completed front toe.

FIG. 6-77. When the top of the toe is flat, draw a centerline.

FIG. 6-78. Round over the top to form a tube.

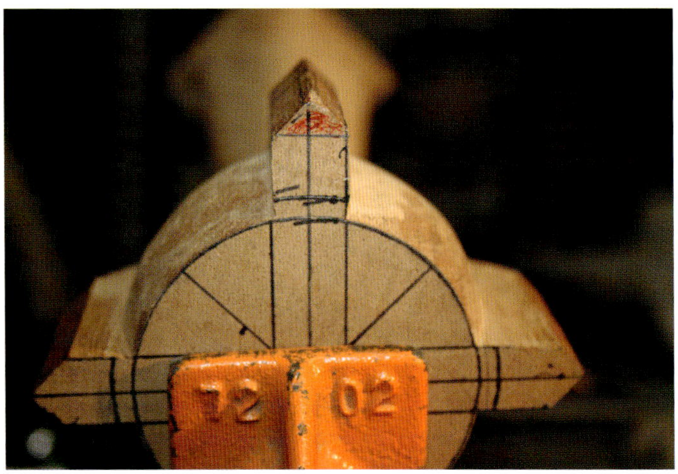

FIG. 6-76. Remove the red triangle on the front toe.

FIG. 6-79. Carve the claw on the front toe.

FIG. 6-80. Mark the front toe's first knuckle height.

FIG. 6-81. From the first knuckle height, create another tubular segment.

FIG. 6-82. Mark the second knuckle height and blend the remainder into the toe segment that runs up the ankle.

FIG. 6-83. Refine each toe segment independently. Scoop on top with a #49 rasp.

FIG. 6-84. Narrow the sides with a #5 12 mm gouge.

FIG. 6-85. Use a file or a flat chisel (or both) to smooth the toe segment.

FIG. 6-86. The bottom two segments of the front toe are complete. Note the crisp intersection line.

The side toes are all that is left to complete the ball-and-claw foot. The only difference in forming a side toe is one cut with the rasp in the second segment that will transition the toe into the ankle. Once that is done, placing the claw and segments and refining them is the same as on the front toe. **Figure 6-88** shows the side toe before being reshaped. With the #49 rasp, remove the red-shaded area to end up with the result shown in **figure 6-89**. Now proceed as before. **Figure 6-90** shows a completed side toe. **Figures 6-91**, **6-92**, and **6-93** show the completed foot from a few different angles.

FIG. 6-87. The front toe is complete. Note how the toe blends into the ankle.

FIG. 6-88. Remove the red section with a #49 rasp. Note that this goes only to the centerline of the toe segment.

This foot is not a simple shape to develop, and it will take some study and practice to get comfortable with the techniques and method. If your expectation is that you will read this description once and then be able to carve a perfect foot, you will be disappointed. However, if you study the method and work to understand it, then have patience and practice the techniques, you will end up with increasingly pleasing results. I have been carving this style of foot with this method for twenty years, and I still find ways to perfect my technique. I love this motif, and I look forward to carving it every chance I get.

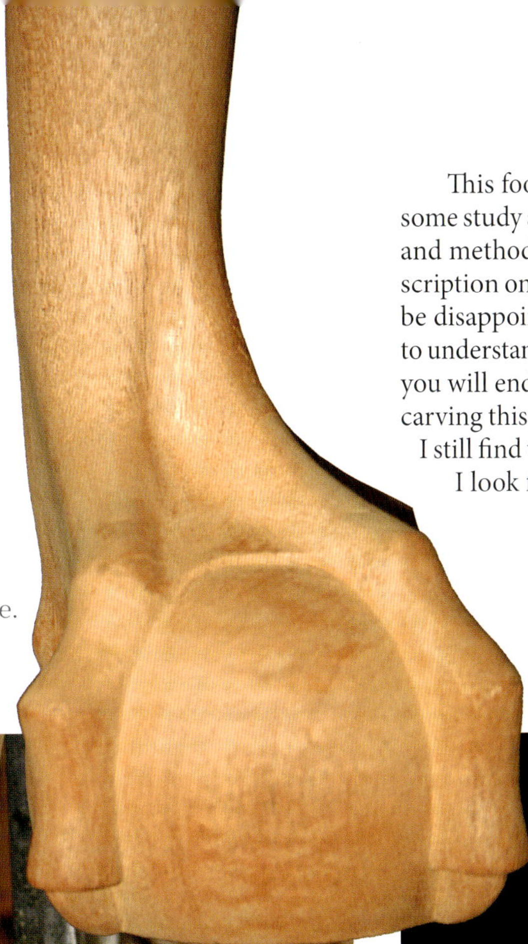

FIG. 6-90. A completed side toe.

FIG. 6-89. The side toe after removal of the red section. Note the rasp marks and how the cut flows into the leg ankle.

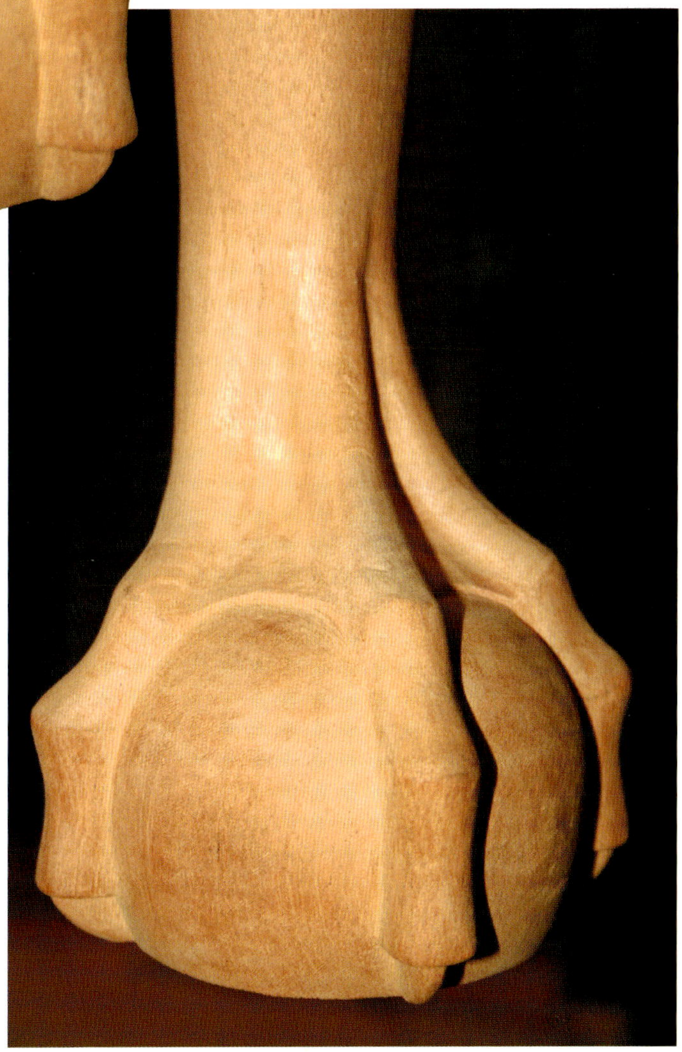

FIG. 6-91. Another view of the completed foot.

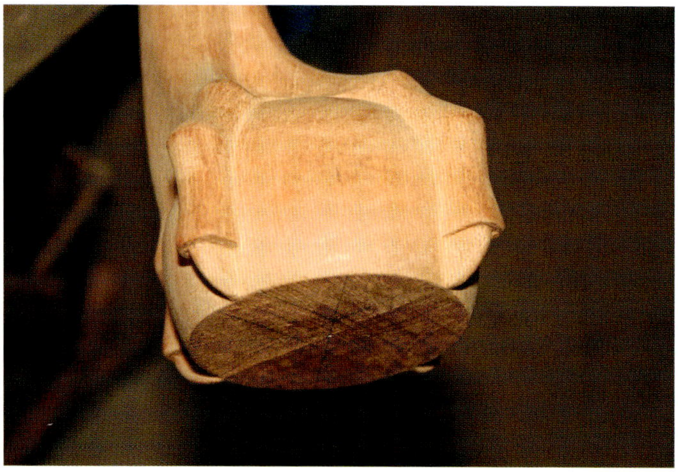

FIG. 6-92. When the foot is complete, look at it from many angles, searching for any irregularities.

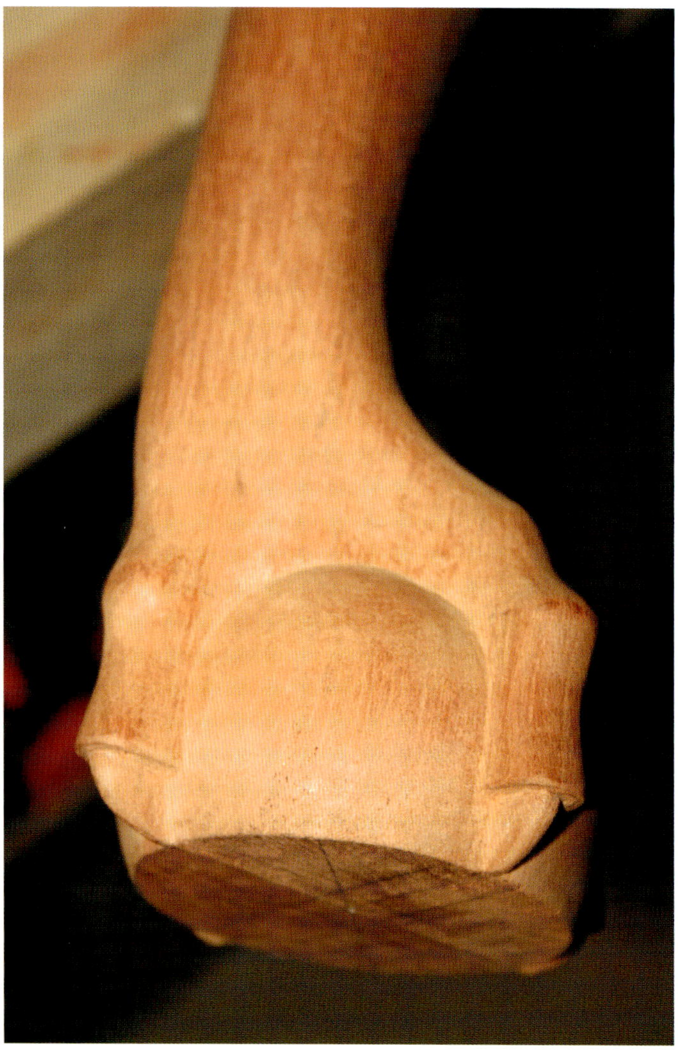

FIG. 6-93. The more the surfaces integrate gracefully, the more convincing that this is really a claw gripping a ball.

Knee Carving

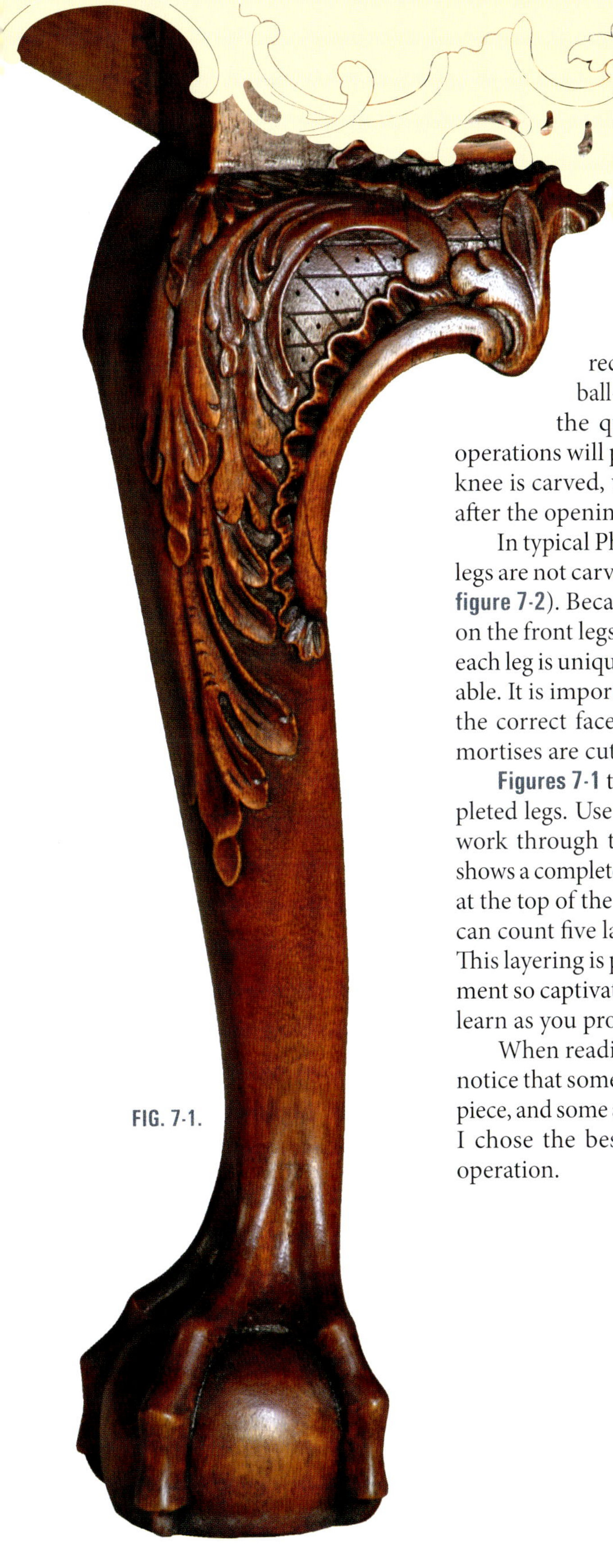

FIG. 7-1.

This chapter will describe how to add the knee carving to the legs. I would recommend carving the knee after the ball-and-claw foot is done, but before cutting the quarter-column opening. This order of operations will prevent excess handling of the leg after the knee is carved, while not putting too much pressure on it after the opening is removed.

In typical Philadelphia style, the back faces of the back legs are not carved, and they do not have a knee block (see **figure 7-2**). Because of this, and the fact that the mortises on the front legs are different on the front and side faces, each leg is unique. That is, none of them are interchangeable. It is important to keep them oriented properly so the correct face is carved on the back ones, and the mortises are cut appropriately on the front ones.

Figures 7-1 to **7-3** show various views of the completed legs. Use these pictures as a reference as you work through the knee-carving details. **Figure 7-3** shows a completed front leg. Starting from the button at the top of the knee at the corner of the post, one can count five layers to get to the leg background. This layering is part of what makes this embellishment so captivating, and it is part of what you will learn as you proceed through this chapter.

When reading through this chapter, you will notice that some of the images are of a mahogany piece, and some are of a poplar one. This is because I chose the best image to show the intended operation.

FIG. 7-2.

FIG. 7-3. A complete front leg. There are five layers from the button to the leg background.

Knee Carving: Adding the Knee Block

It is debatable whether it is better to attach the knee blocks to the legs before or after assembly. There are merits to each, and I have done it both ways. On balance, I think it is better to attach them before on a piece of this size or larger, because the case gets difficult to handle and maneuver. In addition, it is much easier to shape the knee block and blend it to the leg before assembly. The downside is that there is a chance of a gap between the knee block and its rail, and it is possible to break the knee block off during repeated handling and clamping. In theory there shouldn't be a gap, but in practice there is always a chance that things go wrong during glue-up. On this piece I attached the knee blocks before assembly. I did break one off, but it was quite easy to reglue it and touch up the carvings.

All the full scale templates for the knee carvings and knee blocks are on the "Leg Templates" sheet in the insert packet. They are also presented in reduced size in **figure A1-5**.

First attach the knee blocks. The blank for a knee block is pretty small, so it can usually be taken from scraps from other parts. In addition, the thickness can vary depending on stock availability. The only requirement on thickness is that it be flush with the leg and fit underneath the front skirt or side panel. Usually 1½" is thick enough, but it can be thicker if that is the available stock. My point is this: use what is available, as long as the minimum requirements are met. In this case, a knee block blank will be 2½" wide × 2⅛" high × 1½" thick. The grain should run in the vertical direction.

Make a template from the pattern that is labeled "Knee Block Blank." Transfer the pattern to the blank with the proper grain orientation. **Figure 7-4** shows how I oriented two knee block blanks on one piece of scrap stock. I'm not necessarily recommending that you do it this way, but I do not like wasting mahogany, so I try to use every scrap that I can. The extra piece on the left side was attached so that the top face would be parallel to the table. This was needed because the face on the table was not flat and would not have gone through the bandsaw well unless supported. **Figure 7-5** shows that the top edge of the blank needs to be flat. This is the edge that butts underneath the rail.

Use a bandsaw to cut along the bottom profile, as shown in **figure 7-6. Figure 7-7** shows a knee block ready to be attached to the leg. The pencil line in this figure is the profile of the leg at the top of the knee. Remove most of the extra before attaching it to the leg, but make sure to stay proud of the line. The proud portion will be flushed with the leg when the glue is dry. **Figure 7-8** shows the front view of the bandsawn knee block blank.

FIG. 7-4. A creative way to get two knee blocks from scrap. The extra piece on the left is to keep the top horizontal.

FIG. 7-7. The knee profile drawn on the knee block blank.

FIG. 7-5. Make sure the blank will be square to the bandsaw blade.

FIG. 7-8. The knee block front view. This is oriented so that it fits on the right side of a leg.

FIG. 7-6. Use a bandsaw to cut the bottom profile of the knee block.

FIG. 7-9. Use a square to flush the top of the knee block with the bottom of the mortise. When gluing the knee block, make sure its top is aligned with the square.

The knee block needs to be attached to the leg so that the top edge is flush with the location of the bottom edge of the rail. In this project, this line is the bottom of the mortise of whatever leg face is being used. Clamp a square to the leg post (see **figure 7-9**). The square is flush with the bottom of the mortise and at 90° to the post. It will provide a fence to which the knee block top edge can rest while it is being glued. It will be at a right angle to the post, which is the correct position.

With the square clamped in place, apply hot hide glue to both joining surfaces. With the two surfaces touching, move the knee block in small circles to get the "death grip" and butt the top edge flush to the square. At this point just let it alone until the glue is dry. There is no need to clamp. If you are using some other glue, clamp pressure might be needed.

Figure 7-10 shows the leg and knee block after the glue has dried. Use a large, flat chisel to make one straight surface between the two pieces. **Figure 7-11** shows the technique, and **figure 7-12** shows how to check for a straight surface.

Now blend the bottom edge of the knee block into the back face of the leg. Use a #49 rasp and a file for this operation. **Figure 7-13** shows the blending of the knee block and the leg. Strive for a pleasing, continuous curve between the two as viewed from the front. At the same time, clean up bandsaw marks on the knee block. **Figure 7-14** shows the smoothed-out bottom edge of the knee block.

FIG. 7-11. Use a large, flat chisel to blend the knee block and leg surfaces.

FIG. 7-12. The knee and knee block surfaces are properly aligned.

FIG. 7-10. The knee block is now glued to the leg.

FIG. 7-13. Use a #49 rasp and file to blend the underside of the knee block and leg.

FIG. 7-14. Use a small file to remove the bandsaw marks.

FIG. 7-15. Draw a centerline down the length of the leg. Sighting at a low angle helps see any deviations off-center.

Knee Carving: Transferring and Drawing the Pattern

Transferring a carving pattern to a cabriole knee can be more art than science, but by engineering the art a little, this becomes a much-easier process. The templates provide the science, but the art is transferring the flat patterns to the curved knee.

By keeping a few general ideas in mind throughout this process, it will help get through the more difficult portions. One, use the template as a guide, not an absolute. Deviations from the template are inevitable, so become okay with that. Two, it is more important that the drawing on the leg looks good than that it match the pattern in every detail. Three, keep the various elements in the proper spatial relationship. If a leaf has to be shortened or lengthened to place its tip in a good position, that is okay. Finally, remember that even though this is a reproduction, it will not be an exact match; that is to be expected. If your reproduction looks good in its own right, it will be a success.

Another important thing to mention is that it is very helpful, if not mandatory, to have pictures of the finished object. The pictures are the road map that will help with making decisions as the pattern is transferred to the leg blank. If I did not have pictures of this particular object, I would have had no way to create the templates and no guidance on how they were positioned on the blank. So, without the pictures, I would not have been able to carve this knee.

Because this pattern is sufficiently complicated, I used three separate templates to achieve the final drawing: one is for the side and the other two are for the front. The templates will be used to keep individual elements in their proper relative positions and to get close to the final shapes. Then, individual elements will be connected with freehand sketching.

Getting this detailed carving pattern drawn on a cabriole leg is an iterative process and a learned skill. That is, the templates will be used multiple times to get different elements each time. In addition, the templates will need to be moved around slightly to get some elements in the proper position. It is not possible to draw the entire side pattern with one placement, because of the severely curved surface of the leg. The overall strategy is to place anchor elements in the proper places and then connect them with pleasing freehand curves. Among the anchor elements are leaf tips at a known location; for example, the distance off the ground of the lowest leaf. Or where the ruffle goes relative to the side of the leg. Or the distance between mirrored elements from the leg's vertical centerline.

First, draw a vertical centerline on the leg front (see **figure 7-15**). This line starts at the post corner at the top and will run down the center of the leg to the ankle. Sight down the leg at a low angle to locate a few center points and then connect these by hand, drawing small segments from the top and bottom and meeting in the middle. Sighting at a low angle makes it easier for the eye to see any deviations from the center. If the line does not look centered from the low-angle view, erase the section that is off and try again.

FIG. 7-16. This is the carving template for the side of the leg. Note that leaf tips "A" and "B" align with those on the front template.

Make a template from the "Knee-Side-Carving Template" from the insert pages and shown in figure A1-5. **Figure 7-16** shows my side template, and **figure 7-17** shows one of my front ones. The two leaf tips labeled "A" and "B" are the same elements in both templates. I make my templates from box board and cut these detailed ones with carving tools for more-accurate shapes.

Next, make three tick marks on the centerline, as shown in **figure 7-18**. The top one is about 2" down from the post corner and is the "V" of the template from **figure 7-17**. The middle one is about 4" down from the post and is the bottom tip of the template from **figure 7-17**. The bottom one is 7" up from the floor and is the tip of the lowest leaf from **figure 7-16**.

Use the template from **figure 7-17** and place the "V" on the upper tick mark, as shown in **figure 7-19**. Trace around the bottom perimeter and a little bit of the "V," as shown in **figure 7-20**.

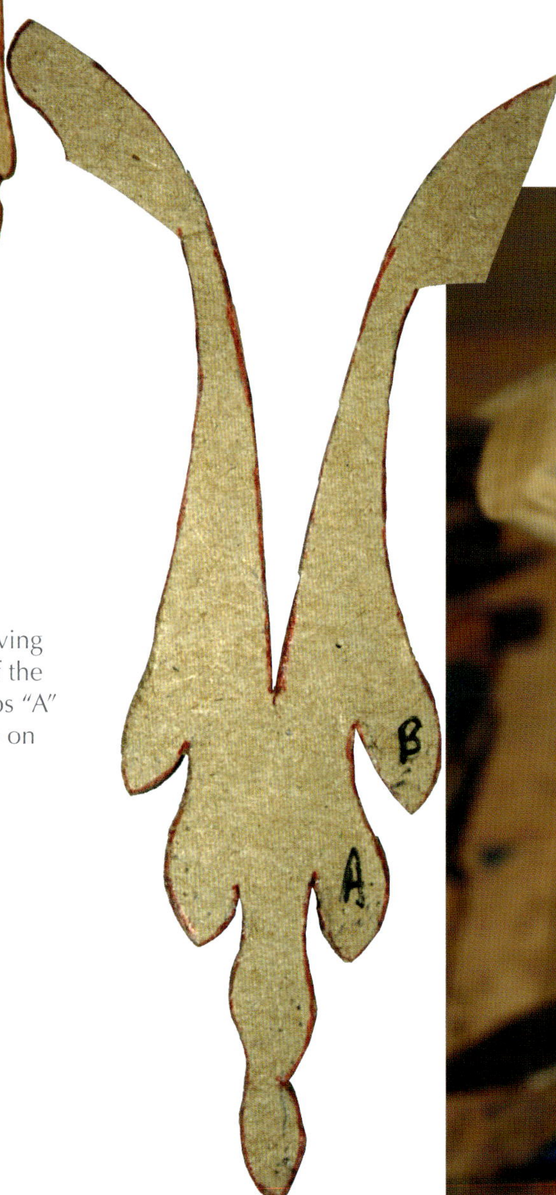

FIG. 7-17. One of two carving templates for the front of the leg. Note that the leaf tips "A" and "B" align with those on the side template.

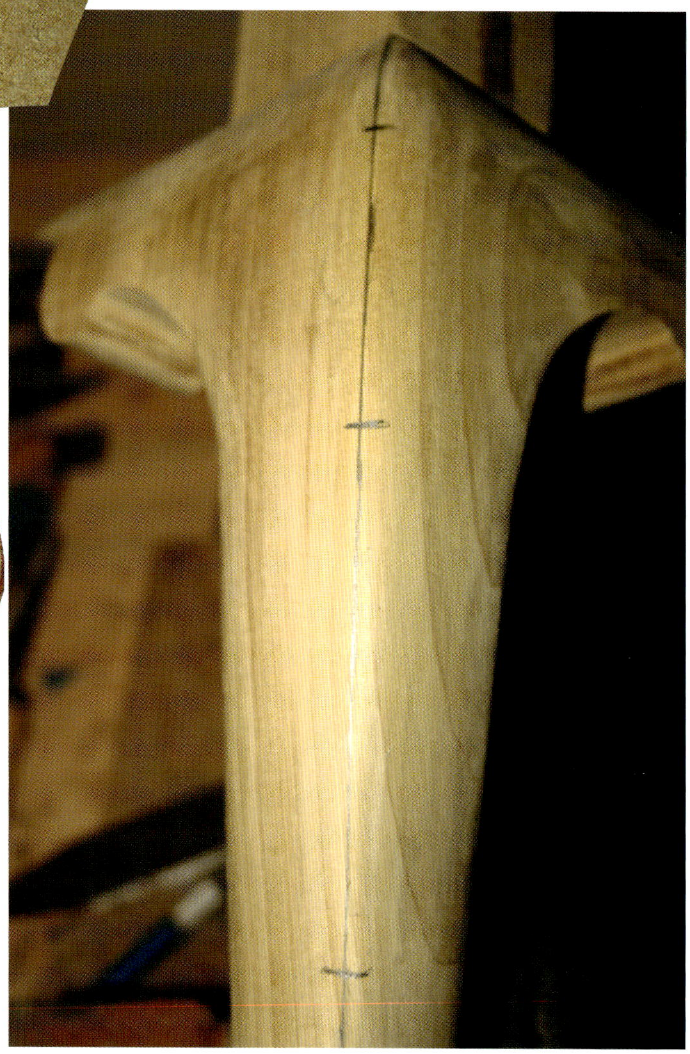

FIG. 7-18. The three tick marks are the vertex of the "V," the lower tip of the front template, and the lower tip of the side template, moving from top to bottom.

Next, use the template from **figure 7-16** and position it as shown in **figure 7-21**. Trace the portion as shown in **figure 7-22**. Use the palm of your hand as a pivot and sweep a smooth arc to connect the top of the "V" with the line of the "button" element (see **figure 7-23**). **Figure 7-24** shows the technique. As part of this operation, also complete the button from **figure 7-22** to **figure 7-23**.

FIG. 7-19. Align the front template, using the top two tick marks.

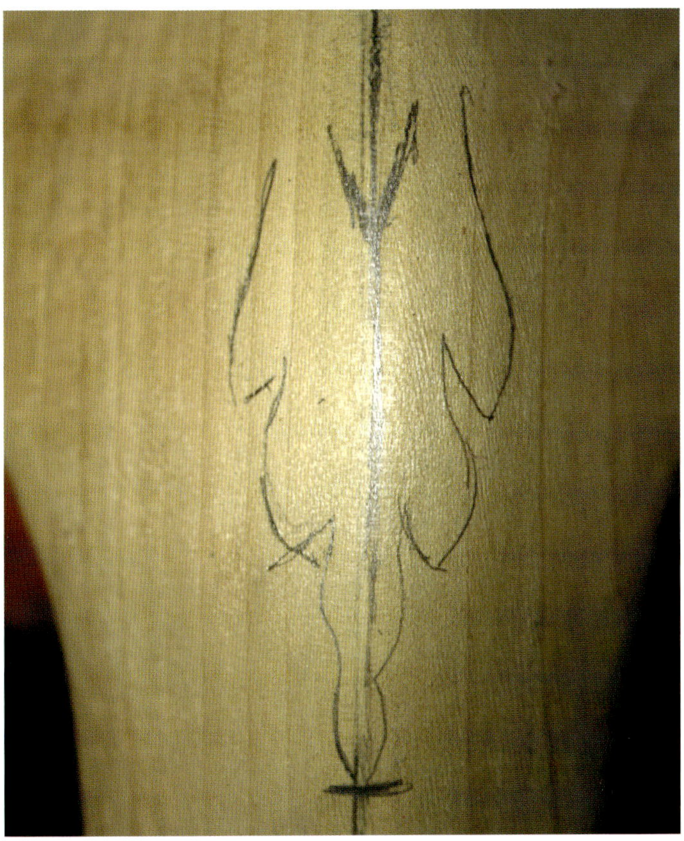

FIG. 7-20. Trace the perimeter of the front template to the leg blank.

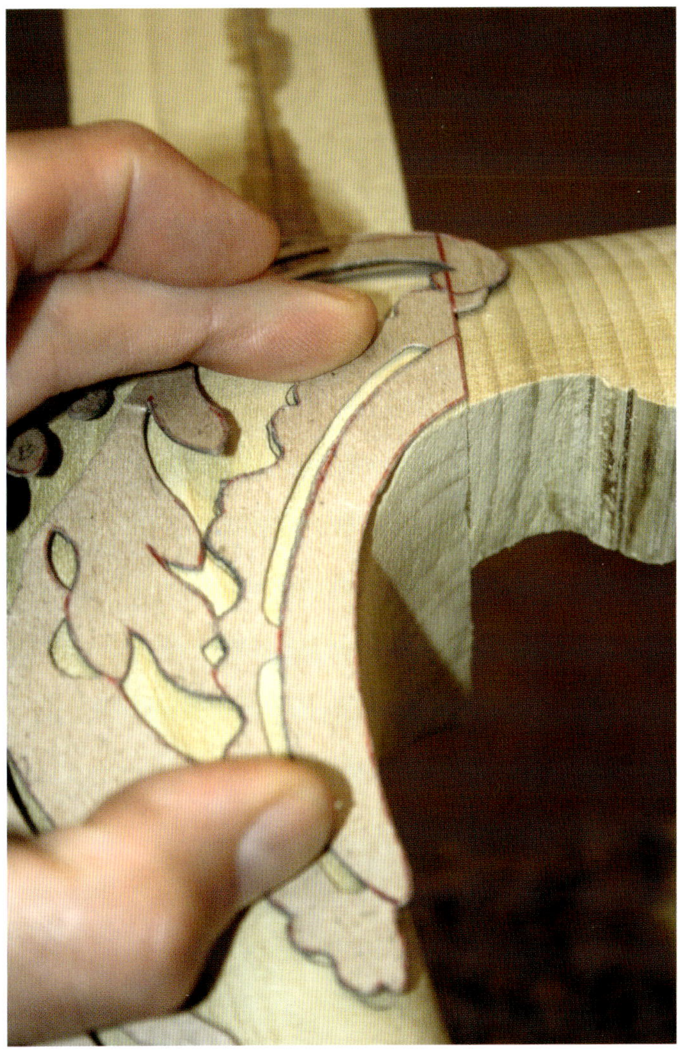

FIG. 7-21. Align the side template. The knee / knee block joint line is a reference.

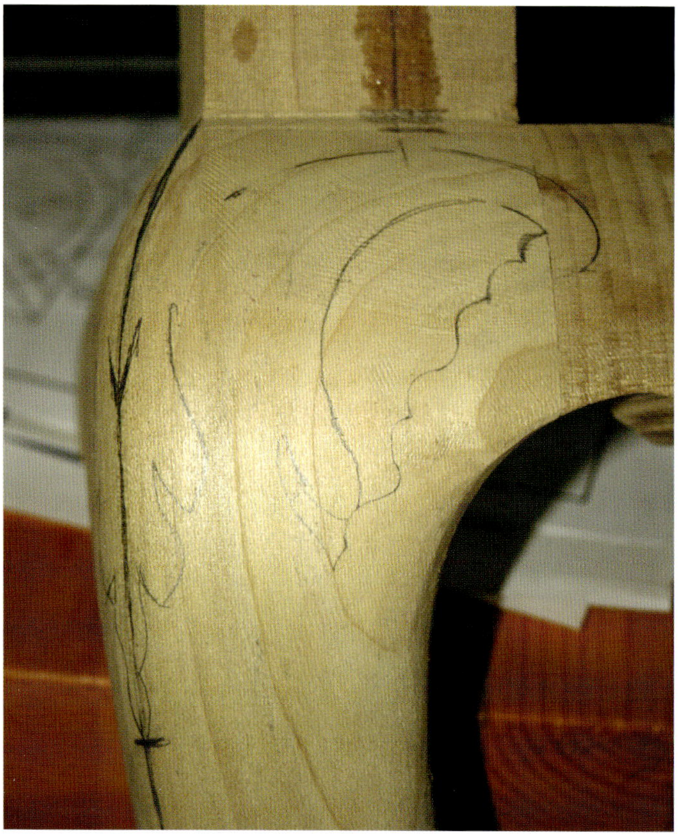

FIG. 7-22. Trace the upper portion of the front template.

Now add the leaf cluster that is to the right of leaf "B." Use the side template from **figure 7-16** and turn it if necessary, as shown in **figure 7-25**. Trace the portion shown in **figure 7-26**. Draw in the connecting lines as shown in **figure 7-27**.

Using the side template, position it as shown in **figure 7-28**. Align the lowest point of the template at the bottom mark drawn previously. Note how the template is not aligned as before; this is a consequence of the flat template on a curved surface, with the constraint that the bottom tip needs to be at the lowest mark on the centerline. Trace the lower portion as shown in **figure 7-29**. Connect the two leaf clusters (see **figure 7-30**). This U-shaped connection should be pointing at the bottom leaf tip on the centerline from the front template. The reason for this is that when carved, this will be the husk of a cornucopia that emanates from the upper cluster.

FIG. 7-23. Freehand-draw the connecting segments.

FIG. 7-24. Hand-draw a connecting curve from the base of the "V" to the top of the C-scroll.

FIG. 7-25. Reuse the side template and position it to get the leaf cluster just to the right of "B." Adjust the template so that the leaf cluster is positioned nicely on the leg. The template will probably no longer align with other landmarks.

FIG. 7-26. The placement of the leaf cluster from the second tracing.

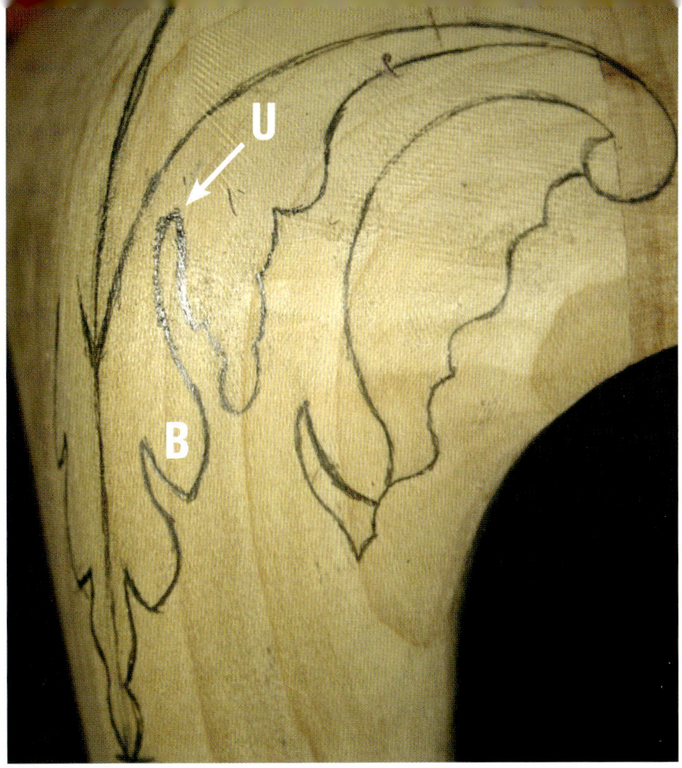

FIG. 7-27. Connect the new leaf cluster to its surrounding elements. Note the tight "U" as the connection between the new cluster and "B."

FIG. 7-28. Use the side template to add the lower elements.

FIG. 7-29. Trace the lower elements.

FIG. 7-30. Connect the two segments from the previous figure with a tight "U."

FIG. 7-31. Use the side template again to get the remaining elements. Turn it as needed.

Now fill in the remaining elements between the lower portion just completed and the upper ones. The side template will again be used for this. Position it so that leaves "A" and "B" more or less align with those drawn on the leg. The template position is in **figure 7-31**, and the tracing is in **figure 7-32**. As before, connect the template segments by hand drawing. **Figure 7-33** shows the results. Note that two more leaf clusters are connected with another cornucopia husk. This is a frequent element in this project, as well as many other Philadelphia pieces. Also note how one leaf overlaps the ones below it.

Next, make a knee block–carving template from the full-sized drawing in the insert pages and referenced in **figure A1-5**. This template has been elongated a bit to account for the curve of the surface. Position the template so that the bottom right corner aligns with the lower portion of the knee block (see **figure 7-34**). Trace the segments as shown in **figure 7-35**, and connect the segments as shown in **figure 7-36**. Note how the button is drawn. A portion of the button perimeter is the outer edge of the knee block.

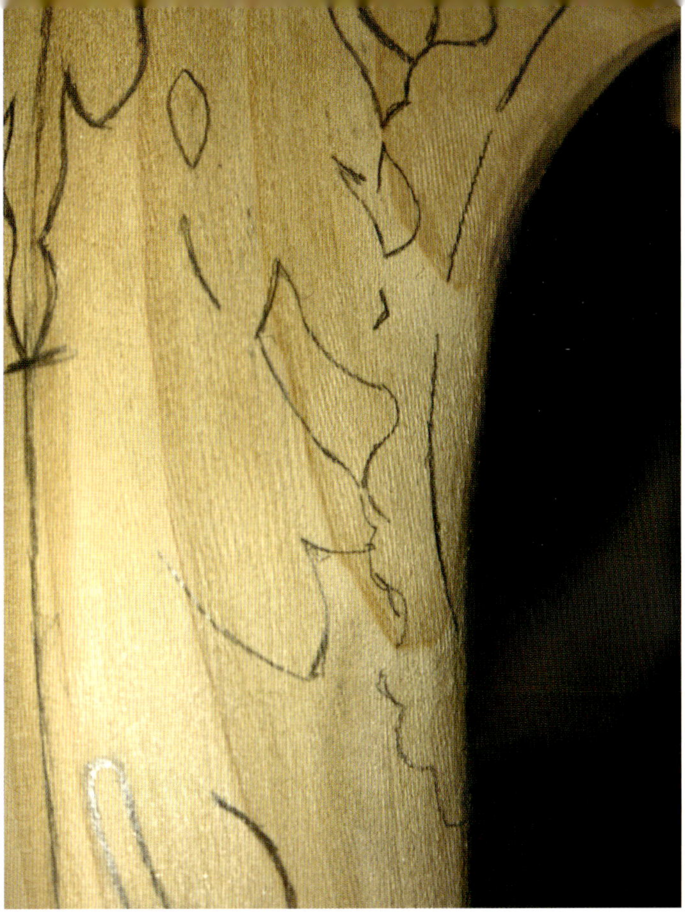

FIG. 7-32. The elements are positioned nicely.

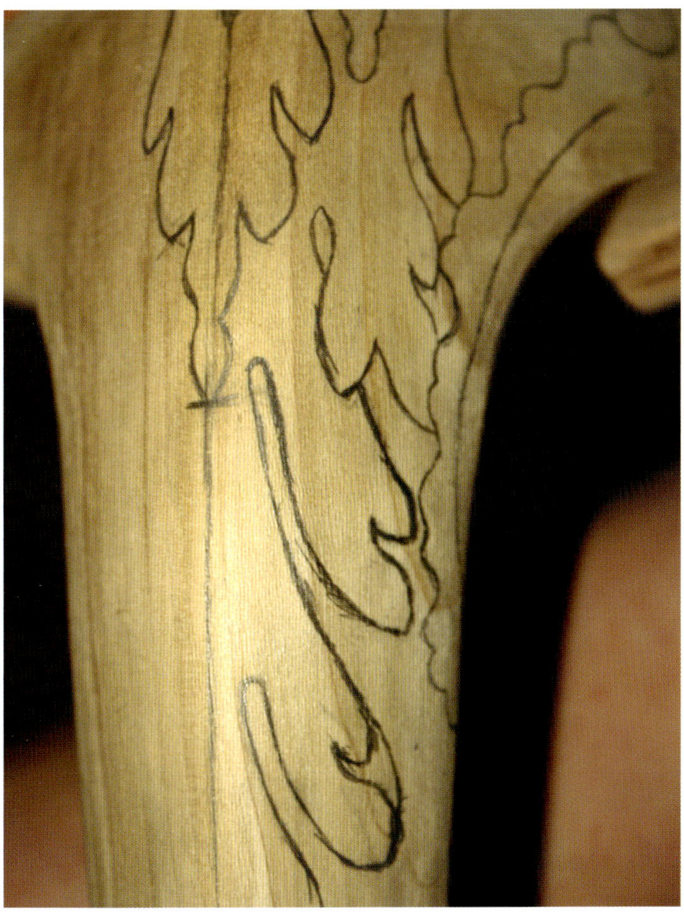

FIG. 7-33. Freehand-draw the connecting segments. Note how one leaf overlaps another.

FIG. 7-34. Use the knee block template. The important alignment is the bottom.

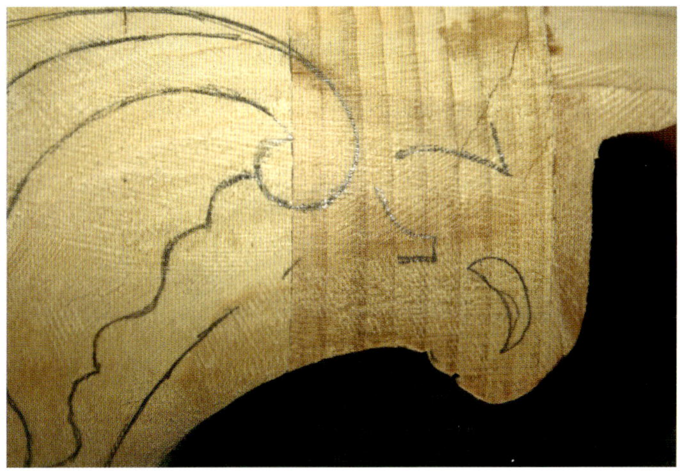

FIG. 7-35. Trace the lower segments from the template.

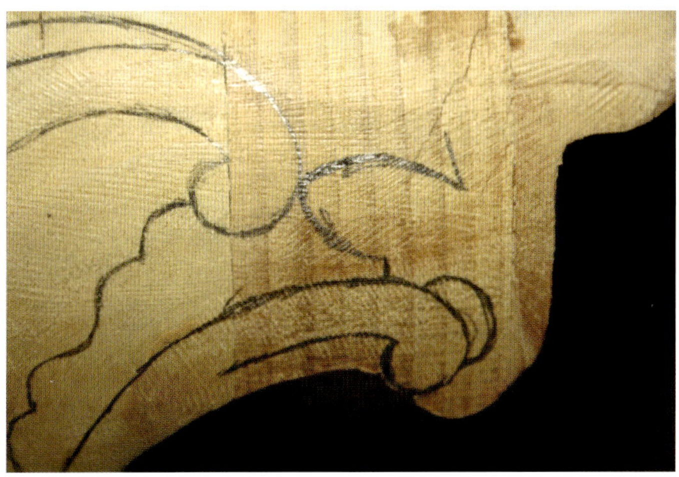

FIG. 7-36. Complete the drawing by hand.

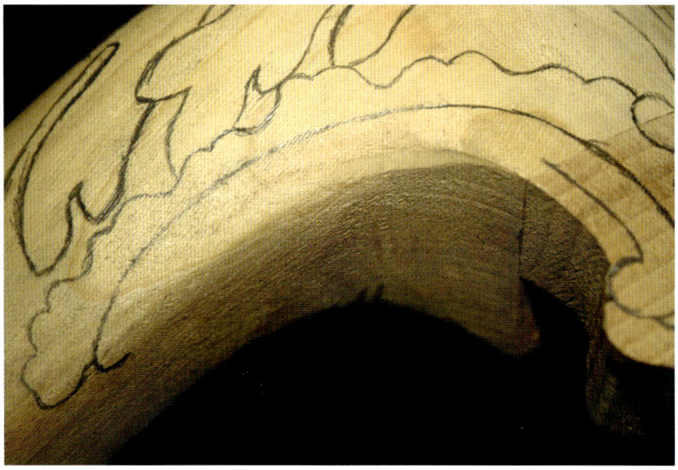

FIG. 7-37. Connect the outer button element arc with the ruffle at the bottom.

This is a good time to connect the button from the knee block to its termination farther down the leg. This needs to be done freehand. **Figure 7-37** shows the two points that will be connected, and **figure 7-38** shows the connection. As a guide, the freehand line should be more or less parallel to the adjacent line that is the other perimeter of the button element. Notice how the termination is a leaf tip. It should have a pleasing curve and flow.

Use the knee block template positioned so that its top edge is aligned with the top edge of the knee block, and trace the top segments as shown in **figure 7-39**. Complete the leaves as shown in **figure 7-40**.

FIG. 7-38. Connect the inner button element arc to the bottom. The two arcs are mostly parallel.

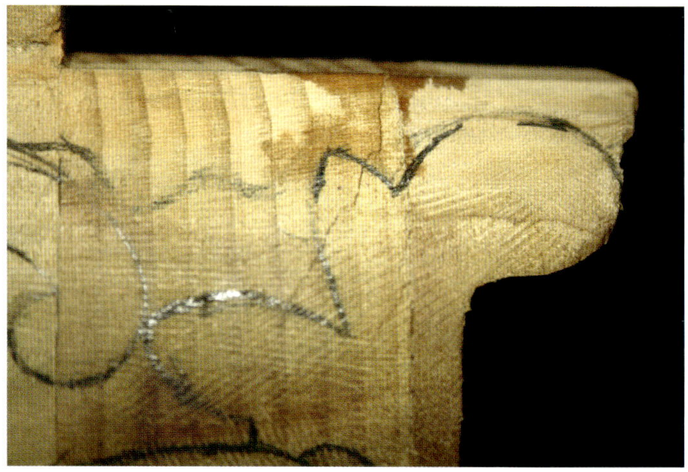

FIG. 7-39. Trace the upper portion of the knee block template.

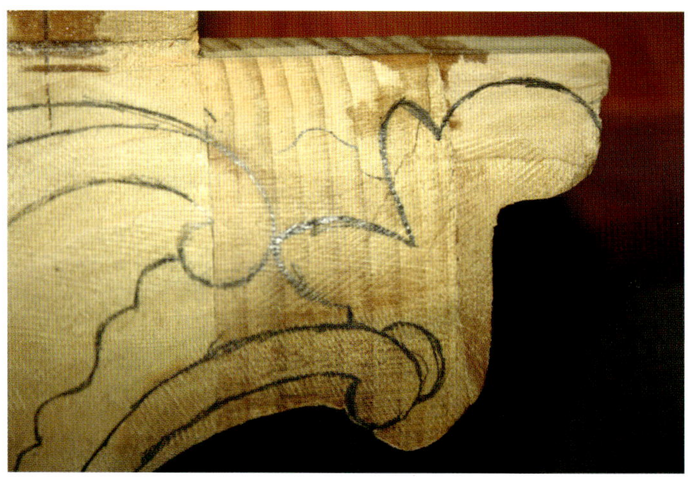

FIG. 7-40. Complete the drawing by hand. Leave a little space on top of the leaf tips.

These elements span the knee, post, and rail. Draw in the ruffle portion that is on the knee and post. This is drawn by hand and is an undulating sinusoid (see **figure 7-41**).

Make a template from the insert pages of the blue drawing in **figure A1-5**. This is the one inside the "V" and butts up to the post corner. Position it as shown in **figure 7-42**, and trace it as shown in **figure 7-43**. **Figure 7-44** shows how to connect the leaf cluster to the circle.

Figure 7-44 also shows two leaves drawn by hand that emanate from the circle at the post and fill in the space over to the ruffle. **Figure 7-45** shows a few other leaves that fill the remaining area.

FIG. 7-43. The top cluster is in place.

FIG. 7-41. Hand-draw the ruffle at the top of the knee block. This fits around the existing elements.

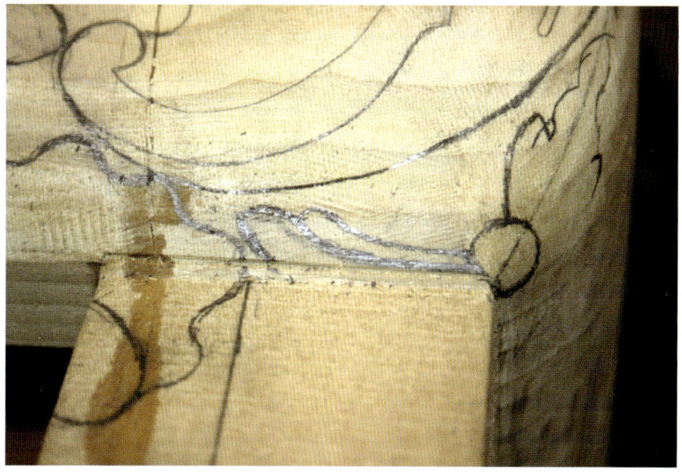

FIG. 7-44. Connect the segments from the tracing. Freehand-draw the two leaves pointing to the knee block.

FIG. 7-42. Use the second front template to establish the leaf cluster at the leg post.

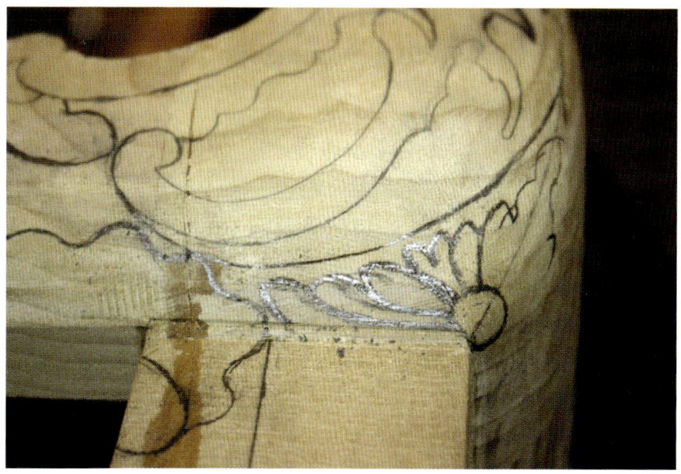

FIG. 7-45. Add three more leaves in the open area.

One side of the leg is now complete. Repeat these steps on the other side. Because the other side is a mirror image, the templates will need to be flipped when used. **Figure 7-46** shows the completed knee pattern. It doesn't have to be perfect, but if it looks unbalanced, or not symmetrical, redo the parts that are off. Be critical of the drawing without being obsessed; if it looks good, it *is* good. Little imperfections are okay, but big ones probably need work. In addition to helping this project, critiquing your work will help train your eye.

This is the most complicated pattern in this project, and on the most difficult surface. All the drawing gets easier from here.

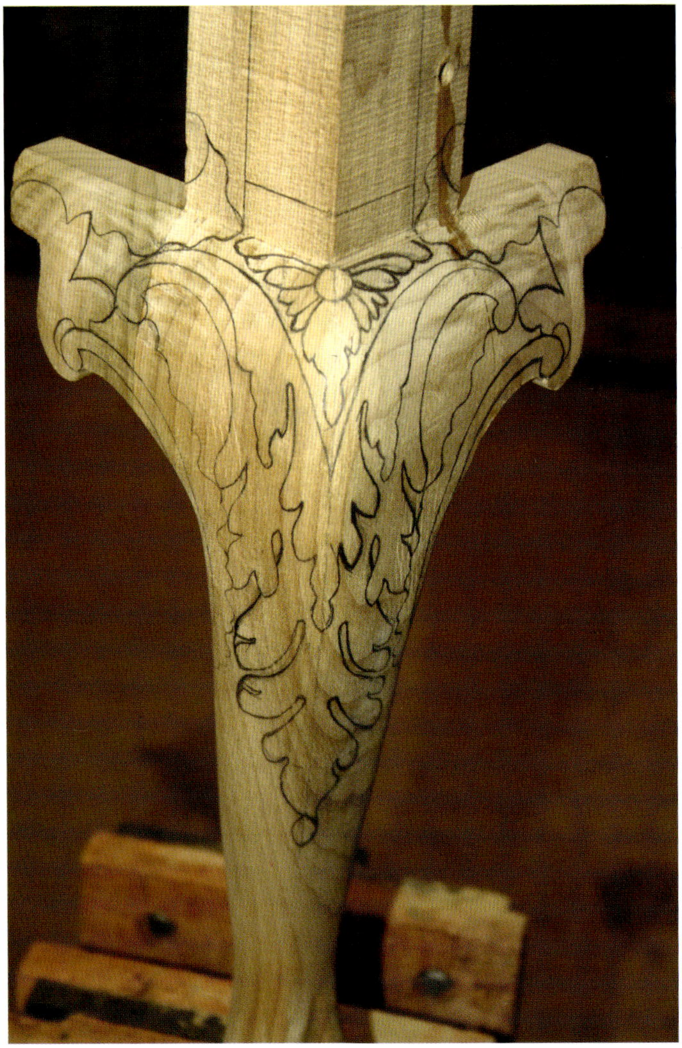

FIG. 7-46. The leg pattern is now complete and ready for carving.

Knee Carving: Carving to the Pattern

Now that the pattern is drawn on the knee, it can be carved. As mentioned, there are five layers to this pattern. Study **figures 7-1** and **7-3** to familiarize yourself with which elements are on top, what is background, and how elements relate to the pattern just drawn. Try to remove some of the detail with your eye and visualize the envelope that encapsulates a leaf cluster or other element. With this image in mind, think about raising the envelope from its surroundings by setting in around it and feathering the immediate background to the base of the set-in cuts. This is how the layers are established.

One mistake that people make is that they carve detail too early in the process. This can cause many problems, including not getting layering correct or not getting elements to flow properly. Another mistake is to work on one area to completion and then move on to the next; this too will cause problems. A better way to work is to make a little progress in one area and then bring the entire piece, or at least the immediate area, to the same level of completion. In this way the levels will appear and the elements will become distinct.

The first step will be to raise the carved area from the background. This is done by setting in around the outermost perimeter by using gouges of varying sweeps and widths. Then bevel into the base of the set-in cuts and, finally, blend the surrounding background. This will give the illusion that the carved elements are sitting on top of the background, which is the goal.

To separate the pattern envelope from the background, set in around the pattern by using conforming gouges (see **figure 7-47**). The areas to be removed are marked with an "X." The set-in cuts for the ruffle were made using medium-width #7 and #9 gouges. A #3 12 mm gouge was used for the long, sweeping arc of the leaf. The leaf tips were cut with #7 6 mm and 10 mm gouges. The set-in cuts should be made so that the pattern is not undercut.

Figure 7-48 shows the main envelope of the pattern in various stages, raised from the background. The area on the left side of the image, between a leaf and ruffle, shows the set-in cuts and the initial bevel into the base of these cuts.

Moving to the right in **figure 7-48**, more of the background has been removed. This was done with narrower #2, #3, and #5 gouges (a narrower width is 5 mm or less). The smaller widths are needed because the spaces are tight. Use a #1 skew chisel to get in the tight corners where leaf tips separate.

Moving still farther to the right, the background is smoothed, with the pattern envelope sitting on top. Smooth the background with small files, rifflers, scrapers, and sandpaper. Feather the area near the pattern envelope into the background about 1" to 2". This is enough distance to make the surface of the background smooth and flowing, which has the effect of convincing one's eye that the pattern is lying on top. **Figure 7-49** shows the pattern raised above the background.

FIG. 7-47. The areas marked with an "X" will be lowered. Use appropriate gouges to make stop cuts around the leaf tips in preparation to separate them from the "X" areas.

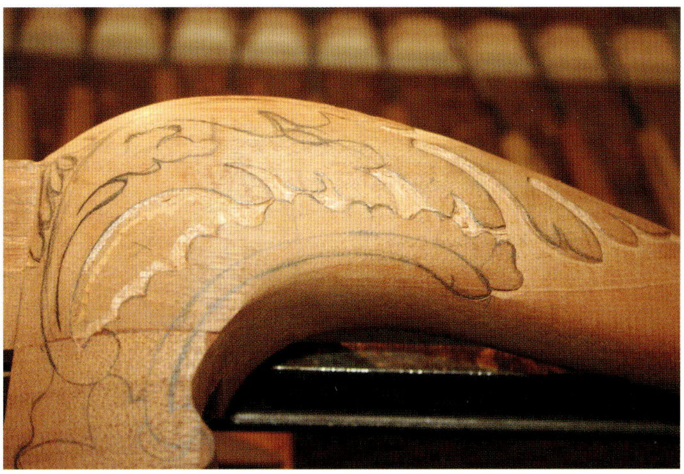

FIG. 7-48. Use appropriate gouges to bevel into the bottom of the stop cuts. Flatter gouges can be used for the gentle curves, and tighter sweep ones are needed for the others.

FIG. 7-49. Remove the areas between the stop cuts. Strive for a smooth final surface. Use rifflers to get into the tight areas.

FIG. 7-50. Make stop cuts around the knee block leaves.

Use the same techniques on the knee block. **Figure 7-50** shows the set-in cuts, and **figure 7-51** shows the smoothed background. Note how the button in the middle has been raised and separated from what will become the ruffle. Stop after the bevel into the stop cut. The goal here is just to make the separation. The surface of the ruffle will be shaped later.

Continuing in the same area, separate the button and leaf as shown in **figures 7-52** and **7-53**. A V-tool can also be used to separate the long arc. I use conforming gouges on tight curves, and flatter gouges (or a V-tool) on longer, flatter curves. One is not necessarily better than the other; it is personal choice and confidence with the tool.

FIG. 7-52. The first step to establish the bottom element that flows from the knee block down the leg is to outline its perimeter with stop cuts.

FIG. 7-51. Lower the background as before.

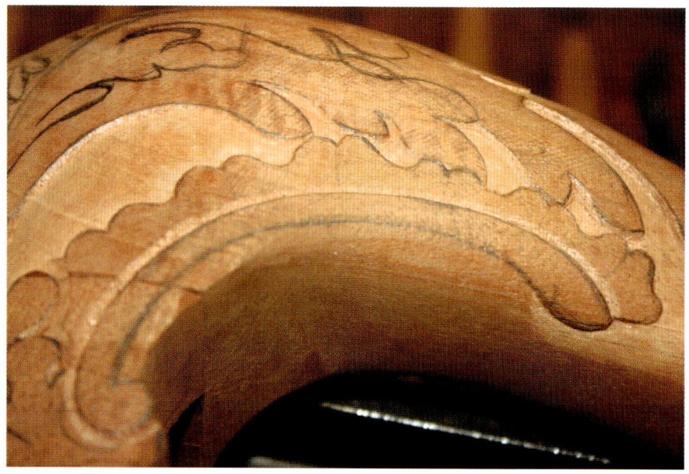

FIG. 7-53. Bevel into the stop cuts with gouges. Use a V tool on the flatter curves if desired.

FIG. 7-54. Extend the ramp from the bevel cuts to just short of the perimeter of the ruffle.

Figure 7-54 shows how to complete the separation of the button and leaf element. Use a #9 10 mm gouge on the backside of the leg. This is the lower side of the image. Note how the #9 cut terminates at the button and how it runs out on the leaf end. On the upper side, lengthen the bevel out close to the perimeter of the ruffle with a #2 12 mm gouge. This ramp, when combined with the rolling hills of the ruffle, will add movement in another direction to the final surface. Finally, note the secondary leaf at the lower end of the element. Make a vertical stop cut with a #7 4 mm gouge to define the secondary leaf tip. Use the same tool to bevel in as shown. Strive for a crisp point at the intersection of the two cuts.

FIG. 7-55. Use narrow #9 gouges to cut concave troughs in the convex lobes of the ruffle.

Next, shape the ruffle. This surface is an up-and-down rolling-hill undulation following the line of the button and leaf element below it. The troughs are centered in the convex portions of the ruffle envelope. Use a #9 7 mm gouge to begin the troughs, as shown in **figure 7-55**. As shown in the image, leave a small, 1⁄16" flat perimeter along the outside edge.

Use a flat chisel to round the ridges on either side of a trough to form a convex surface (see **figure 7-56**). Deepen the troughs with a narrower #9 gouge and blend any newly created ridge. The goal is to create a smooth up-and-down surface that is slanted from the edge of the ruffle down to the leaf stem. I use several radiused scrapers of various diameters to smooth the rolling-hill surface. Iteratively deepen the troughs and blend the ridges until the valleys are sufficiently deep so that there is a nice difference in height between the highs and lows. To get a dramatic falloff from the ruffle perimeter, use a #9 5 mm gouge pointed straight down, and quickly scoop to level at the base. As the troughs and hills are being created, some cleanup is needed at the wall. Use a corner of a flat chisel or a skew chisel to straighten the wall at the base of the hills and valleys.

Use a flat chisel to ease the back edge of the button and leaf element. **Figure 7-57** shows the initial cut. Smooth this surface with more chisel cuts and blend the remaining facets with small files and sandpaper. Cut in the secondary leaf tip with a #7 4 mm gouge. **Figure 7-58** shows the smoothed surface with the secondary leaf. Use a #9 7 mm gouge to connect the inside curve, as shown in **figure 7-59**. This completes the separation of the button and leaf element from the leg.

FIG. 7-56. Round over the ridges of the gouge cuts to form convex surfaces on the concave lobes.

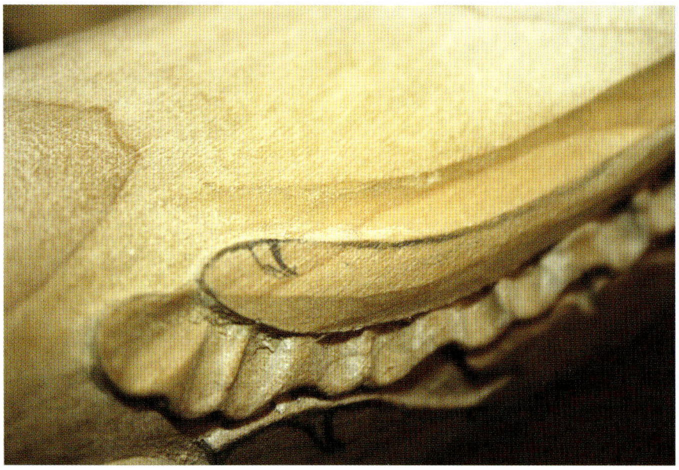

FIG. 7-57. The first step in rounding over the back side of the leaf.

FIG. 7-58. Smooth the surface with small files of rifflers. Cut in the secondary leaf tip.

FIG. 7-59. Use a #9 7 mm gouge to connect the button to the leaf tip. First, make a stop cut around the button.

Now that the main carved pattern is layered on top of the background, layer the top leaf cluster on the one below it. This is achieved using the same techniques; that is, set in around the perimeter, bevel into the set-in cuts, and blend the background. **Figure 7-60** shows intermediate progress. The upper leaf cluster lies on top of the lower one, in a manner similar to the overall pattern lying on top of the background. On the basis of the color differences of the lower section, one can see that the surface is almost smooth after approximately an inch of feathering from the raised element. Smooth the remaining facets of the background, as shown in **figures 7-61** and **7-62**. Use rifflers to get into the tight areas between leaf tips. It's amazing that removing such a small amount of wood can have such a dramatic visual effect! It is the smoothness and uniformity of the background that accounts for this illusion.

FIG. 7-60. Layer one leaf cluster on top of another. Make stop cuts around the top cluster and bevel into them.

FIG. 7-61. Feather and smooth the background with chisels and rifflers.

FIG. 7-63. The centerline will be a trough cut. Each side line will be the backbone of the cornucopia, whose open end is at the "U."

Repeat the layering process on the other side. **Figure 7-63** shows the lower portion layered on both sides of the centerline. Detail can now be added to the lower leaf cluster. Note the three lines. The middle one will be a tapered trough that is narrow at the top and widens as it moves down the leg. The lines on either side of the center will be crest lines for cones that emanate from the tip of the top cluster and terminate at the U-shaped separation down the leg. Also note the two scoops at the bottom center of the image. Use a #9 10 mm gouge to create a ridgeline that connects the outer edges on opposite sides. The knee-carving patterns are mirrored on the front legs. This orientation is for the right leg; **figure 7-64** shows the opposite orientation for the left leg. This is a small point, so if they both go in the same direction, no one will notice and it will look fine.

FIG. 7-62. Another view of the layering.

FIG. 7-64. The opposite orientation of the lower leaf tip.

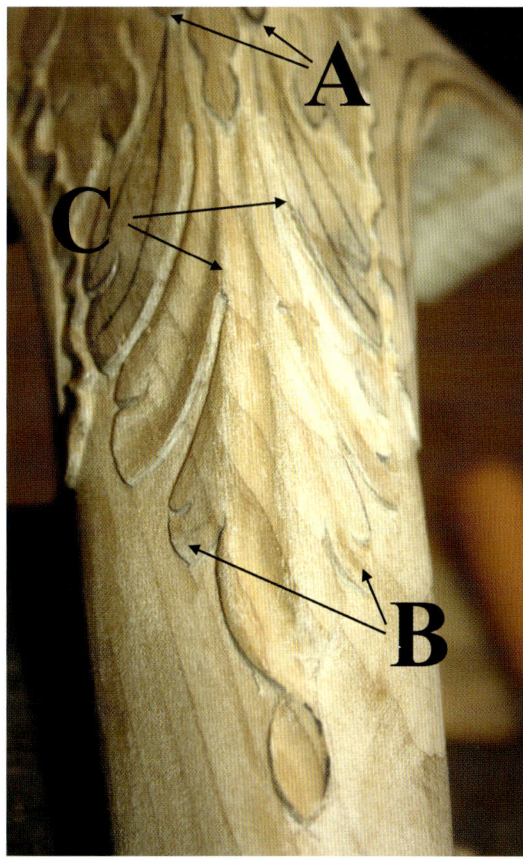

FIG. 7-65. The lower cluster is mostly done. Note how the high and low areas taper as they progress up the leg.

Figure 7-65 shows progress in shaping the lower section. Note that the surface continually alternates between up and down, moving from side to side. The low sections are formed with #9 gouges of appropriate widths. Remove the ridges formed by the gouge cuts with a flat chisel, and blend the convex and concave surfaces with round rifflers and radiused scrapers. **Figure 7-66** shows some initial gouge cuts and the resulting ridges.

The troughs narrow as they taper, moving up the leg in **figure 7-66**. Switch to a #11 2 mm gouge for the center and a #11 1 mm gouge for the sides. Referring again to **figure 7-65**, the troughs on the sides form the low side of a cone that emanates from the leaf tips "A" at the very top of the image. The side troughs also flow into the center of the leaves "B" and help form the cones "C."

Figure 7-67 shows the lower section almost complete. Note how each of the four cones labeled "A" flows into leaf separations.

FIG. 7-66. The troughs start as gouge cuts. The edges formed by the gouge cuts are then rounded.

FIG. 7-68. The leaf tip is defined.

FIG. 7-67. Four cones, or cornucopias, terminate at a "U."

FIG. 7-69. The leaf tip is established. The center will be a trough.

Now work on the leaf cluster in **figure 7-68**. The pencil line shows how to separate the leaf tip from the cluster. Use a #7 6 mm gouge to define the leaf tip with a vertical stop cut. Then use the same tool to bevel into the stop cut, as shown in **figure 7-69**. The curved line drawn down the center of the cluster will be a #9 10 mm gouge cut. The result of this cut is shown in **figure 7-70**. As is usually the case, any cross section of a leaf cluster is going to be an alternating up-and-down, rolling-hills surface. Since the center of this cluster is a valley, its sides will flow into hills. Round the ridges formed by the gouge cut and smooth the surface with files and scrapers. **Figure 7-71** shows this section complete.

Figure 7-71 also shows leaf "A" overlapping the one below, which is leaf "C." This is accomplished by starting at the "eye" labeled "B." This is a relatively deep #11 2 mm gouge cut. The right side of this cut is part of the edge of the leaf that is on top. The left side is part of the edge of the leaf underneath. To complete the illusion, the underneath leaf's right edge—labeled "C"—needs to visually connect to the left edge of the "eye." **Figure 7-72** shows the "eye" (labeled "A") before the surrounding leaves are shaped.

Returning to **figure 7-71**, the secondary leaf "D" is formed with a vertical #7 4 mm gouge stop cut and beveling into it with the same tool. A similar secondary leaf will be added to leaf "E." Also note that leaf "D" rounds down on its left-hand edge a little. The continually flowing surfaces in several directions are what adds life to the leaves. There should be no flat surfaces anywhere on any of the leaves.

Next, isolate the uppermost leaf cluster closest to the post. **Figure 7-73** shows the section in question. Use a V-tool to establish the wall of the "V" that surrounds the leaf cluster. Since this might get tight in spots, some of the leaf tips might need to be moved a bit to accommodate the wall.

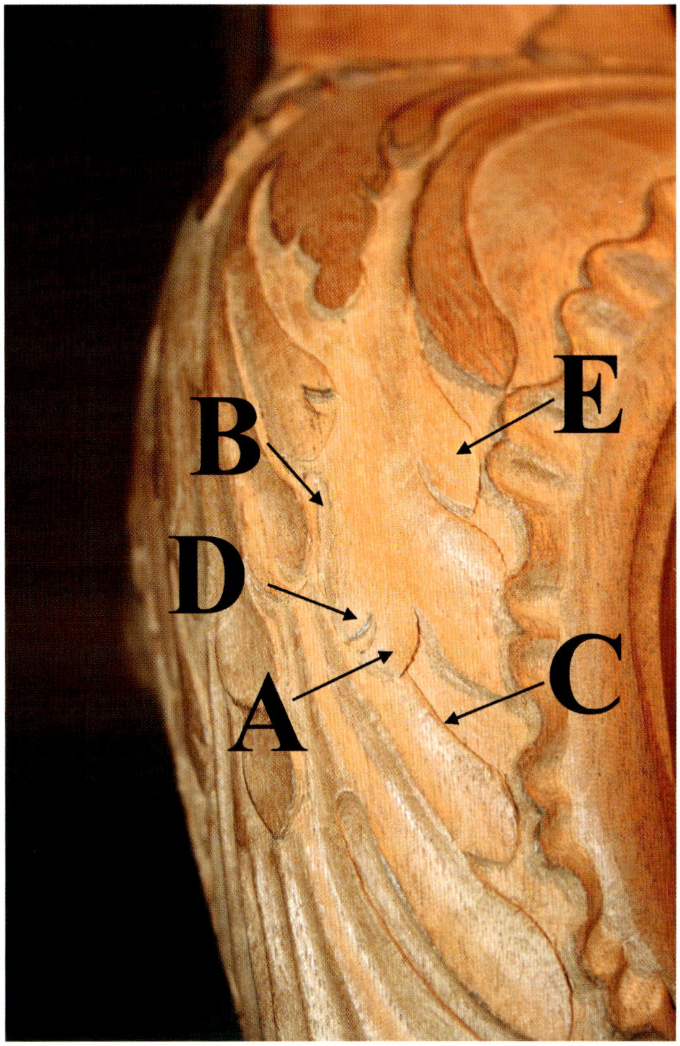

FIG. 7-71. The "eye" at "B" allows the overlap of leaf "A" on leaf "C."

FIG. 7-70. Use a #9 10 mm gouge to cut the trough.

FIG. 7-72. A better view of the "eye." This separates two leaves and is made with a #11 2 mm gouge.

When the wall is established, use narrow gouges of appropriate sweeps to form the leaf tips with vertical stop cuts. A #7 4 mm and #5 5 mm gouge should work for most of them. Bevel into the stop cuts and clean out the area between the leaf tips and the wall of the enclosing "V." **Figure 7-74** shows one side of the cluster separated from the wall. Repeat the same steps on the other side of the cluster.

Figure 7-74 also shows how to separate the central button from the leaf cluster. Use a #7 6 mm or a #5 5 mm gouge to set in vertically around the perimeter of the button. With the same tool, bevel into the bottom of the stop cut, as shown.

Now feather the ridge into the surrounding background, leaving the leaf tips high. The goal is to have the button sitting on top of a smooth surrounding leaf cluster. **Figure 7-75** shows the raised button.

FIG. 7-73. The top leaf cluster emanates from the corner of t he post.

FIG. 7-74. Isolate the leaf cluster from its background and separate the button from the cluster.

FIG. 7-75. Raise the button by lowering the background around it. Feather and smooth the background.

Figure 7-76 shows the early stages of detailing the upper leaf cluster. First, isolate the subcluster "A." Use the same set-in, bevel, and smooth techniques as before. Note that the leaves "B" are lower than their neighbors. The scoop at the tip of cluster "A" is made with a #9 7 mm gouge. Note how the left side of the gouge cut, labeled "C," flows into the side of the cluster.

Continue detailing the upper cluster. Use a #9 5 mm gouge to scoop the center, as shown in **figure 7-77**. Round over the ridges formed by the gouge cut, which will be high, and drop the edges of the outer leaves, as shown in **figure 7-78**. Note the rolling-hill surface moving from "A" to "B."

Use a #9 5 mm and #9 7 mm gouge to scoop each leaf (see **figure 7-79**). The ridge left by two adjacent gouge cuts will be the line that defines each leaf and separates one from another. Strive to make these curved lines smooth, which will be visually pleasing. **Figure 7-80** shows late progress.

FIG. 7-77. Scoop the center of the front cluster.

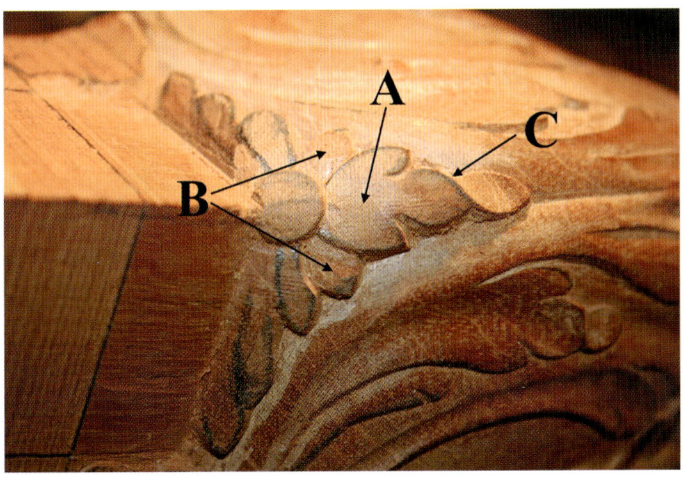

FIG. 7-76. The line "C" forms opposite sides of two leaf sections.

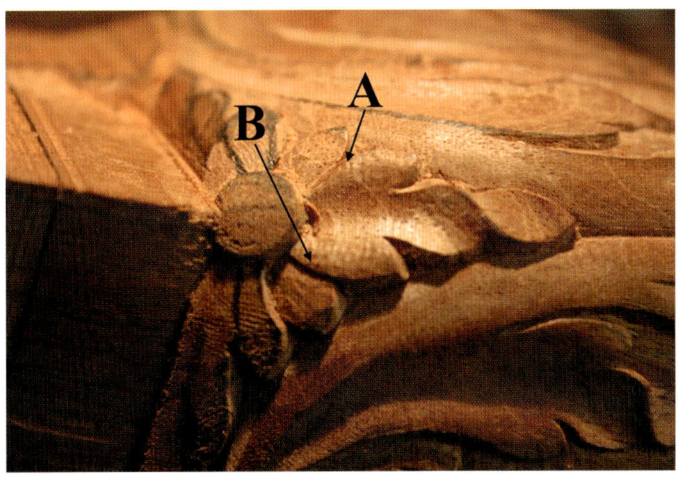

FIG. 7-78. Round over the ridges formed by the gouge cuts.

FIG. 7-79. Use narrow #9 gouges to scoop the individual leaves.

FIG. 7-80. The upper leaf cluster is almost complete. The leaf edges are the intersection of two gouge cuts.

Finally, ease the edges of the button so the surface is slightly curved in all directions, as shown in **figure 7-81**.

Now detail the knee block; **figure 7-82** shows early progress. Use a V tool to separate cluster "A." Then use a #9 10 mm gouge to make the cut labeled "B." Excavate the area "C" that separates cluster "A" from the C-scroll.

Figure 7-83 shows more refinement of the knee block. Note how the meeting of the two gouge cuts labeled "A" forms a smooth, curved line that shapes both leaves. Note also how the bottom corner, labeled "B," is rounded to tuck in under the C-scroll. This corner falls off not only side to side, but also top to bottom. Further note the #9 5 mm gouge cut labeled "C." This cut gives a two-level step from the leaves to the background.

After all the previous steps on both sides of the knee are completed, the carving is substantially complete. What remains is the ruffle that is part of the knee and rail, and the hatched pattern on the background. The ruffle will be left until after assembly so that the pattern will bridge both the leg and rail seamlessly. The hatched pattern will be done next.

The hatched pattern is created from two sets of parallel lines that are at some angle to each other. I don't know what this angle is because I drew them by eye, connecting different landmarks and spacing them to capture the spirit of the original. I also tried to make the few lines on the knee block appear to be an extension of ones on the knee. **Figure 7-84** shows the hatch lines in place.

Use a V-tool to cut along the lines shown in **figure 7-85**. Be careful to avoid tear-out, especially at the corners. Crisp corners are part of what adds to the elegance of this embellishment. Cut the ones across the grain first, then cut the ones with the grain. This should help avoid tear-out. Also, make the cuts slowly to feel how they are going. If they don't feel right, cut in the other direction. Another technique that will help is to start at a corner and cut into the diamond. This should give adequate support for the corner. After the hatch lines have been carved, use a small awl or nail to make little holes in the center of each diamond.

Study the pictures of the finished knee in **figures 7-1** and **7-3** as a guide as you carve yours. I will point out the details that haven't been covered. There are small cutouts on the cornucopias. These are made with a #7 4 mm gouge. First, make a vertical stop cut perpendicular with the line of the cornucopia stem. The orientation of the tool is concave down. Then use the same tool to bevel into the convex side at a steep angle. These details come in pairs, so make another one close to the first. Furthermore, there are two to three pairs along the stem of the cornucopia. Move a visible distance away and make another pair. If there is enough length, make a third pair.

There are accent marks in the ruffles. These are made with a #11 1 mm gouge or a V-tool. They are short little ticks that will break up the surface and cast a shadow. In addition, they will become dark when you're adding age to the finish, and stand out nicely against a much-lighter background.

There are also accent marks along the length of many of the leaves. I am somewhat liberal with these, independent of what is on the original, because I think they add a nice touch. These too will go dark when finished, and help make the carvings look a little more alive.

FIG. 7-81. The button is rounded. Remove the corners with a gouge or chisel. Smooth the surface with a file. Be careful not to damage the post corner.

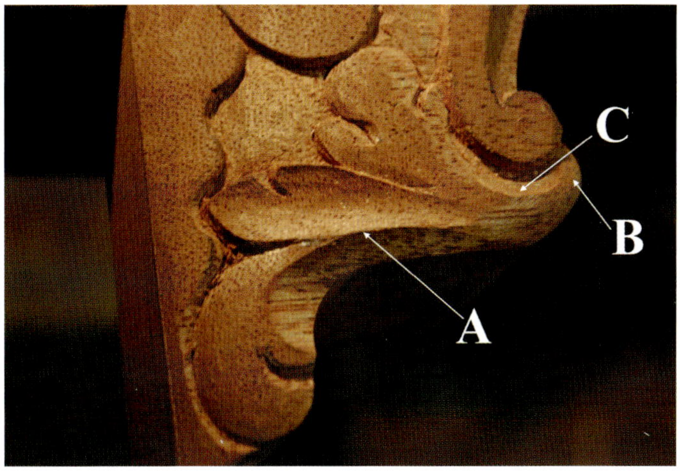

FIG. 7-83. Detail leaf "A" with a #9 10 mm gouge. Corner "B" tucks under the button. "C" is a #9 cut that is part of the leaf and sits above the excavated area.

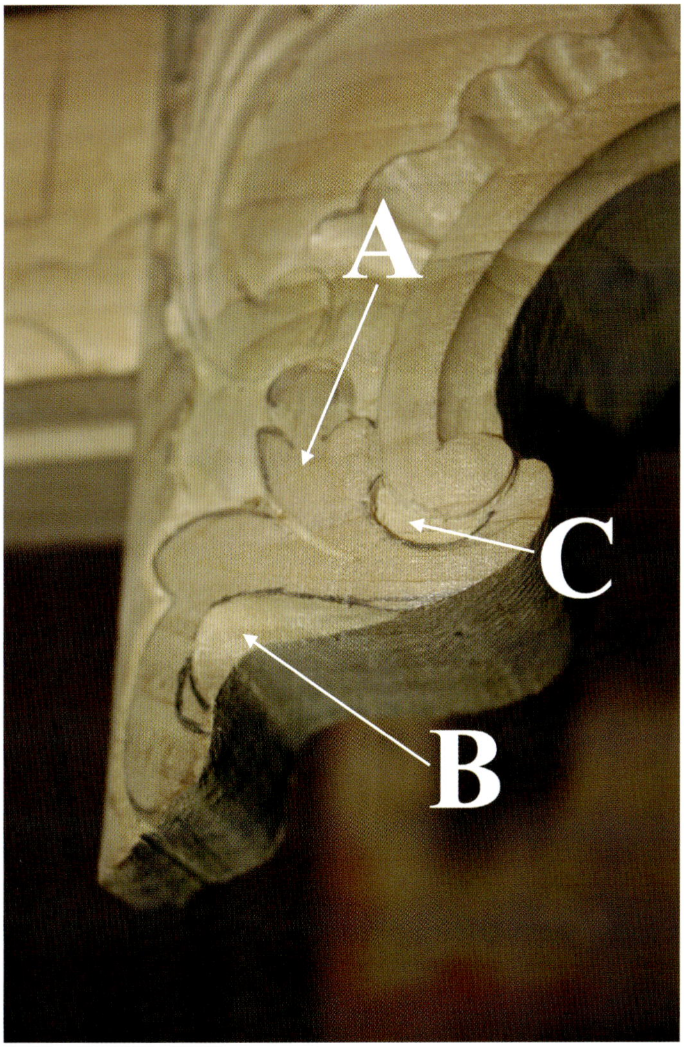

FIG. 7-82. Separate leaf "A" with a V tool. Define leaf "B" with a #9 10 mm gouge. Excavate area "C."

FIG. 7-84. Draw two sets of parallel lines. The ones on the knee block should be extensions of those on the knee.

FIG. 7-85. Use a V-tool to cut along the hatch lines. Cut across the grain first. To avoid chipping a corner, start at a corner and cut into a diamond.

Side Rail

This chapter will describe how to carve most of the side rail. The parts that flow from the rail to the leg and knee block will not be done now but will be completed after the case is assembled. This will be part of the integration carving. **Figures 8-1** and **8-2** show the finished side rail.

Side Rail: Preparation for Carving

At this point the side rail should have the joints cut, but not the bottom profile.

Make a template from the full-sized drawing "Side Panel Carving" in the insert section and referenced in **figure A1-1**. This is one-half of the full pattern. **Figure 8-3** shows my version of this template. Note that there is some spillover across the centerline and over the end line. This is to help keep the lines and elements better connected.

Mark the centerline on the rail blank. It is always good to reference things off a centerline because it helps keep things balanced. Align the template to the centerline and trace around the cutouts. Flip the template, realign it to the centerline, and trace the cutouts again. When this is done, connect the template segments with smooth curves. Refer to the template drawing or the finished rail to understand how to connect the lines. **Figure 8-4** shows the side pattern drawn on the blank. I first traced the lines with a pencil and made any adjustments that were needed. When I was happy with the pencil drawing, I went over the lines with a pen. This makes the lines more visible and less subject to erasure when handling it.

FIG. 8-1. The completed carved side rail of my reproduction.

FIG. 8-2. Note how the surfaces and elements interact.

FIG. 8-4. Transfer the pattern to the side panel.

FIG. 8-3. Create the side-pattern-carving template.

Side Rail: Carving to the Pattern

The first step will be to raise the carved pattern envelope from the background. One of the things that I noticed when I studied the original was how shallow the carved rails were; the height off the background was about 1⁄16". This shallow depth gives a sense of lightness and delicacy. It also isn't a lot of depth to work with. Fortunately, the depths within the carved envelope can be deeper. As long as the outside is shallow, the eye will not see the extra depth within the envelope. Despite that I've mentioned the shallowness of the envelope, don't be a slave to this. If you need a little more depth in some places, deepen it. It can be mitigated by feathering it into the surrounding background.

Start by using appropriate-sized gouges to make stop cuts along the perimeter, as shown in **figure 8-5**. Bevel into the base of the stop cuts, as shown in **figure 8-6**. Use flatter gouges, files, scrapers, and sandpaper to blend and feather the background (see **figure 8-7**). Strive to create a flat, smooth surface. In reality this is a flat, angled surface. If it is smooth enough, the eye will not see the angle. The carved area will appear to be lying on the surface, which is the goal.

Figure 8-8 shows the fully raised envelope. On the basis of the background color, it is easy to see how far from the envelope the feathering goes. **Figure 8-9** shows the shallow depth of the carved envelope relative to the surrounding background.

Cut the bottom profile with a bandsaw. Leave the flat sections where the knee blocks will attach. **Figure 8-10** shows the bottom profile cutout. Use small files to clean up the bandsaw marks and smooth out the curves if needed.

FIG. 8-6. Raise the carving envelope from the background.

FIG. 8-5. Set in around the outside perimeter.

FIG. 8-7. Smooth the background with scrapers, rifflers, and sandpaper.

FIG. 8-8. Feather the background as far as needed to get a flat-appearing surface.

There are four little leaves tucked into the four concave lobes of the ruffle. **Figure 8-11** shows one of these leaves labeled "A." Draw the pencil line shown to leave a 1⁄16" perimeter. Make a stop cut, as shown, and bevel in to its bottom. Note that the high spot is the outer edge of the round portion. The surface falls off in all directions from here. Use a riffler to smooth and round the surface.

Now start to isolate individual elements inside the envelope. Excavate the sections shown in **figure 8-12**. Make stop cuts around the perimeter of the teardrop sections and use narrow gouges to remove the middle portions.

Figure 8-13 shows two C-scrolls isolated. Note that the teardrop perimeter was left intact.

FIG. 8-9. The carving envelope is raised from the background. Note how shallow it is.

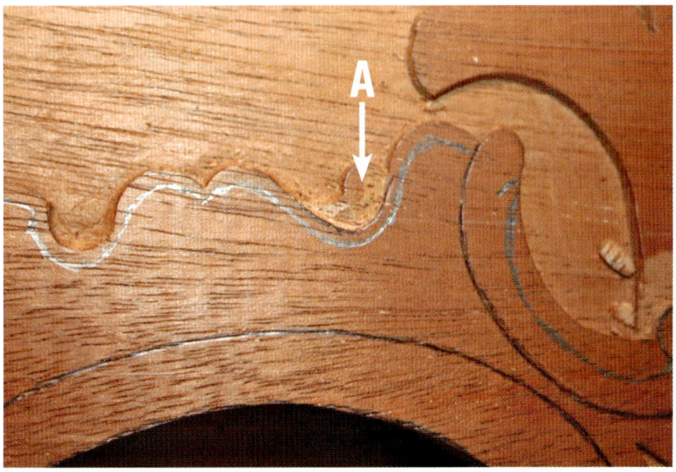

FIG. 8-11. The leaf "A" is tucked into the ruffle.

FIG. 8-12. Excavate these elements.

FIG. 8-10. Cut out the rail profile with a bandsaw.

Use a #9 7 mm gouge and a #9 5 mm gouge to make the cuts shown in **figure 8-14**. Round over the ridges formed by the gouge cuts, and blend the convex and concave portions into a smooth, undulating surface. **Figure 8-15** shows the result. Note the ¹⁄₁₆" flat perimeter. Also note how the surface angles to the bottom of the C-scroll.

Next, detail the C-scroll. Continue the circular portion from the outside edge to about the halfway point, as shown in **figure 8-16**. Starting at point "A," draw arc "B" parallel to the outside edges of the C-scroll. This arc is in the center of the scroll. It also connects at the analogous point on the other side of the C-scroll. Isolate the rounded portion (see **figure 8-16**) with a #7 4 mm gouge.

FIG. 8-15. Round over the trough edges to form a smooth, undulating surface.

FIG. 8-13. Separate the C-scrolls from their adjacent elements.

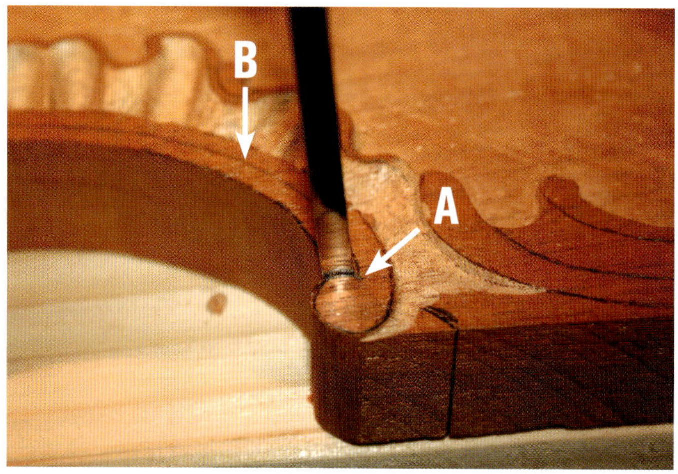

FIG. 8-16. Define the C-scroll button with a #7 4 mm gouge.

FIG. 8-14. Begin the ruffle troughs with a #9 5 mm gouge.

FIG. 8-17. Use a #9 10 mm gouge to cut into the C-scroll button stop cut.

FIG. 8-18. Intermediate progress between the two C-scroll buttons with the #9 gouge.

Now use a #9 10 mm gouge to scoop the inside half between the two circular ends, as shown in **figure 8-17**. **Figure 8-18** shows intermediate progress, and **figure 8-19** shows the operation complete.

Round over the backside of the C-scroll, as also shown in **figure 8-19**. Use a flat chisel for the initial cuts and smooth the surface with a small file or riffler. **Figure 8-20** shows the completed C-scroll.

Now work on the central plume. **Figure 8-21** shows the initial #9 7 mm gouge cut, and **figure 8-22** shows it extended. Note how the gouge cuts flare into two at the top of the plume. **Figure 8-22** also shows the separation of the side clusters from the center stalk and the leaf "A" in its cluster. The side clusters tuck underneath the center one, as shown by "B." This is achieved by making the side cluster lower than the center one where they meet.

FIG. 8-19. Begin to round over the backside of the C-scroll with a flat chisel.

FIG. 8-21. Begin to shape the central plume. Separate the two sides with a central gouge cut.

FIG. 8-20. The completed C-scroll. Note the crispness of the cuts and lines.

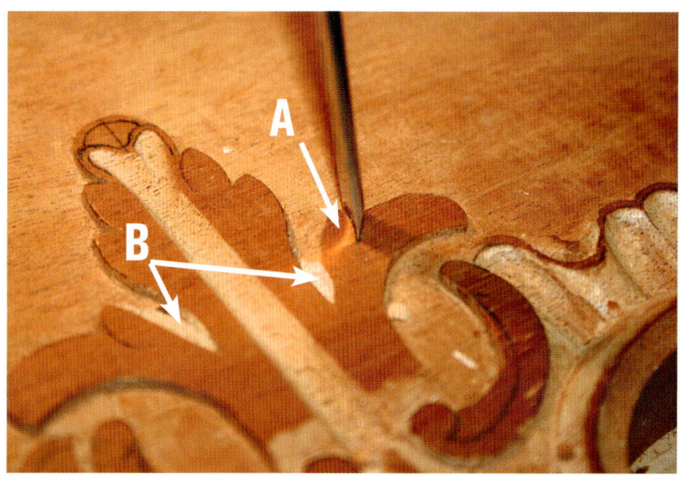

FIG. 8-22. Separate the two side leaf clusters.

FIG. 8-23. More of the central plume elements are separated.

FIG. 8-24. The top of the central plume.

Figure 8-23 shows more progress in detailing the central plume. The overall cross-sectional shape of the center cluster is low in the middle, flowing up and over, moving to the sides, and then falling off a bit on the outer edges. Note how the sub-leaves are separated from the main stalk.

Scoop out the center section of the top leaf in the central cluster, as shown in **figure 8-24**. Use narrow #9 gouges for this.

Figure 8-25 shows the completed central plume, as well as several elements below it. There are a lot of details shown in this image, so study it to understand how the individual elements fit together. As you look at the image, note that the elements labeled "A" are similar to C-scrolls, except that one end is a leaf. Also note how the interior gouge cut tapers to a point at the base of the secondary leaf "B." Further note that the leaf tip labeled "C" falls off in all directions. Finally, strive for smooth surfaces that transition continually from high to low without unwanted facets. The more your surfaces flow gently from one to another, the better your carving will look.

Figure 8-26 shows another view and angle of the lower central area. Note how the bottoms of the teardrops are flat. Note also that the central teardrop's perimeter is raised and tapers into the central trough at "A." On the bottom side labeled "B," there is a wide, gentle scoop that carries the bottom of the teardrop to the bottom perimeter. In addition, the sides flow into the cusps at the points "C."

Figure 8-27 shows the side panel carving substantially complete. Note that the elements that will transition to the knee block and leg post are not done at this point. What remains are to add accent marks with a #11 1 mm gouge and to punch holes around the C-scrolls with an awl. See **figure 8-2** of the finished side for placement of these details.

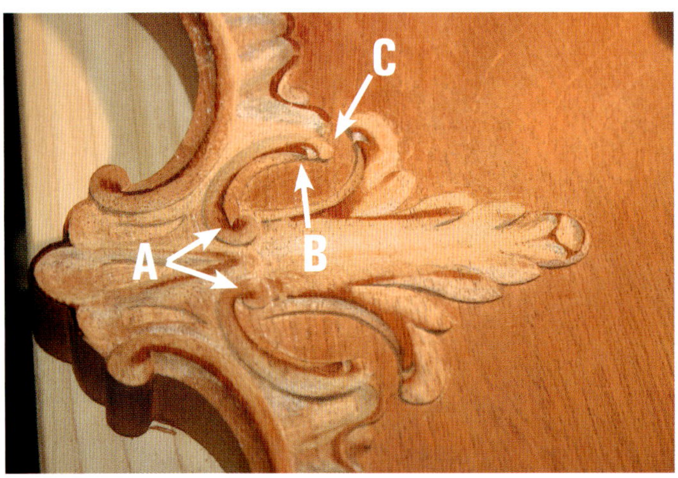

FIG. 8-25. The completed central plume. Study how the elements interact.

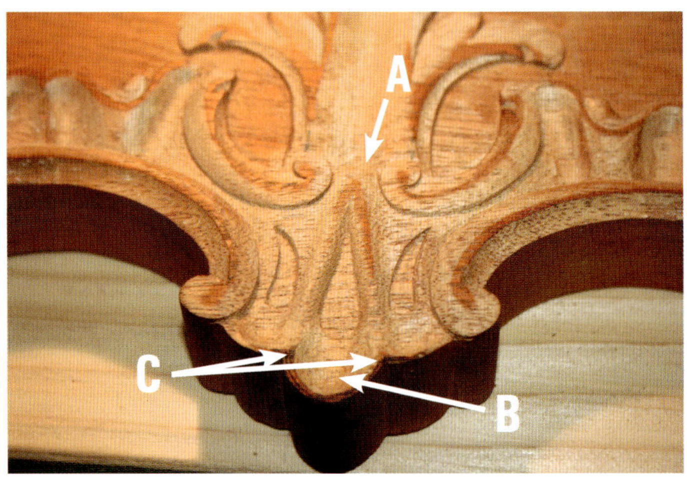

FIG. 8-26. The completed lower central area. Note how the high areas define the central element.

FIG. 8-27. The mostly completed side panel. The areas that connect to the knee blocks and post will be done in the integration-carving phase.

Chapter 9
Front Rail

This chapter will describe how to carve most of the front rail. The parts that flow from the rail to the leg and knee block will not be done now but will be completed when the case is assembled.

Figures 9-1 and **9-2** show the finished front rail. Note that the background of the surface between the pattern perimeters is an undulating surface. This is achieved by separating the various elements with relatively steep bevels into the stop cuts,

FIG. 9-1. The completed front rail on my reproduction.

FIG. 9-2. The carving is quite shallow but has visual depth. The light and dark contrasts enhance the depth.

then feathering and blending the surrounding surface relatively quickly with respect to distance from the element. The undulating background is what is left after feathering all the areas around the elements and smoothing the remaining surface.

In **Figure 9-2**, the top most element in the center just under the drawer is very close to the drawer opening. Be careful not to break the drawer opening line. If this line is broken, it will not be straight, and that will be quite visible.

Front Rail: Preparation for Carving

At this point the front rail should have the drawer opening and all the joints cut, but the bottom profile is not cut. **Figure 9-3** shows the shape of the front rail when it is ready for carving.

Make a template from the full-sized drawing "Front Skirt Profile & Carving Template" in the insert packet and referenced in **figure A1-3**. Note that this is one-half of the full pattern. **Figure 9-4** shows my version of this template. Note that there is some spillover across the centerline and over the end line. This is to help keep the lines and elements better connected.

FIG. 9-3. The lower front face frame pieced together. The front rail is ready for carving.

FIG. 9-4. Make a full-sized template.

Mark the centerline on the rail blank. It is always good to reference things off a centerline because it helps keep things balanced. Align the template to the centerline and trace around the cutouts, as shown in **figure 9-5**. Flip the template, realign it to the centerline, and trace the cutouts again. When this is done, connect the template segments with smooth curves. Sometimes it is a bit unclear which lines connect. Look at the template drawing or the finished rail to understand how to connect the lines. **Figure 9-6** shows the center section complete. I first traced the lines with a pencil and made any adjustments that were needed. When I was happy with the pencil drawing, I went over the lines with a pen. This makes the lines more visible and less subject to erasure when handling it.

Figure 9-7 shows the right-hand side of the rail. The horizontal pencil line is where the knee block will attach. This line needs to be straight and square to the side. Note also how part of the C-scroll dips below the height of the knee block area. These are slight complications at the construction phase, but they add to the overall visual appeal. All the parts are better integrated, and it becomes harder to tell where one part ends and another begins.

FIG. 9-5. The template is transferred to the front rail.

FIG. 9-6. Connect the template segments. Flip the template and draw the other side.

FIG. 9-7. The horizontal line locates the knee block.

FIG. 9-8. Cut the front rail profile with a bandsaw.

Now that the pattern is drawn on the rail blank, use a bandsaw to cut the bottom profile. **Figure 9-8** shows the rail after the profile has been cut. Clean up the bandsaw marks (see **figure 9-9**) with small files of various shapes. **Figure 9-10** shows a cleaned-up section. When the entire bottom profile has been smoothed, it is ready for carving.

FIG. 9-9. The edges have saw marks.

FIG. 9-10. Remove the bandsaw marks with small, shaped files.

Front Rail: Carving to the Pattern

Several of the elements on the front rail are the same or very close to those on the side rail. Thus they will be carved with the same techniques.

FIG. 9-11. Raise the carving envelope. Set in around the outside and bevel into the stop cuts.

The first step will be to raise the carved pattern envelope from the background. One of the things that I noticed when I studied the original was how shallow the carved rails were. The height off the background was about 1⁄16". This shallow depth gives a sense of lightness and delicacy, but it also isn't a lot of depth to work with. Fortunately, the depths within the carved envelope can be deeper. As long as the outside is shallow, the eye will not see the extra depth within the envelope. Although I've mentioned the shallowness of the envelope, don't be a slave to this. If you need a little more depth in some places, do it. It can be mitigated by feathering it into the surrounding background.

Start by using appropriate-sized gouges to make stop cuts along the perimeter and beveling into their base, as shown in **figure 9-11**. Use flatter gouges, files, scrapers, and sandpaper to blend and feather the background (see **figure 9-12**). Strive to create a flat, smooth surface. In reality this is a flat, angled surface, but if it is smooth enough, the eye will not see the angle. The carved area will appear to be lying on the surface, which is the goal.

FIG. 9-12. Smooth the background. Do not carve into the top edge, which is the drawer opening.

FIG. 9-13. The depth of the raised carving envelope is very shallow.

Also note in **figure 9-12** that the feathering does not affect the drawer opening. This line should remain intact, so that the line of the opening remains straight. If this line is breached, it could be a visual distraction because it may not be parallel to the drawer.

Figure 9-13 shows the shallow depth of the carved envelope relative to the surrounding background. Using the same techniques, complete raising the carved pattern envelope.

Now start to isolate individual elements inside the envelope. Excavate the sections shown in **figure 9-14. Figure 9-15** shows more sections complete.

Establish one of the lower C-scrolls by setting in around the perimeter and beveling into the bottom of the cuts. **Figure 9-16** shows the C-scroll isolated. One of the techniques I use on the longer, flatter curves is to drag the corner of a #2 12 mm gouge along the curved line. The corner of the gouge is shallow, so not a lot of force is needed. This makes it easy to move the tool accurately and quickly.

Figure 9-16 also shows the initial scoops that are part of the ruffle. Note that there is a conforming line about 1⁄16" from the outside perimeter. Draw this line by hand prior to carving the troughs. Leave this area high. The undulating surface of the ruffle is inside the 1⁄16" line. Use #9 gouges of appropriate widths for these cuts. Round over the gouge-cut edges to form convex surfaces. The up-and-down surface should also angle from the perimeter toward the base of the C-scroll. **Figure 9-17** shows the undulating surface complete.

Figure 9-17 also shows the demarcation lines for the C-scroll. The long arc approximately bisects the width of the scroll and terminates at the extension of the circular arcs on each end. Make a stop cut with a #7 4 mm gouge, as shown in **figure 9-18**. Do this on both sides.

FIG. 9-14. Excavate the interior elements.

FIG. 9-15. More interior progress.

FIG. 9-16. Use #9 gouges to create the troughs.

Next, use a #9 10 mm gouge to scoop the inside portion of the C-scroll. **Figure 9-19** shows how to start, and **figure 9-20** shows the operation complete.

Round over the back side of the C-scroll. Use a flat chisel for the first few cuts (see **figure 9-21**). Blend the facets into a smooth surface with a small file or riffler. Note that the outside edges of each circle are relieved a bit. The high spot on each circle is at the center. **Figure 9-22** shows the right end complete and the left end almost complete.

FIG. 9-17. Round over the trough edges to form a smooth, undulating surface.

FIG. 9-19. Use a #9 10 mm gouge to isolate the button.

FIG. 9-18. Establish the C-scroll button section.

FIG. 9-20. The two C-scroll buttons are connected with a pleasing concave surface.

FIG. 9-21. Begin to round over the other side of the C-scroll.

One of the more unusual details on this piece is a series of punched holes along the outside edges of some elements. These are done by eye. Make these with an awl, as shown in **figure 9-23**. Tap the awl lightly with a mallet. **Figure 9-24** shows a series of the holes complete. Also note the tick marks that accent the ruffles and define lines in the leaves. These are made with a #11 1 mm gouge.

Another unique detail to this piece is an "S" figure. There are several of these in the background area. Each "S" is two cuts with a #9 5 mm gouge of opposite orientation that meet in the middle. **Figure 9-25** shows a few of these "S" details and how the gouge is used. Look at the picture of the finished piece for placement of these. I probably don't have exactly as many as on the original, because my judgment said some would not

FIG. 9-22. Smooth the back surface of the C-scroll with rifflers.

FIG. 9-24. The result of the series of holes. These will set off the outlined elements.

FIG. 9-23. Use a small awl to make a series of holes along the perimeter of some of the elements.

FIG. 9-25. Create the figure "S" with a #9 5 mm gouge.

FIG. 9-26. Various details.

fit in the space allotted. This is not an issue, in my opinion. It is better to leave something out than to force an element that does not fit.

Figure 9-26 shows the completed middle section of the front rail. The area labeled "A" is a scoop with a #9 that wraps around to "B." "C" and "D" are high and blend smoothly into the adjacent low areas. The surface "E" is high and falls off in all directions. The surface "F" is a leaf that is tucked into the surrounding element. This is formed by making stop cuts on the surrounding element and then beveling into the bottom of the stop cuts. Keep the outside edge high toward the center and smooth the surface.

Still referring to **figure 9-26**, the upper element "G" is high along its vertical centerline and falls off into the troughs of the side leaves "H." Each of the leaf tips is separated by a vertical gouge cut of appropriate sweep, followed by a bevel into that cut, usually with the same tool.

Study the picture to understand how each of the elements relates to the others. High areas are next to low ones and vice versa. All the elements are formed with techniques previously described. The more you study the picture and visualize how the elements relate, the more your eye will start to better see how to form them. Also keep in mind that shape comes first and detail last.

Figure 9-27 adds the left and right sides of the front rail as a reference.

FIG. 9-27.

Quarter Column

Quarter columns were used on many high-end case pieces. They are a unique and elegant way to dress up an otherwise plain-looking leg post or case corner. A quarter column consists of three parts: a turned base, a turned capital, and a middle section. The capital is at the top, and the base is at the bottom. In most examples the middle section was fluted, but on the especially elaborate pieces the middle section was carved, as is this one. Each of the three elements is one-quarter of a circle; hence the name quarter column. **Figure 10-5** shows my completed column in place. Look for the lines between the three individual pieces.

Figures 10-1, **10-2**, **10-3**, and **10-4** are pictures of the column of the original. Study these and use them as a reference for all of the discussion in this chapter.

Excavate the Column Opening in the Leg Post

The quarter column opening is 13" tall, and the horizontal cross section is 1¼" square. The opening is carved in the two front leg posts. Set a marking gauge to ⅞". Use the inside face as a reference, and score a line on the leg post. **Figure 10-6** shows the technique. Score a second line, using the side face as reference. **Figure 10-7** shows two lines just above the knee, and **figure 10-8** shows the entire opening. The bottom of the column opening is ⅝" up from the top of the knee.

FIG. 10-1. The column on the original.

FIG. 10-2. Note the joint line between the capital and the center portion.

FIG. 10-3.

FIG. 10-4.

FIG. 10-5. Quarter column on my piece. Note that it is three pieces.

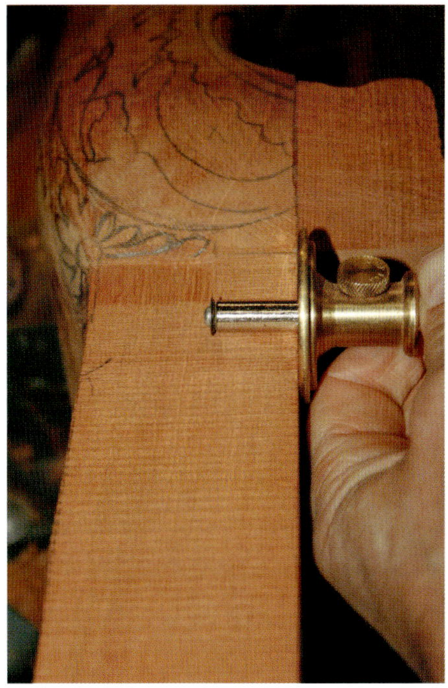

FIG. 10-6. Use a marking gauge set to 7/8" and the inside post face as a reference.

FIG. 10-7. The bottom portion of the quarter-column opening is marked.

FIG. 10-8. The entire column opening is marked.

Use a handsaw to cut along the top and bottom lines at 45° (see **figure 10-9**). Be careful not to go beyond the side lines. With the saw cuts complete, the material can be aggressively removed with a larger flat chisel and mallet. There is a lot of material to remove, so it will take many iterations. **Figure 10-10** shows early progress; **figure 10-11** shows intermediate progress. Stay a little away from the marking gauge line for now.

To excavate the material below the marking gauge lines, use a #9 15 mm gouge to hog out the middle, as shown in **figure 10-12**. Continue with the #9 until very little material is removed with this tool. Use the flat chisel to get closer to the marking gauge lines, as shown in **figure 10-13**. Be careful not to dip below the marking gauge lines. The goal is to end up with a square corner cut out of the leg post.

Use a smaller #9 gouge to get closer into the corner. Use the flat chisel to get closer to the inside corner. **Figure 10-14** shows additional progress. Note that the inside corner is starting to approach square. Continue shaving thin pieces with the flat chisel. **Figure 10-15** shows late progress. Eventually, use the marking gauge line to guide the chisel on its final cuts.

Verify that the inside corner is square. **Figure 10-16** shows that more material needs to be removed close to the inside corner. The square indicates where material needs to be removed. Use a large, flat chisel to straighten out the surface. **Figure 10-17** shows good progress, but there is still a bit in the middle to go. **Figure 10-18** shows a square inside corner.

FIG. 10-9. Use a handsaw to cut the top and bottom surfaces. Don't go past the vertical opening lines.

FIG. 10-10. Use a flat chisel to remove material into the top and bottom cuts.

FIG. 10-11. The front section is removed down to the 45° surface.

FIG. 10-12. Use a #9 15 mm gouge to remove material below the 45° surface.

FIG. 10-13. Use a flat chisel to carve closer to the opening lines.

FIG. 10-14. The inside corner is approaching square.

FIG. 10-15. Iteratively get closer to the opening lines with a flat chisel. Use the marking gauge line to make the final cut.

FIG. 10-16. The inside corner is not square. This shows where to remove material.

FIG. 10-17. There is a high spot in the middle.

Turn the Base and Capital

The capital and base elements are turned from the profiles in **figure A-4**. I build up the turning blank from four sections 1¼" square and about 3"–3½" long. This length accounts both for the capital and base, plus about ⅛" extra for each piece. This will allow enough flexibility to get a good fit in the opening when all three pieces are in place. These four sections are fastened with hot hide glue into a 2½" square blank that is then turned. First, glue two sets of two, then glue the pairs to get the square. **Figure 10-19** shows the glued-up blank ready for turning.

FIG. 10-18. After the adjustments, the inside corner is square.

FIG. 10-19. Glue four capital and base sections together in preparation for turning.

This turned blank will yield four bases and four capitals. When the turning is complete, heat the profiled blank in the oven to about 140°F to soften the hide glue. Break the elements apart and clean up any residual glue with water. Because each segment was square to start, a quarter of the turned element will fit without modification in the column opening.

An alternate way would be to start with a 2¾" blank of solid stock of sufficient length.

The extra width is to account for the saw kerfs when the piece is cut in quarters after turning. Turn the base and capital profiles, then cut the turned item into four parts. The sawn faces might need to be squared, which is a dicey operation with a small piece.

Theoretically, both these methods would yield the same result. However, the built-up-block method is far superior in my opinion, because all the cutting and fitting come before the turning, so the quarters will fit with no more work. Because of the much easier and better results, I wouldn't even consider the solid-block method.

Figures 10-20 and **10-21** show a base and a capital, respectively, after turning. **Figure 10-22** shows the turned blank before the glue is softened and the pieces are separated.

FIG. 10-20. One base section after turning.

FIG. 10-21. One capital section after turning.

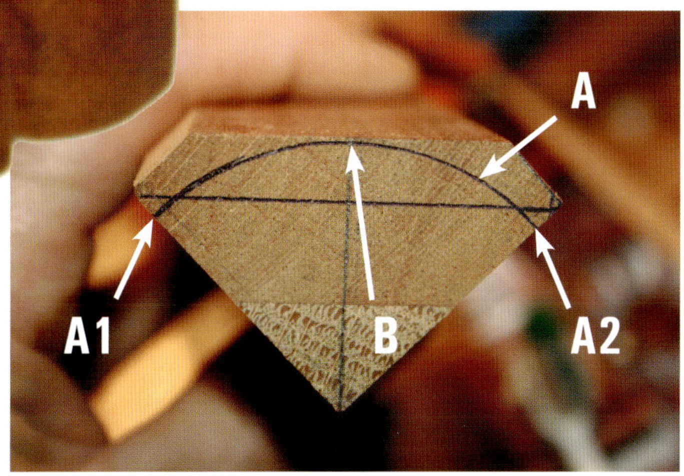

FIG. 10-23. Layout and guide lines for shaping the middle section.

FIG. 10-22. The turned capital and base block before separating the components with heat.

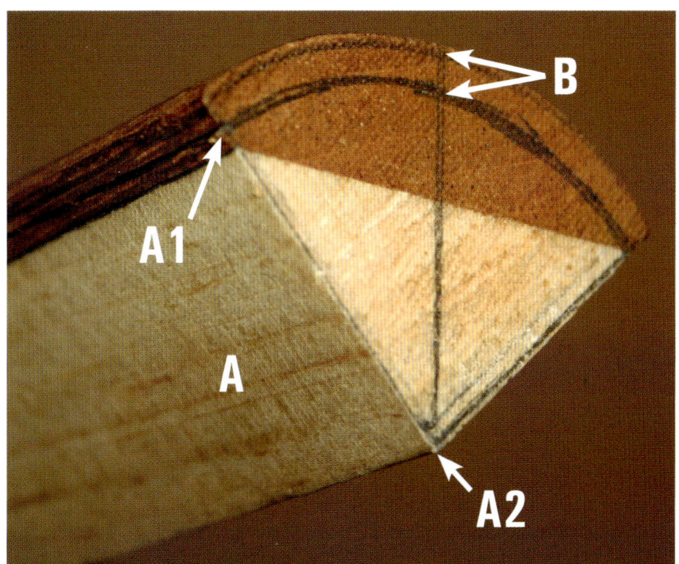

FIG. 10-24. The length "B" is the carving-envelope depth.

Shape the Middle-Element Blank

I make the middle section without turning. The arc "A" in **figure 10-23** is one-quarter of a 1⅛" radius circle. The background of the quarter column will be at the 1" radius, and the extra ⅛" is for carving. Draw a similar arc on the opposite end. Connect the end points "A1" and "A2" with their corresponding points on the opposite end. Carry the centerline "B" to the opposite end. The centerline will remain high the entire length of the piece. With these lines and arcs as a guide, use a #49 rasp to remove the material outside the arcs. **Figure 10-24** shows the middle section shaped and ready for carving.

Build Up the Quarter-Column Stock (Optional)

If a piece of solid stock is used, it needs to be 1¼" square by the desired length. However, a thinner piece of stock can be used if you make a composite piece, as shown in **figures 10-23** and **10-24**. The face "A," which is determined by the points "A1" and "A2" in **figure 10-24**, is between the back corner and the end of the arc. This face will be seated against the column opening and hidden. The corresponding face on the other side of the back corner will also be hidden. Thus, only the ⅛" carving area—labeled "B"—plus a little more is visible. This area needs to be primary wood; the rest is hidden and can be anything.

Use yellow or white glue for this operation. When the hide-glued base/capital blank is heated, the yellow glue will remain intact.

Figure 10-25 shows how a quarter section is extracted from the sandwiched stock. Use a table saw with the blade set at 45° to make the cuts shown. **Figure 10-26** shows a square corner. Make adjustment cuts, keeping the back corner square, until the sides are 1¼" from the back corner to the end points of the 1¼" radius arc.

FIG. 10-26. Check that the column blank is square.

FIG. 10-27. Fit the three sections prior to carving the middle section.

FIG. 10-25. Technique for creating a quarter section from a composite buildup.

FIG. 10-28. The middle section is proud of the capital and base. The extra material will be carved.

Fitting the Base, Capital, and Uncarved Middle Section

At this point, the opening is cut in the leg post, the base and capital are turned, and the middle section is an uncarved, rounded, 1⅛", radiused quarter cylindrical section. Fit the three pieces in the opening, as shown in **figure 10-27**. Cut the base and capital to length, then cut the middle section to fit.

Note how the various pieces relate to the opening. The widest points of the base and capital are the only areas that reach to the outside edge of the opening. These are at the top of the capital and the bottom of the base. Also notice that the uncarved middle section is proud of the bottom of the capital and the top of the base. This is the ⅛" carving section. **Figure 10-28** shows this in more detail. By fitting these three pieces now, there will be no height adjustments when the carving is complete. In addition, the carving pattern can now be made to fit the fixed-height blank.

Carve the Middle Section

Set a marking gauge to 1" and use the back edges to score lines on both sides of the middle-section blank. **Figure 10-29** shows the technique. This line is the depth of the carving and the height of the background surface. With a scribed line, it will be much easier to get a more uniform background surface and a consistent carving height.

Make a template from the full-sized pattern titled "Quarter Column" from the insert packet and referenced in **figure A1-4**. This template has been sized to be wide enough to accommodate the curvature of the quarter section.

The two columns are mirror images, so there is a left and a right orientation. Referring to **figure 10-5**, the orientation is such that the plume of leaves emanates from the upper-side corner. **Figure 10-5** is of the right column, and the plume originates from the upper-right corner. On the left side, it would originate from the upper-left corner. Keep this in mind when transferring the pattern to the blank.

Figure 10-30 shows the bottom alignment of the template. Note that the leaf tip goes to the very bottom of the blank. The originating plume starts at the top edge. "Stretch" or "shrink" the template as needed. If the blank and template are mismatched, force these two end points and make up the difference in the middle stems. It doesn't matter if these are a bit shorter or longer; it will look fine either way. **Figure 10-31** shows the column pattern drawn on the blank.

FIG. 10-29. Set a marking gauge to 1" and score lines on each side. This sets the background surface.

FIG. 10-30. Align the template to the bottom of the middle section.

Raise the carving envelope by lowering the background around the pattern to the scribed lines on the sides. Use gouges of appropriate widths and sweeps and the same techniques as in the previous carvings. In addition, clean up the background with rifflers, scrapers, and sandpaper as needed. Remember that a smooth and clean background will greatly improve the look of your carving. **Figures 10-32** and **10-33** show the carving envelope raised and the background smooth. Be mindful that the background is a circular, cylindrical surface. Sight down the blank from an end at a low angle. The background surface should look like it is all part of the same circular cylinder. In addition, the background should be the same radius as the bottom of the capital and the top of the base. These surfaces will be blended when the three column pieces are glued into the leg post opening.

FIG. 10-32. The carving envelope is raised above the smooth background.

FIG. 10-31. Trace the carving pattern to the column middle section.

FIG. 10-33. More of the raised carving envelope.

Isolate the central portion of one of the flowers drawn in **figure 10-33**. Draw the outside circle shown in **figure 10-34**. This ring remains high when the flower is complete. Set in around the circular center with a #5 5 mm gouge, as shown in **figure 10-34**. Bevel into the base of the cut, as shown in **figure 10-35**. Deepen the area around the center and then bevel back to the outer circle. **Figure 10-36** shows the results.

Now isolate the flower from the stems on each end. **Figure 10-37** shows one of the stems lowered around the leaf tips. Set in around the leaf tips with a #7 or #5 gouge and bevel into the cuts along the stem. Repeat this on the stem on the other side of the flower.

There are five leaf petal clusters to each flower. Separate the petal clusters now. **Figure 10-38** shows the clusters separated. Set in with #5 and #7 gouges to match the arc of each cluster. Bevel into the stop cuts from the side that will be lower.

FIG. 10-36. Blend the surface to the outside circle.

FIG. 10-34. The larger circle will be the high spots around the flower.

FIG. 10-37. Lower the stem to the left of the flower.

FIG. 10-35. Separate the flower's central dome.

FIG. 10-38. Separate the flower sections.

Each cluster is a convex surface falling off in all directions from a high spot near the center. Study **figures 10-39**, **10-40**, and the completed version in **figure 10-5** for the details of leaf separation. Make sure each of the leaf tips is distinct and well defined. Gouges that are good for leaf tips are #5 5 mm, #5 8 mm, #7 6 mm, and #7 10 mm. When cutting the leaf tips, and especially when using the #7 gouges, be careful to orient the trailing corner of the gouge so that it points to the center of the flower. This will give a more realistic and pleasing look.

Round over the flower's central cylinder into a dome. Remove the corners with a flat chisel or a #2 or #3 gouge. Use a #7 6 mm gouge to round the dome. Blend the facets with a small file or riffler. **Figure 10-41** shows the completed flower.

Make a small hole in the middle of the dome with an awl. Tap the awl with a mallet, but don't hit too hard, to avoid splitting the dome. Add accent cuts with a #11 1 mm gouge. The long accent cut on each leaf cluster has a series of holes along the line of the cut. **Figure 10-42** shows these gouge cuts and holes.

The lower leaf cluster is made of two subclusters. **Figure 10-43** shows the bottom left cluster with its leaves drawn. **Figure 10-44** shows the leaves detailed. The overall shape of both subclusters is convex. Note that they both emanate from underneath the flower above it. **Figure 10-45** shows the right subcluster shaped. Study **figures 10-1** through **10-5** for the details of these two lower clusters.

The connecting stems above each of the flowers are similar. The spine of each is high and runs diagonally from top to bottom. **Figure 10-46** shows the spine line drawn on one of the stems. **Figure 10-47** shows it carved. Each side of the stem is shaped with a #7 10 mm gouge.

FIG. 10-40. Another view of the individually shaped leaves.

FIG. 10-41. Round over the central dome. Smooth the convex leaf surfaces.

FIG. 10-39. Shape and model the individual sections.

FIG. 10-42. Use a small awl to make holes in the leaf accent lines.

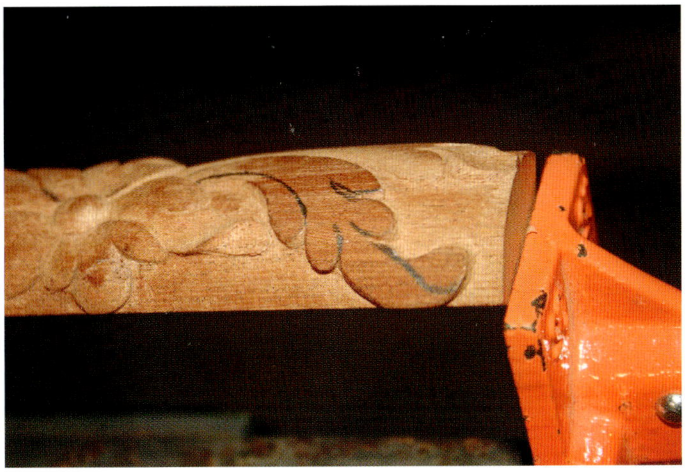

FIG. 10-43. Draw the individual leaves in the lower leaf cluster.

FIG. 10-44. The bottom lower leaf cluster is detailed.

FIG. 10-45. The top lower leaf cluster is detailed.

FIG. 10-46. Draw the centerline of the connecting stem.

FIG. 10-47. The stem centerline remains high. Each side is shaped with a #7 10 mm gouge.

The upper leaves and flowers are done in a similar manner. Study the pictures of the finished column for the details. **Figures 10-48** and **10-49** show the upper flower and leaf cluster detailed.

The middle section is now substantially done. Compare your version to the original and to mine. Look for any details that are missing, and add them.

FIG. 10-48. The upper leaf cluster is detailed.

FIG. 10-49. Another view of the detailed upper leaf cluster.

Moldings

There are three moldings on this dressing table. The Greek key and cove moldings are applied, and the guilloché (*ghee-YOWSH*) molded edge on the top is carved from the solid. These three embellishments look good together because their sizes are nicely integrated.

The Greek key molding is an unusual addition to a Philadelphia dressing table. It is applied just below the cove molding, which is immediately under the top. **Figure 11-1** shows the molded top and the two applied moldings as seen from the right front corner. **Figure 11-2** shows these profiles from the back. In addition, the drawing titled *Molded Elements in Place* in **figure 11-3** shows a cross-sectional view of all three together. Note how the vertical edge of the cove molding is in line with the vertical wall of the top's fillet. This means that these two surfaces look like one surface, with a $\frac{5}{8}$" semicircular bead sitting proud. Further note that the smaller $\frac{1}{8}$" semicircular bead at the bottom of the cove molding is proud of the Greek key.

FIG. 11-1. The Greek key and cove moldings are applied. The guilloché molded edge is carved from the solid.

Because of these relationships, it is important that the top overhangs the case in a reasonably exacting way. The overhang on the front and sides is $1\frac{3}{16}$". This allows for the $\frac{7}{8}$" deep cove and the $\frac{5}{16}$" deep semicircular edge. Note that the $\frac{5}{16}$" thickness of the molded section of the top is because the height of this section is $\frac{5}{8}$". The overhang on the back is $\frac{1}{2}$" and is less exacting because there are no moldings or molded edge on the back.

FIG. 11-2. The three moldings as seen from the back.

FIG. 11-3.

Molding Elements
(All Drawings Full Scale)

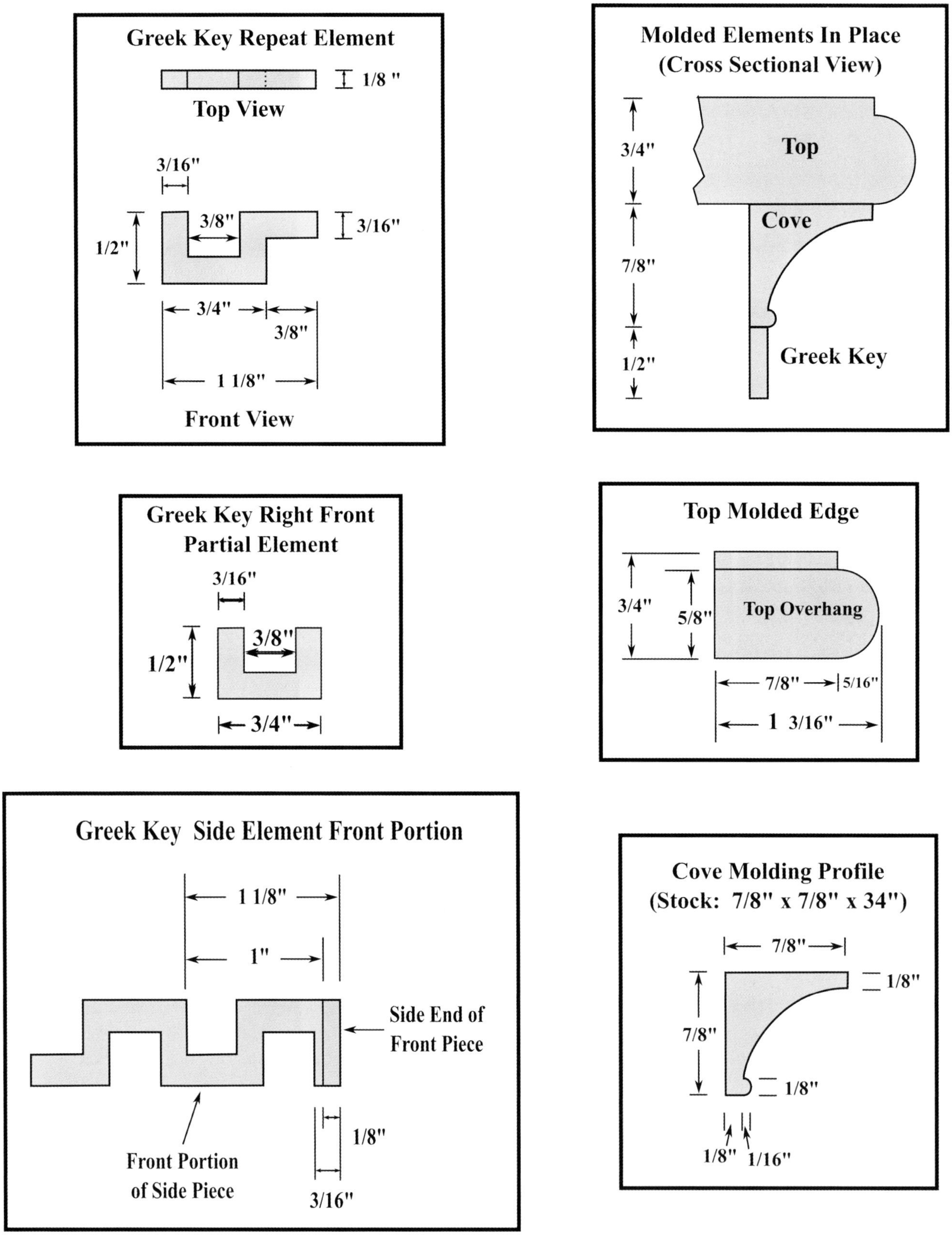

The order of operations for putting these pieces together is the following: the top goes first, then the cove molding, and finally the Greek key. The two applied moldings are three pieces each.

Make each of these independently, but be careful to get the top sized appropriately before carving the molded edge. As in many cases, implementation and theory aren't always the same. However, if you are reasonably careful, you will be off by only a little. And if you are off a little, it is pretty easy to make an adjustment. If the top is a little short or long, thin or thicken the cove stock so the ⅝" semicircle is completely proud.

To minimize the chances of incorrectly sizing the top, it is a good idea to make the cove molding first and then dry-fit the two side pieces to the case. Now measure the width of the case plus the two moldings. Add ⅝" (2" × 5⁄16") for the carved portion to get the width of the top.

The depth is not as critical because of the overhang on the back. If the back overhang is a little more or less than ½", it doesn't matter. Use whatever portion of it that is needed to get the proper relationship in front between the top and cove molding.

The only sizing issue for the Greek key molding is that the bottom of the cove molding is sufficiently thick to allow the bead to be proud.

With this overview in mind, it is time to start making moldings. I would strongly advise making a test section for the top guilloché pattern. A 3" (wide) × 6" (long) × ¾" (tall) piece of stock will be plenty. This will be good practice for the layout and carving. In addition, it will give you a reference model when working on the case top.

Greek Key Molding

The Greek key molding is applied as three pieces: one symmetrical piece in front and an asymmetrical one on each side. The symmetrical front piece begins and terminates with an upward-pointing opening. The asymmetrical side pieces have a downward-pointing opening on the front end and whatever happens when the repeating pattern is flushed with the back of the case. The openings in the Greek key alternate between up and down on the straight sections and as it wraps around the corners. The side pieces and front pieces meet in a butt joint with the joint on the side.

The Greek key stock thickness is ⅛". Thus the front piece is the full width of the case plus ¼", allowing for ⅛" overlap on each side. In this case the front piece would be 33⅝" (33⅜" for the case plus ¼").

The pattern for the Greek key is based on a repeated element that is 1⅛" long, and a couple of variations of that element. The right-front partial piece is ¾" long and terminates the right side of the front piece with an upward-pointing opening. The other variation is ⅛" shorter. It is the front most portion of each of the side pieces. This is a different orientation of the repeated element, but with the leading leg ⅛" thinner. This ⅛" will be replaced when the side piece butts into the front ⅛" thick front piece. In this way, all the legs are 3⁄16" wide. **Figure 11-3** shows the full repeated element and the two

FIG. 11-4. Set a marking gauge to 5⁄16". Score the depth openings from the top and bottom edges.

variations. The "right-front partial element" is used once on the right-hand end of the front piece to make it symmetrical with the left end.

On the original there are twenty-eight full elements and one "right-front partial element." The repeated element is based on multiples of a 3⁄16" base element. The width and height of any segment is 3⁄16". The openings are twice that length, or ⅜". Because the height of the Greek key is ½" and the width of a segment is 3⁄16", that means the opening is 5⁄16" high.

This might sound a bit complicated when explained in words, but the pattern is straightforward and the drawings should make it clear. Study the drawings to fully understand the pattern before transferring it to the stock.

One of the issues with a rigid geometric pattern such as this is that rarely, if ever, does the theory meet the practical. In this case, there are twenty-eight repeated elements that are 31½" (28 × 1⅛"), plus ¾" for the "right-front partial." This gives a length of 32¼". Recall that this case is 32⅜". With the ¼" overhang, the overall length that is needed is 32⅝". In this case, the front Greek key piece is ⅜" too short.

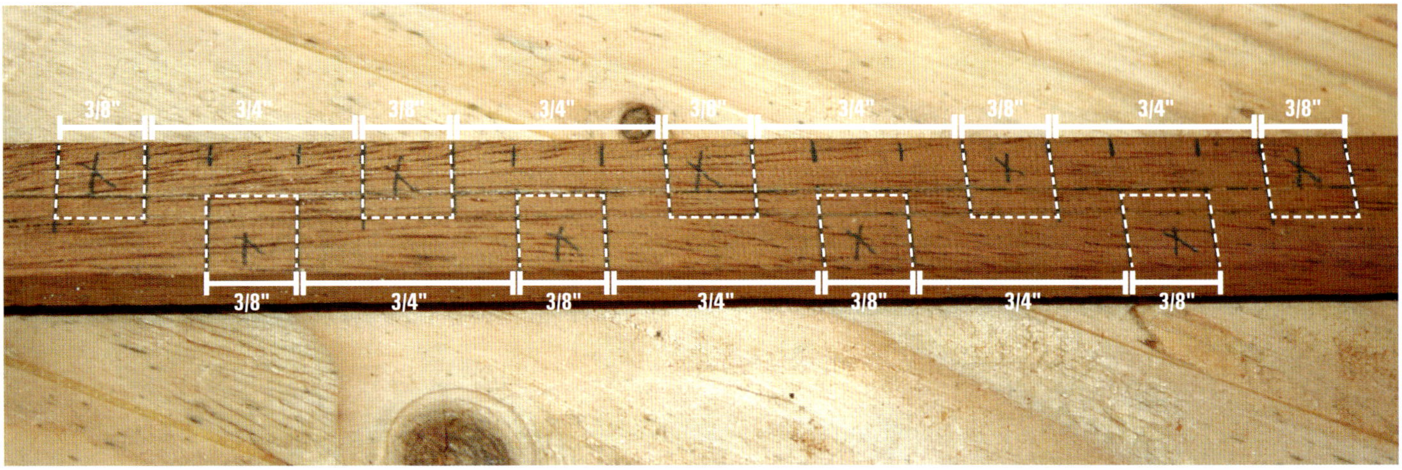

FIG. 11-5. Typical layout for the center portions of any of the three pieces.

So the front piece needs to be "stretched" 3/8". Distribute the 3/8" over the entire length of the piece, 1/32" at a time. The 1/32" is arbitrary; I picked it because it is the smallest reasonable number that divides evenly into 3/8". In this case there are twelve 1/32" segments that need to be added.

The strategy will be to add one 1/32" to twelve openings distributed more or less evenly along the length of the front piece. There are on the order of fifty-six openings, so every fourth opening will be lengthened by 1/32". If possible, don't add any length to the end openings. With this distribution it will be next to impossible to see any differences, and the pattern will look fine.

If the Greek key piece needs to be "shrunk," use a similar technique to subtract 1/32" from the number of openings that are required to remove the distance needed.

When you are comfortable with the design of the Greek key components, transfer the layout to the wooden stock. The stock for the Greek key pieces is 1/8" thick by 1/2" wide. Cut each piece a little longer than needed; the extra length will be removed after it is installed. For the front piece, leave a little extra on each end.

Set a marking gauge to 5/16" and lightly score two lines the length of the stock (see **figure 11-4**). These lines are the depths of the openings and are measured from the top and bottom edges. **Figure 11-5** shows a theoretical layout of the center portion of any of the three pieces. Remember to adjust the 3/8" openings to "stretch" or "shrink" the front piece as needed. Because the side pieces do not have a mating piece on the back, it is not as important to worry about how the pattern terminates at the back. Adjustment on the sides would be needed only if there was a small portion of the pattern at the back. This is a judgment call as to what is visually unacceptable. An example of something that might be unacceptable would be if there was a 1/32" wide sliver after an opening. In this case I would add or subtract that sliver from somewhere in the middle.

FIG. 11-6. Nibble the openings with a bandsaw.

FIG. 11-7. Remove the bandsaw marks with a small file and a guide board.

FIG. 11-8. The left front corner. The leading edge of the side piece is only 1/16" thick.

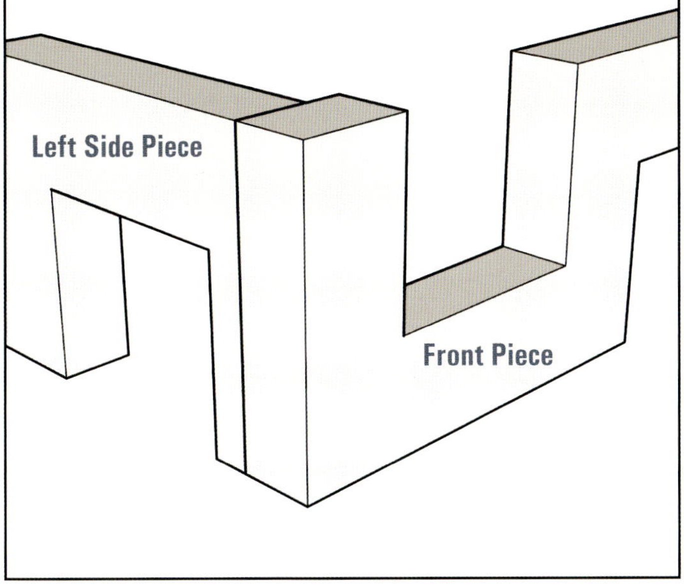

Use a bandsaw to cut the openings. Make repeated cuts perpendicular to the long edges to nibble away each opening. **Figure 11-6** shows a complete opening and one in progress. This is the most efficient way.

Because the openings are only 3/8" wide and the Greek key pieces are sufficiently long, it is difficult for most, and impossible for some, to turn the stock 90°. One could use a handsaw, but it would take a long time and probably not be as accurate. Cutting just the sides of the openings with a saw and chiseling the horizontal line would also take a lot more time and would probably split the wood. Thus I prefer the nibbling method.

After all the openings have been cut, the bandsaw marks need to be removed. Use a backing block and a small file for this operation. **Figure 11-7** shows the technique. Strive for an exact square opening. The backing block is needed to prevent the fragile Greek key stock from breaking. It is also useful for aligning the file square to the stock. Be careful not to overcut the sides at the bottom and not to gouge the bottom when filing the sides.

Figure 11-8 shows a diagram of the left front corner. Note the 1/16" leading end on the left. This will butt into the 1/8" thick front piece to form a 3/16" leg.

There are more than a hundred openings, so the cleanup will take awhile, but it is necessary for a refined look. When the cleanup is complete, the Greek key is ready to be applied to the case. The cove molding needs to be cut and applied before the Greek key, so put these pieces aside for now.

FIG. 11-9. Score lines on the top 5/16" from the edge. Score a line on the vertical face 1/16" from the top.

FIG. 11-10. There is no fillet on the back edge.

Prepare the Top for the Guilloché Pattern

The top is a single piece of 3/4" thick stock that overhangs the case by 1 3/16" on three sides and 1/2" in back. Three-quarters of an inch of the overhang accounts for the cove molding immediately below the top. The remaining 5/16" of the overhang is the semicircular envelope for the guilloché pattern that is proud of the cove molding. Size the top to fit your case with these overhang additions.

After the top has been sized to fit your case, cut a 5/16" wide by 1/8" deep fillet on the two sides and the front. This will "raise" the center section above the molded edge. Create these lines with a marking gauge, square, and knife. **Figures 11-9** and **11-10** show these lines cut into the top perimeter; **figure 11-10** is a view of the back. Note that there is no fillet along the back edge. It is visually important to have crisp lines and square sides to the fillet. This will give a lighter and more elegant look.

Use a flat chisel and small router plane in several iterations to cut the fillet. **Figure 11-11** shows the technique and result. Use a second board of equal thickness to the top to support the router plane on its free edge.

Next, use a circle template to draw ⅝" diameter semicircles on the ends, as shown in **figure 11-12**. This figure also shows several straight lines. These lines divide the horizontal surfaces in half and the vertical ones in quarters. They will be used as guides to form the semicircular shape.

Use a block plane to bevel the corners between the centerline on the horizontal surface and the nearest quarter line on the adjacent vertical one. **Figure 11-13** shows the technique, and **figure 11-14** shows all the corners beveled. Use a file and sandpaper to complete the rounding. **Figures 11-15** and **11-16** show the rounding complete.

FIG. 11-11. Use a small router plane to create the rabbet.

FIG. 11-13. Use a block plane to bevel between two adjacent guide lines.

FIG. 11-12. Use a circle template to draw a ⅝" semicircle. The guide lines split the edge into four sections.

FIG. 11-14. The beveled corners begin to approximate the semicircle.

FIG. 11-15. Round the beveled corners with files and sandpaper.

FIG. 11-16. The completed semicircular edge. It is now ready for carving.

Laying Out and Carving the Guilloché Pattern

After the ⅝" diameter semicircular surface has been shaped on the two sides and front, draw the guilloché pattern on this surface.

This rigid layout has the same problem as the Greek key molding; that is, there are not an integral number of divisions in the needed length. So the pattern needs to either be *stretched* or *shrunk*. Determine the difference that needs to be added or removed. In this case, it will not be off by more than one-half of the repeat length of ½", so there can be at most eight 1/32" adjustments to make. Distribute the difference in 1/32" increments as evenly as possible, staying away from the ends.

The pattern in **figure 11-17** is meant as a guide; it is not a template. The vertical layout lines are ½" apart, and the first line from each end starts at 5/16". Draw the lines as described and shown in **figures 11-18** and **11-19**, accounting for any stretching or shrinking. There are multiple ways of visualizing this pattern, but it helped me to think of it as a series of "S" surfaces. A typical "S" surface is the shaded section of **figure 11-17**.

Use a circle template to draw a 3/16" diameter circle on each of the layout lines, as shown in **figure 11-18. Figure 11-19** shows a few of the circles drawn in place.

FIG. 11-18. Use a circle template to draw 3/16" circles on each of the vertical guide lines.

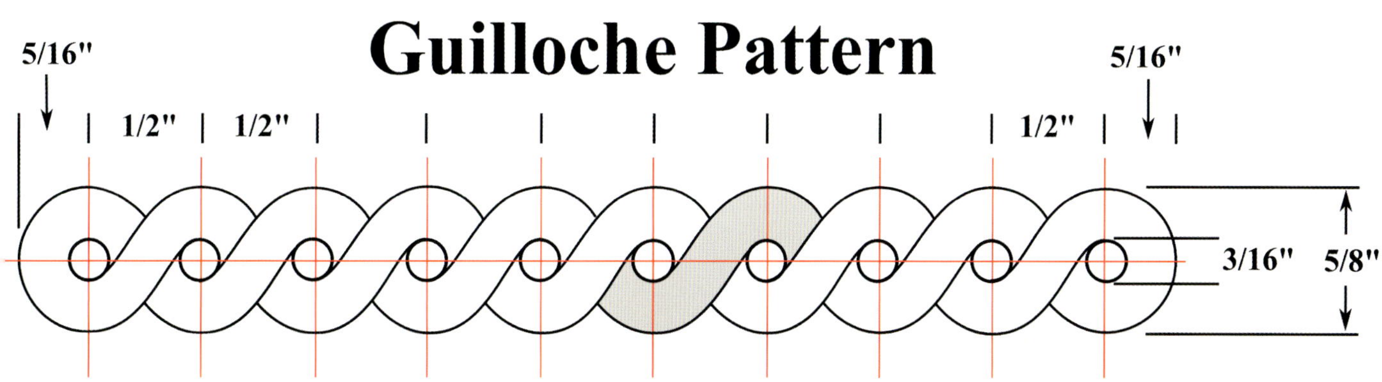

FIG. 11-17. This is the theoretical pattern for the guilloché. The repeating "S" is one way to visualize it.

Each of the circles will be the center hole of the pattern. Use a #8 4 mm gouge (see **figure 11-20**) to establish the perimeter of a hole and remove the initial portion. Deepen the hole with a 3⁄16" twist drill. Drilling the hole is easier and quicker than carving it deeper. I used a hand drill for this because the top is too big and cumbersome to use a drill press. **Figure 11-21** shows the technique.

Three additional layout lines are needed: one on the top and two on the bottom. On the top side, draw a layout line 1⁄8" from the fillet wall, as shown in **figure 11-22.** On the bottom side, use a marking gauge set to 5⁄16" to score a line, as shown in **figure 11-23.** This line is the equivalent of the fillet wall on the top. Also on the bottom side, draw a line 1⁄8" closer to the edge than the scored line. This is the equivalent of the 1⁄8" line on top.

FIG. 11-19. Some of the circles drawn in place.

FIG. 11-21. Use a 3⁄16" twist drill to deepen the holes.

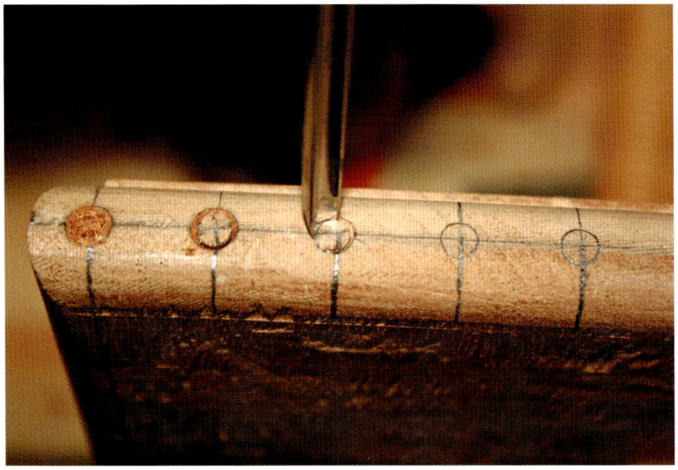

FIG. 11-20. Use a #8 4 mm gouge to define the circles.

FIG. 11-22. On the top side, draw a line 1⁄8" from the base of the fillet.

Now draw the curved lines on the top side, as shown in **figure 11-24**. Draw the additional curve labeled "A" in **figure 11-25**. This completes one of the curves on top. Note that the additional curve "A" intersects the S curve to the right, halfway between the small circle centerlines and set back from the fillet wall by ⅛". Note also the curve above the ⅛" layout line is symmetrical about its centerline and butts into the base of the fillet wall.

Repeat this drawing along the remainder of the perimeter. **Figure 11-26** shows the result. Note how the S curve flows into the corner on the right side.

Draw the analogous curves on the bottom side, as shown in **figure 11-27**. The curves on the bottom are mirror images of the ones on top. These lines determine a series of "S" surfaces. On the top portion, the lines indicate that the surface to the left flows under the one on the right. On the bottom portion, the surface on the right, labeled "A" in **figure 11-27**, flows under the one on the left, labeled "B."

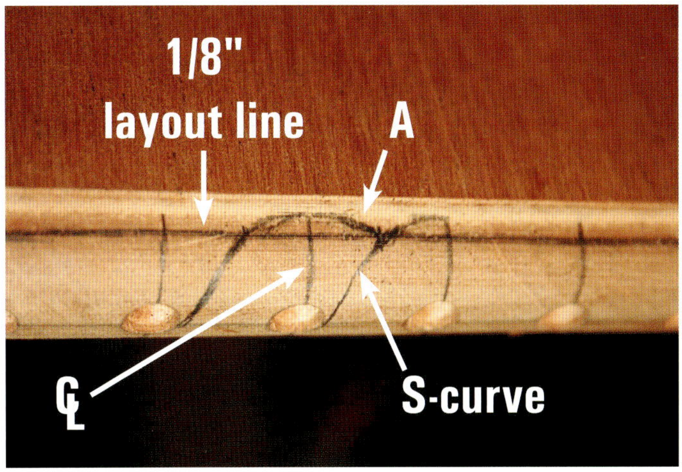

FIG. 11-25. Extend the "S" with curve "A."

FIG. 11-23. Use a marking gauge set to 5⁄16" and score a line on the bottom face.

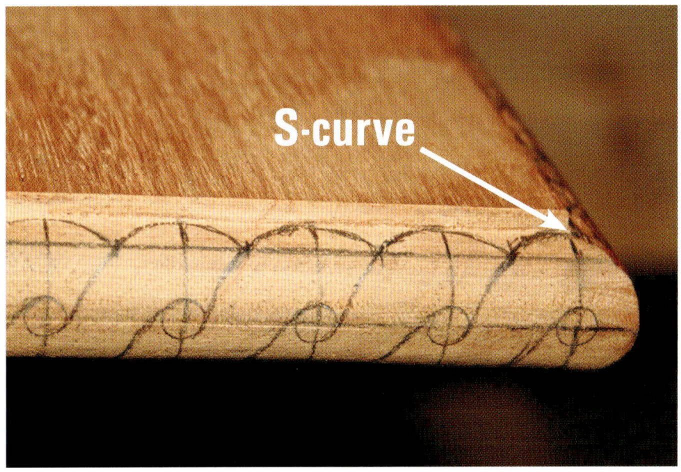

FIG. 11-26. Complete drawing the S curves.

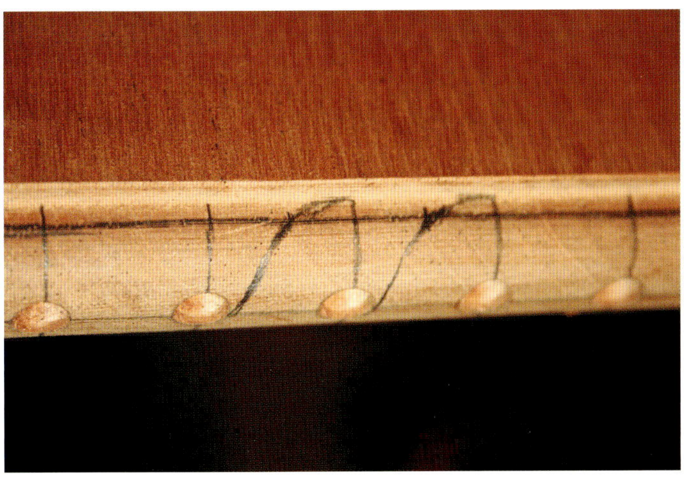

FIG. 11-24. Draw the top portion of the "S."

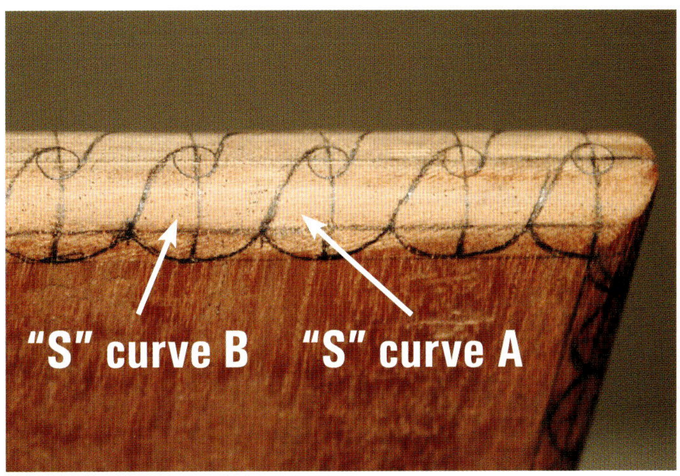

FIG. 11-27. S curve "A" flows under S curve "B."

There is a "V" shape produced at the intersection of two adjacent S curves; establish these first. **Figure 11-28** shows the vertex line of the "V" and how to define it with a ½" straight chisel. Use the same flat chisel to round the tops of the S curves, as shown in **figure 11-29**. **Figure 11-30** shows the results.

Next, use a #7 16 mm gouge to separate the S curves, as shown in **figure 11-31**. Start the cut with a corner of the gouge at the intersection of a centerline and the base of the fillet wall. Rotate the tool along the penciled guide line to the inflection point where the concavity of the curve changes. Switch the tool orientation and blend the remaining cut into the small circular hole.

You will probably be a bit timid to start, but after a few cuts you should become more comfortable as you get a feel for the motion of the gouge and the flow of the curve. To aid understanding and efficiency, make several of these cuts on consecutive sections. **Figure 11-32** shows the idea.

Use a flatter gouge—a #2 or #3, for example—to make bevel cuts from the left into the stop cuts along the S curve. **Figure 11-33** shows a few of these. These cuts make the top of the S curve on the left tuck under the one on its right.

Carve the "S" surfaces as best you can, then smooth them with rifflers and sandpaper to achieve the results shown in **figure 11-34**. Note that the right surfaces tuck underneath the left ones on the bottom. This is the opposite of the flow on the top.

There are approximately 125 of these S curves around the perimeter. Your latter ones will probably be better than the early ones, so try a few on the side toward the back until you get your rhythm.

Once all the S curves are shaped and smoothed, carve a narrow trough down the center of each surface. This sounds simple to do, and conceptually it is. However, it is more difficult to implement than it sounds, since it is important to get smooth and uniform curves. One of the downsides of a highly repetitive pattern is that it is easy to see differences between repeats of the pattern, even if they differ only a little, so it is important to make all of them as similar as possible.

Draw a centerline on each of the "S" surfaces. These lines need to follow the surface edges as accurately as possible. Start by making short tick marks on various points along the "S" surfaces, as shown in **figure 11-35**. The intent here is to get the directions correct in key transition areas. Next, connect the ticks to get the result shown in **figure 11-36**.

Use a #11 2 mm gouge to carve along the centerline. **Figure 11-37** shows a beginning technique. Because the curvature of the arc is almost always changing, the tool needs to change direction continually. You will get the best results if you can do this in one motion, but this is difficult to do and requires practice. To make this task easier, do part of the curve in one motion and the remaining part in another; sometimes changing your position relative to the board to make the second cut easier.

FIG. 11-28. Mark the centerline of the "V" with a flat chisel.

FIG. 11-29. Round the tops of the S curves with the same flat chisel.

FIG. 11-30. A couple of the S-curve bottoms are established.

FIG. 11-31. Use a #7 16 mm gouge to define the S curves on top.

FIG. 11-32. For efficiency, make several iterations of the same cut in succession.

FIG. 11-33. Dive the surface to the left into the one on the right.

FIG. 11-34. Smooth the surfaces of the S curves with rifflers and sandpaper.

FIG. 11-35. Draw small segments along the centerlines on each of the S-curve surfaces.

FIG. 11-36. Connect the individual segments.

FIG. 11-37. Use a #11 2 mm gouge to cut along the centerline.

Figure 11-38 shows the top portions of several "S" surfaces. Note that there are no egregious discontinuities in these gouge cuts. When making the second cut, it is important to have it start in the same direction that the first one ended. If this is done well, it will not be detectable that two cuts were made; it will look like one.

Set the #11 2 mm gouge in the trough at the end of the first cut, as shown in **figure 11-39**. Point "A" shows the location in a different trough. Note how the gouge is pointing in the direction of the line immediately in front of it. In mathematical terms, the direction of the tool should be in line with the slope of the curve at any point. **Figure 11-40** shows the results of a few second cuts. Repeat these techniques on the remaining "S" surfaces.

As mentioned, begin in a less visible spot than the front. Your technique and results should get better after you do a few of them.

FIG. 11-38. Several cuts on the top portions of the S curves.

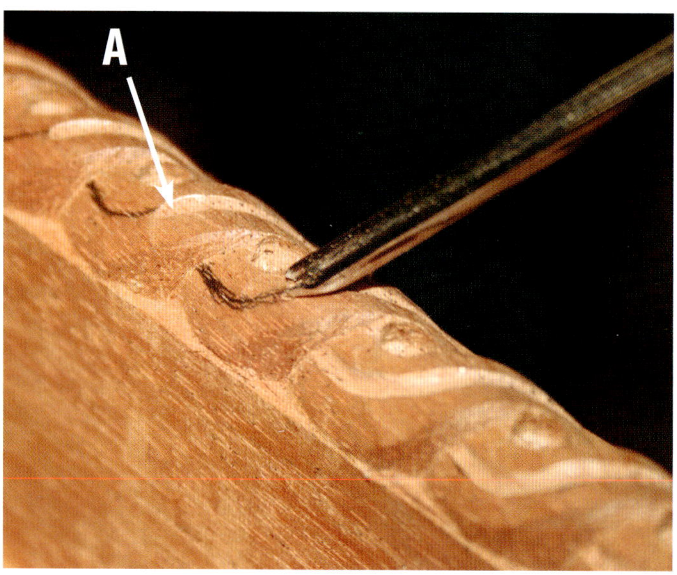

FIG. 11-39. Begin the bottom portion by starting in the trough from the top.

FIG. 11-40. Several #11 cuts are complete.

Cove Molding

The cove molding fits immediately below the top. It is attached with glue and brads and is made in three pieces, with mitered corners in front. The front piece is mitered on both ends, and each of the two side pieces are mitered in front and flush with the back face of the back leg post. Be sure to make each piece a little longer than needed, to allow for any adjustments or mistakes.

There are a couple of choices on how to select stock for a molding such as this. One, use a sufficiently long piece of stock to accommodate all three components. This might be preferred if molding planes are used. Two, use one piece of stock for each component. Three, spoon two profiles together on a larger piece of stock. Theoretically, the third choice is the most economical, because there is less waste, but it takes a bit longer because there is an extra step or two.

In principle I prefer choice 3, because I try to be very conscious of waste. To me, wood in general, and mahogany in particular, are valuable resources that should not be wasted. So I take the extra time to search my scrap pile, looking for a discarded piece that can be turned into something useful and lasting.

Figure 11-41 shows the cove-molding profile and two cutting sequences. Sequence A uses $\frac{7}{8}$" × $\frac{7}{8}$" stock. Sequence B uses 1$\frac{1}{8}$" × 1$\frac{1}{8}$". In two or three steps, one gets to the same point, either 2A or 2B, respectively. From here forward the steps are the same.

Through step 3 in **figure 11-41**, I would use a table saw. The stairsteps shown in step 3 assume a $\frac{3}{16}$" kerf on the table saw blade and will require four cuts of varying heights. Note that cut number 1 is such that it isolates the bead.

FIG. 11-41.

Cove Molding Extraction Sequence

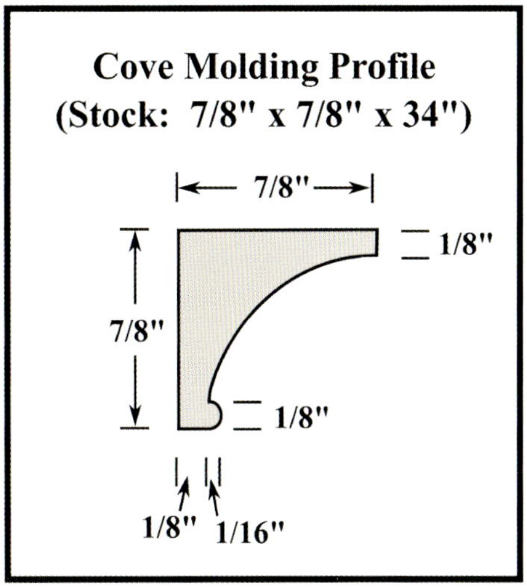

1A. Trace the profile on the stock end.

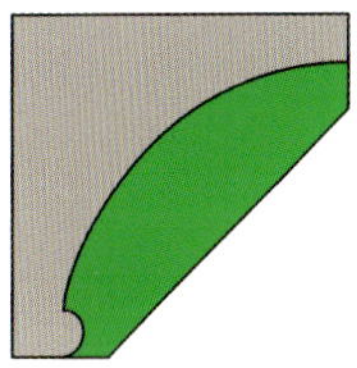

2A. Cut off a 45° angle lengthwise.

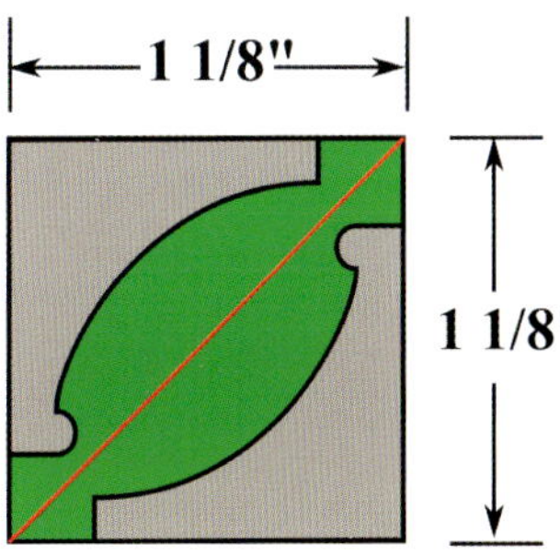

0B. Trace two profiles on the end of bigger stock.

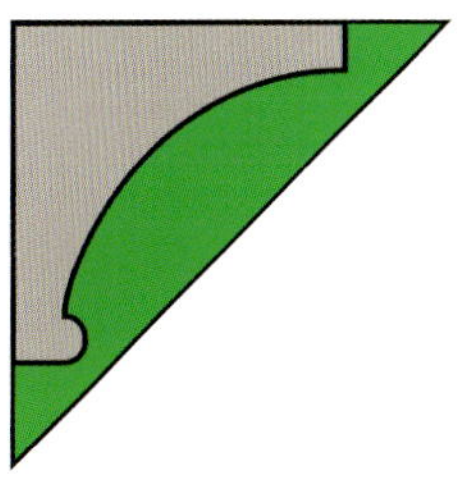

1B. Cut at 45° to get two pieces.

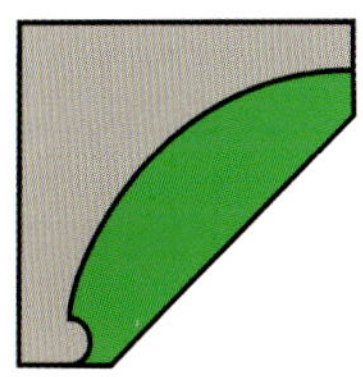

2B. Remove the two corners at the 7/8" line.

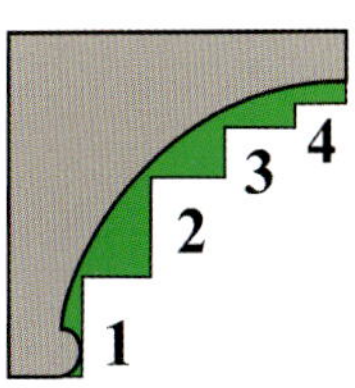

3. Approximate the cove with a stair step.

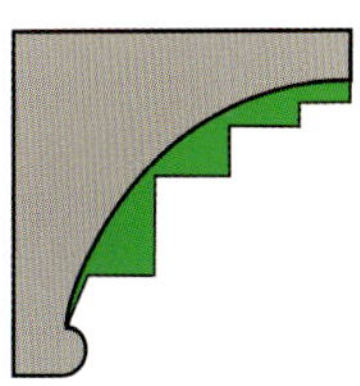

4. Round over the bead.

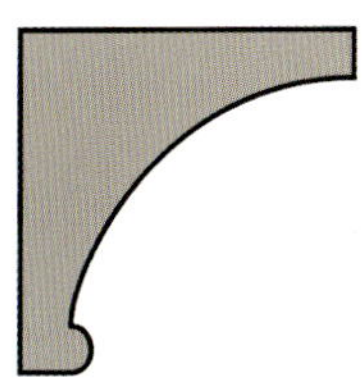

5. Carve the cove.

Use a ⅛" concave scratch stock to shape the bead. Because scratch stock works best when minimal wood is removed, use a #7 12 mm gouge to shape part of the cove on top of the bead. This will leave minimal material to be removed on both sides of the bead. Step 4 in **figure 11-41** shows what remains after the bead is shaped.

Use wider #7 gouges to carve the remainder of the cove. Carve as close to the curved line as possible. When this is done, remove the facets with a French curved scraper. Coarser sandpaper draped over larger convex-contoured sanding blocks also smooths and shapes the cove nicely. Finish up with finer-grit sandpaper until the surface is smooth to the touch.

Applying the Cove Molding

The cove molding should not be applied until the case is fully assembled. The following description of installing the cove molding assumes the case is fully assembled.

To install the cove molding, turn the assembled case upside down on a flat surface. The flat surface will be used as a reference when fitting and positioning the cove-molding pieces. Gravity will also help in this position. When working upside down, be careful to cut and apply the molding in the proper orientation. It is easy to get confused and cut it wrong. The bead is on the bottom, so when installing it on the upside-down case, the bead will be facing up!

Use a table saw to cut a 45° angle for an outside corner on one end of both side pieces and one end of the front piece. Because the sides are mirror images of each other, be careful to account for this when orienting the angled cuts. Cutting the second miter on the front piece is the only delicate operation in applying this molding.

To determine the final length of the front piece, dry-fit one corner by using the 45° end of it and its mating side piece. Clamp each piece in place. Use a 0.5 mm pencil to mark the back face of the front on the opposite side where the case ends. This is line "A" in **figure 11-42**. Orient the 45° cut to accommodate an outside corner. **Figure 11-42** also shows the 45° cut on the front, as well as its mating side.

When making this final 45° miter cut, sneak up on it. That is, cut a little proud of the line to start. Test-fit it between the two side pieces. It should be a little long. Take a little more off and test again. Repeat this process until the front piece fits as best as possible.

When I apply a molding like this, I attach it to the case with headless brads and glue the mitered corners to each other. I glue the corners so I can get a good-looking joint line. I use brads because it is difficult to get a good glue joint to the case while keeping the miters aligned. This also eliminates any wood movement issues that might exist.

Figure 11-43 shows one corner nailed and glued. Drill a small through hole for the brad to avoid splitting the molding stock. Place brads as needed, approximately every 6".

Note the protrusion labeled "Mitered Corner Mismatch" in **figure 11-43. Figure 11-44** shows a modeled version of the same concept. The curves do not align properly along the miter joint. This happens because the cove is hand-carved, and the surface is rarely exactly the same over any measurable length.

A crisp, aligned miter joint line is desired. This mismatch will be adjusted to get a crisp joint line and blended to get a pleasing cove. Use a small file to remove the extra material immediately next to the joint down to the miter line. This will create a feathered facet between the miter joint line and the cove, some short distance away. **Figures**

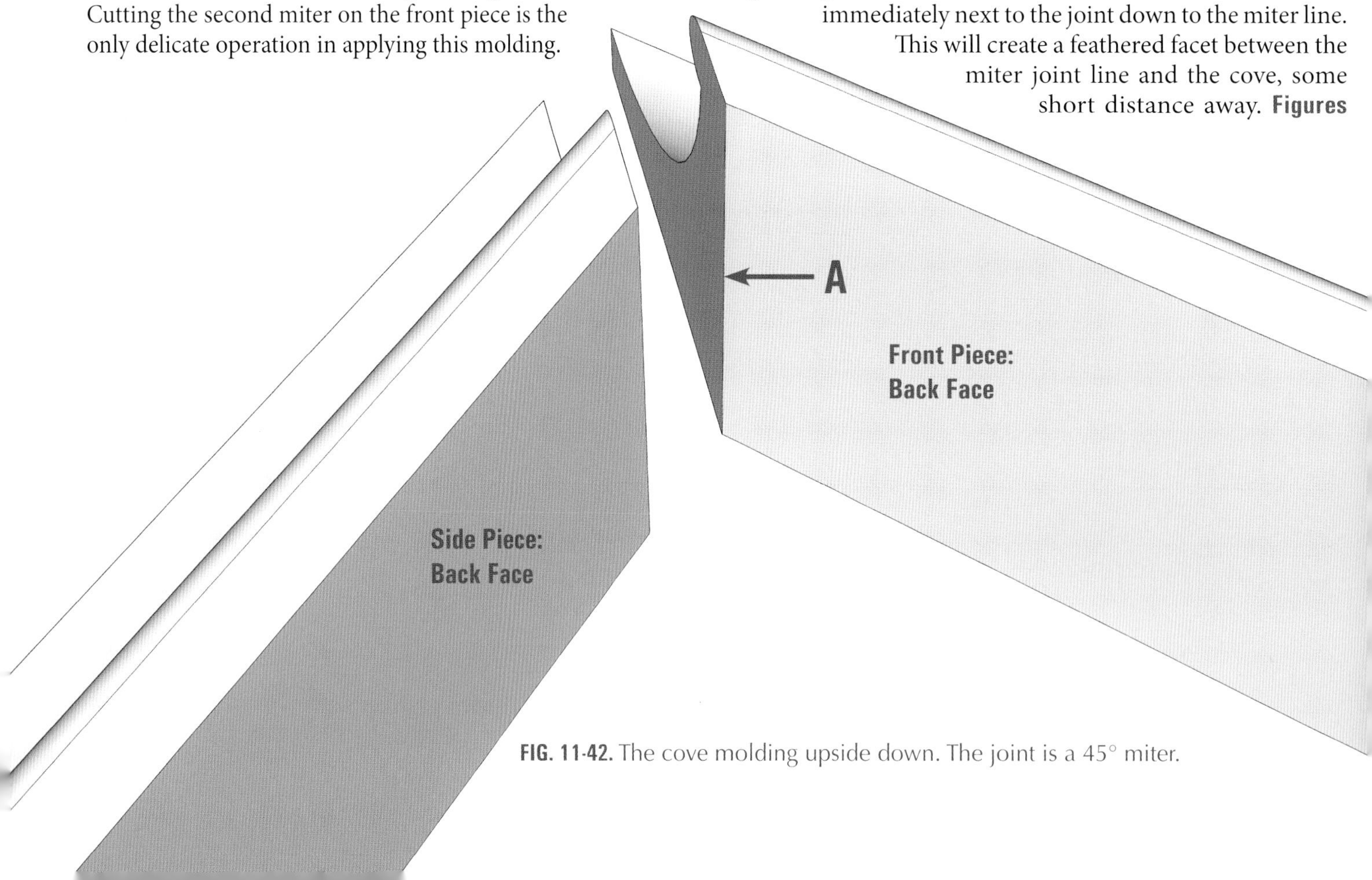

FIG. 11-42. The cove molding upside down. The joint is a 45° miter.

FIG. 11-43. Nail the cove molding with headless brads. Drill a pilot hole so the stock won't split.

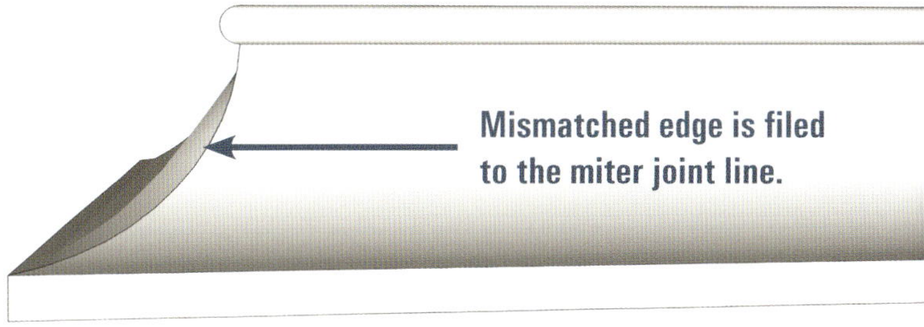

FIG. 11-45. Use a file to remove the extra material down to the joint line.

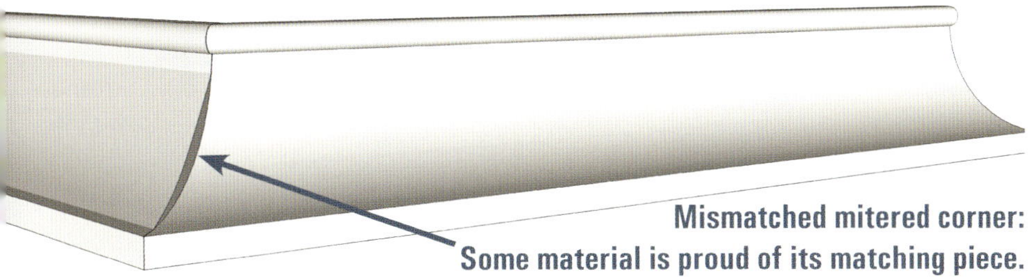

FIG. 11-44. The profile at the corner is mismatched.

11-45 and **11-46** show two views of the mismatched area after the initial blend with the file.

Blend the remaining material into the cove farther away from the joint line with a #7 16 mm gouge. Clean up the facets left by the gouge with a French curved scraper and sandpaper around a convex sanding block to get a smooth surface. **Figure 11-47** shows the model version of the completed cove, and **figure 11-48** shows the same thing in wood.

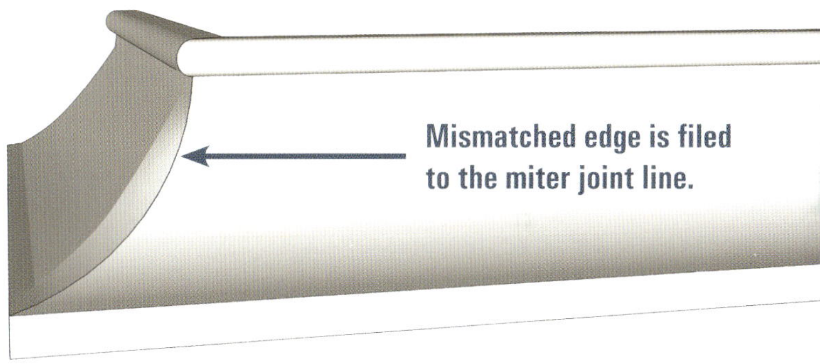

FIG. 11-46. Another view of the first removal of the extra material.

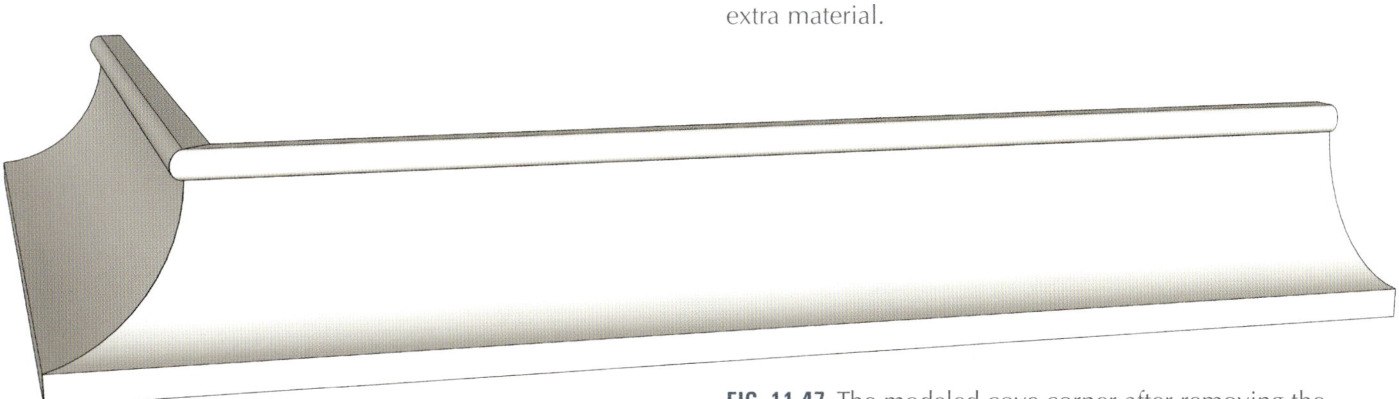

FIG. 11-47. The modeled cove corner after removing the mismatched material.

FIG. 11-48. The completed cove corner.

FIG. 11-49. Extend the cove molding beyond the back. Cut it close and flush it with sandpaper.

Cut the back ends of the side pieces flush with the back of the case. **Figure 11-49** shows an applied side piece ready to be cut. Use a handsaw to cut it close, then flush the molding to the back with sandpaper on a flat sanding block.

Apply the Greek Key Molding

The Greek key molding is applied with glue. Each of the legs is sufficiently small that even a headless brad could split the wood. The biggest challenge in gluing this molding is getting sufficient pressure in enough spots to secure it without gaps. Because the molding is delicate, there is little to no strength in it. Clamp pressure in one area does not radiate very far from the contact point; thus, many clamps are needed.

Figure 11-50 shows the clamping scheme. I used several pinch clamps to hold the molding piece in place. Clamp a board to the bench to use as a fence. Place several equal-length blocks along the length of the piece. Apply pressure to the back of the case to force the molding to the case.

Because the front piece extends beyond the case and covers the side pieces, glue the side pieces first. Recall from **figure 8-11** that a side piece has a 1⁄16" wide leading vertical leg, and the initial opening is pointing down. With this in mind, align the front edge of a side piece flush with the front of the case. The piece should be long enough to extend beyond the case in back (see **figure 11-51**). When the glue has dried, use a handsaw to cut the piece flush with the case.

FIG. 11-50. Glue and clamp the Greek key molding with several pinch clamps and pressure blocks.

FIG. 11-51. The Greek key extends beyond the back. Cut it flush when the glue is dried.

After the two side pieces have been applied, attach the front piece. Align the front as shown in **figure 11-52**. Note that the opening points toward the cove molding, which is above it. Note also that it is placed such that the outside vertical leg is approximately 3⁄16" wide. In theory this leg should be 3⁄16" wide, but things are rarely perfect. Adjust the front piece so that the left and right outside legs will be as close to equal as possible.

Glue the front piece in place, using the same clamping scheme as for the sides. **Figure 11-53** shows the front piece glued in place. When the glue is dry, cut the extra length flush with the side piece.

FIG. 11-52. The front portion is long. Butt the side piece into the front piece.

FIG. 11-53. Cut the front piece flush to the side Greek key when the glue is dry.

Integration Carving

Pin the Joints and Flush the Legs and Rails

The case joints are pinned on the sides and back, but not the front. My guess is that the front was not pinned for aesthetics. The back joints can be pinned after the back subassembly is complete. The sides are pinned after the entire case has been glued. Pin the joints midtenon vertically and centered 5⁄16" from the joint line. **Figure 12-1** shows the placement of the pins on the side. Note that the lowest pins are sufficiently above the carving on the post.

Figure 12-2 shows the placement of a pin. Use a ¼" brad point drill bit to make the dowel pin hole. The hole needs to be deep enough to go through the tenon and into the post on the opposite side, about ¼". **Figure 12-3** shows the hole being drilled. Put glue in the hole and some more on the dowel pin and drive the pin into the hole with a hammer (see **figure 12-4**). Hammer it until it bottoms out. You can tell when the pin hits the bottom of the hole by the dead sound the hammer makes.

FIG. 12-1. The case joints are pinned on the sides and back, but not the front.

FIG. 12-2. Locate the pin on the leg. Center it in the tenon, both left to right and top to bottom.

FIG. 12-3. Drill a 1/4" hole deep enough to go into the other side of the mortise 1/4" or more.

When the glue has dried, cut the pin flush with the leg post face, as shown in **figure 12-5**. The leg post should be a little proud of the rails and panels. Flush these up with a block plane and shoulder plane, as shown in **figures 12-6** and **12-7**. Use the shoulder plane near the knee because it can get closer than the block plane. Be careful with the shoulder plane near the knee not to mar the knee itself. Adjust the plane iron to be flush with the side of the plane body on the knee side.

The leg posts are taller than needed and need to be cut flush with the rail tops. Use a straight edge aligned flush to the rail top and score a line on the leg posts, as shown in **figure 12-8**. Use a handsaw to remove the extra material on the leg post, as shown in **figure 12-9**.

FIG. 12-4. Put glue on the dowel pin and in the hole. Drive the dowel with a hammer.

FIG. 12-6. Use a block plane to flush the leg post with the side board.

FIG. 12-5. When the glue is dry, cut the dowel flush with the leg post.

FIG. 12-7. Use a shoulder plane to get closer to the knee.

FIG. 12-8. Use a straight edge and knife to mark the leg posts flush with the top of the side.

Use the side template shown in **figure 12-10** to trace the portions above the knee block and on the leg post. Freehand the curve "A." This is the continuation of the ruffle from the knee and knee block. **Figure 12-11** shows the template tracing.

Set in around the drawing, as shown in **figure 12-12**. Bevel into the stop cuts with a #5 5 mm gouge. **Figure 12-13** shows this step. Be careful not to cut into quarter-column corner "A." Blend the beveled cuts to flatten the background (see **figure 12-14**). The color difference on the background surface shows the blended area.

FIG. 12-9. Cut the leg post flush with the top of the side with a handsaw.

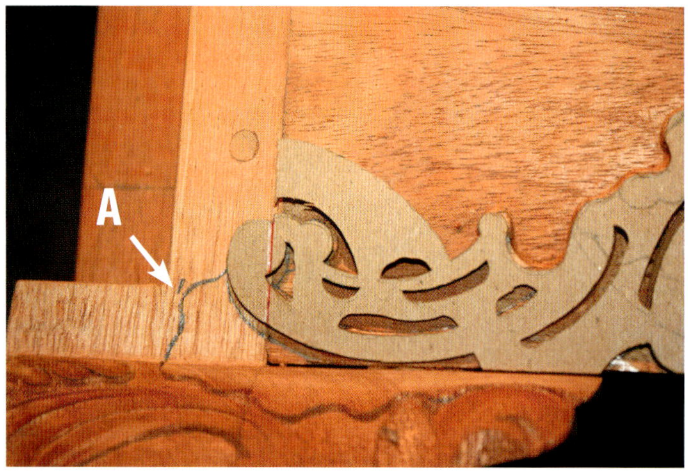

FIG. 12-10. Freehand-draw the ruffle "A" to connect the side template with the knee and knee block.

Integration Carving

Most of the carving can be done on all the pieces independently before glue-up. However, the transition areas between the legs, knee blocks, and rails are best done after the case is assembled. The reason for this is that the patterns can be much better aligned and integrated when everything is together.

There are six places that require integration carving: both knees on the front and the two sides. None is needed on the back face. The pattern is the same for each instance. Although the following discussion is going to use the left front corner as an example, it is probably a good idea to start on one of the sides at the back. This assumes that the first one might not be your best effort. It is better to learn and practice on the ones that are less visible and do the front two last.

FIG. 12-11. The carving elements have been transferred to the post and side.

FIG. 12-12. Set in around the C-scrolls with a #5 5 mm gouge.

Also shown in **figure 12-14** are the #9 5 mm gouge cuts that are the beginning of the concave portions of the ruffle. Round over the ridges with a flat chisel and blend them into the concave troughs with bullnose scrapers to form a smooth, undulating surface. Deepen the troughs and blend again until the ruffle looks as shown in **figure 12-15**.

Separate the central element shown in **figure 12-16**. Make stop cuts on curves "A" and "B" and then bevel into those cuts. In addition, isolate the bottom curve "C" and blend the background into the base of the stop cut.

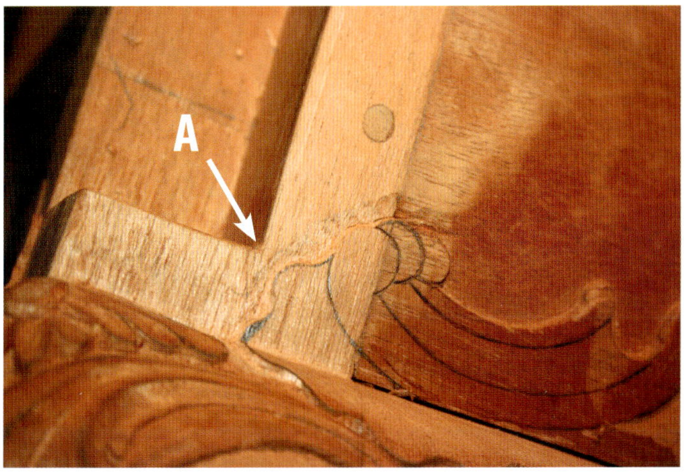

FIG. 12-13. Bevel into the C-scroll stop cuts. Stay away from the corner of the opening.

FIG. 12-15. Round over the ridges of the gouge cuts to form hills.

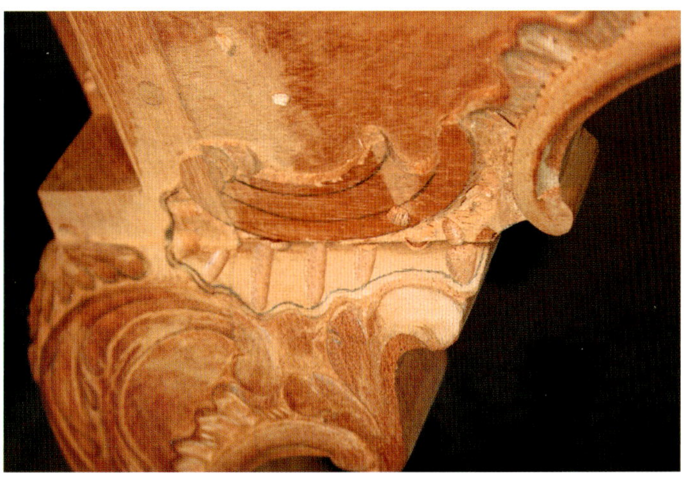

FIG. 12-14. Use a #9 5 mm gouge to make troughs that will be the low points of the ruffle.

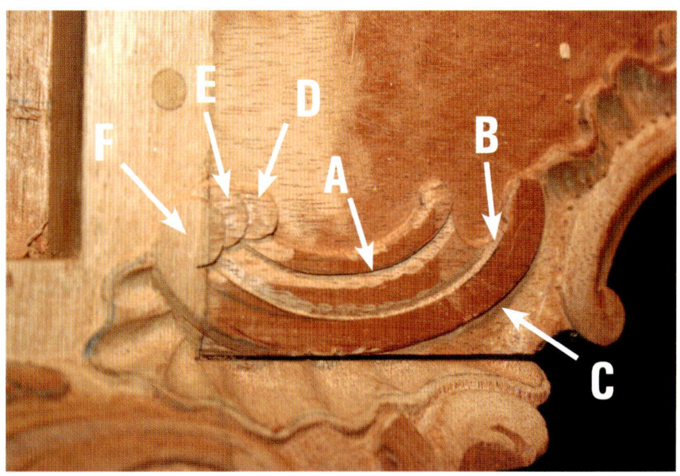

FIG. 12-16. Separate the elements. Note the layered disks "D," "E," and "F."

Also shown in **figure 12-16** is the layering of the disks. "D" tucks under "E," which in turn tucks under "F." Create this effect by setting in around "F" and beveling into this cut, staying within the constraints of "E." Leave some of each disk proud of the background. If too much of a disk gets removed, lower the background around it. Smooth the background to remove any facets that were created. Make analogous cuts to tuck "D" into "E."

Start to detail the lower leaf shown in **figure 12-17**, using a #7 4 mm gouge to define a subleaf "A." Use the same #7 4 mm gouge to open the top side of the subleaf (see **figure 12-18**). Further refine the leaves, as shown in **figure 12-19**. Use a flat chisel to round over the back of leaves "A" and "B," as well as both sides of "C." Blend the facets with a riffler. The color difference in **figure 12-19** shows what to leave high and what is removed.

Use a #7 4 mm gouge to make a series of cuts labeled "A" in **figure 12-20**. With the concave side of the gouge opening toward the narrow end of the middle element, make a stop cut perpendicular to the surface. With the same gouge, make a steep bevel into it from the convex side. Label "A" in **figure 12-21** shows this better. These details come in pairs along the surface, and each pair is separated by some distance. See the figures to approximate the separation distance.

Label "B" in **figure 12-20** shows accent marks along the surface of the ruffle. Use a #11 1 mm gouge for these. These lines will break up the light as it hits the surface, and give it depth. If done properly, the finish can amplify these marks to increase visual depth.

Figure 12-21 shows the integration carving on one section complete. Note the details labeled "A."

These are in pairs and made with a #7 4 mm gouge.Do the other five the same way.

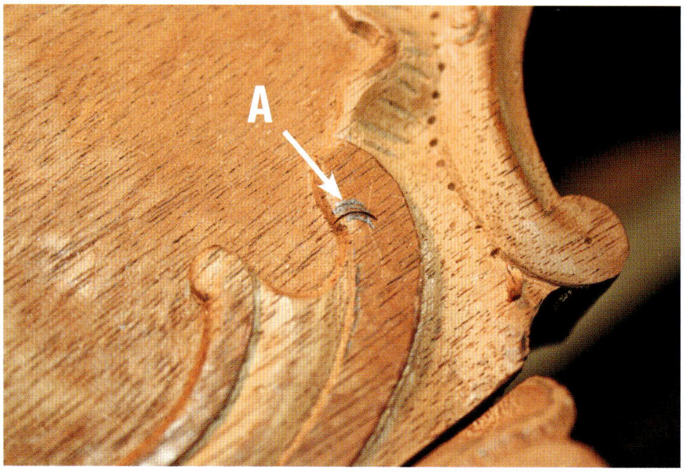

FIG. 12-17. Create a secondary leaf. Start with a #7 4 mm gouge.

FIG. 12-18. Bevel into the stop cut to isolate the secondary leaf tip.

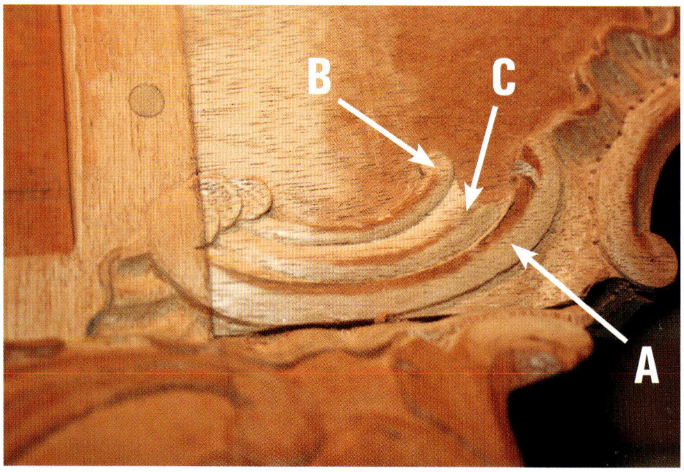

FIG. 12-19. Round over the individual surfaces.

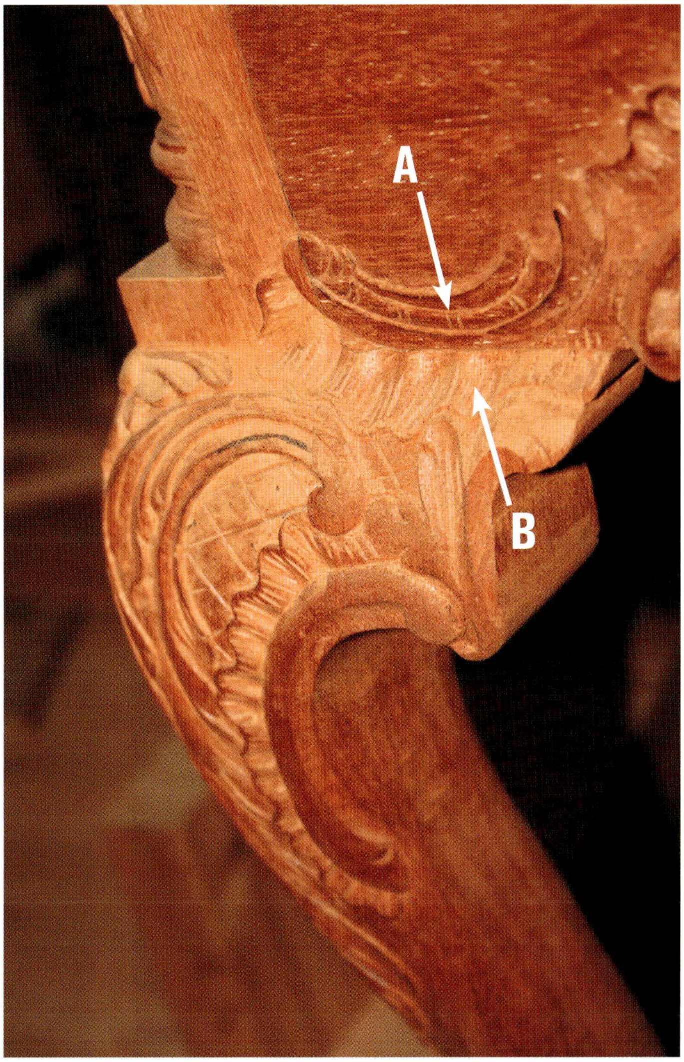

FIG. 12-20. Detail element "A" with a #7 4 mm gouge. Detail the ruffle lobes with a #11 1 mm gouge.

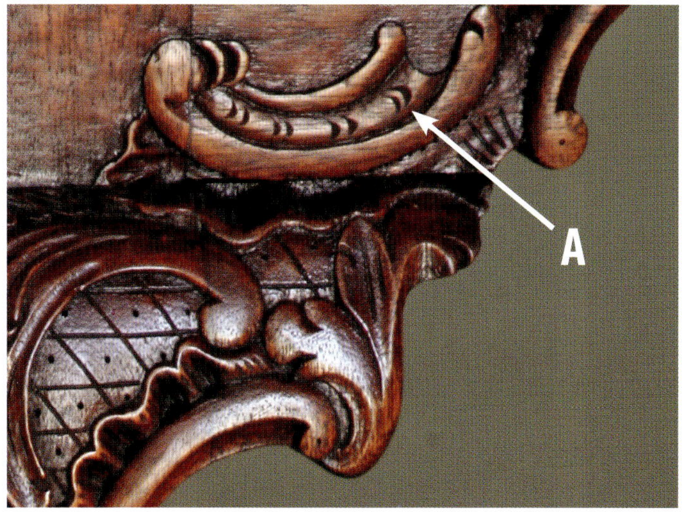

FIG. 12-21. These detail cuts come in pairs.

Finishing

1. Surface Preparation
2. Wash Coat of Shellac
3. Dye: Single, Layered, or Blended
4. First Aging Step: Remove Color from High Spots
5. Shellac Buildup with Intermittent Sanding
6. Polish with Alcohol / Shellac / Oil Pad / Rag
7. Glazing with Gel Stain
8. Final Polish, Wax, or Both

Why I Use Only Shellac

The only finish I use for period pieces is shellac. This is my finish of choice because it is easily repairable, reasonably forgiving, less toxic than others, and gives great results.

I especially like the fact that all the shellac layers bond into one. This occurs because the alcohol in the top layer melts the layer below, and the two become one. This is important because when one sands through the shellac to bare wood, it is easy to build it back up without stripping it all off.

When applying multiple coats of varnish or polyurethane, each coat is its own layer, and the bond between them is mechanical, not chemical, as is shellac. When one sands through a layer of varnish or polyurethane, a hole in that layer is created. This hole has an edge that is visible and difficult to remove without removing the entire layer. This problem is nonexistent with shellac.

Lacquer has the same bonding property as shellac, but the solvent—lacquer thinner—is very toxic, and I would not use it in my basement shop. Although denatured alcohol is not harmless, it is nowhere near as toxic as lacquer thinner. And for a few extra dollars I could use 100% ethanol and avoid any toxicity.

Because of the bonding property of shellac, small scratches, blemishes, and water rings are easily fixed. Put some alcohol on a rag with a drop or two of baby or mineral oil and rub with a little pressure. You will see the defect disappear or get visibly better. Repeat until the repair is complete.

I also like that shellac dries very fast, so many coats can be applied in a short amount of time. Consider the four drawer fronts of this project. If shellac is applied to all four in succession, the first one is ready for another coat when the current coat has been applied to the fourth. In this case, several coats can be applied in one sitting.

Shellac Ratios and Application

I mix my own shellac from dry flakes and denatured alcohol. I have tried various mixture ratios over the years but settled on 1:5 (one part shellac to five parts alcohol) by volume early on. I use this ratio for a wash coat, buildup, and repair. I think it is somewhere between ½ and 1 pound cut, but I have never measured it. I like the volumetric measurement because it is very easy and I don't need a scale. I can use any size of measuring container, and I don't even have to know how big it is.

I use extra blonde and very dark shellac almost interchangeably. Because I like darker colors much more than lighter ones, a little extra darkness doesn't bother me. Besides, my shellac is so thin that not a lot of color is added in any one coat.

I apply shellac with a ¾" Taklon—synthetic bristle—brush. The synthetic bristles hold less shellac than a comparably sized natural-bristle brush, making it easier to spread in a short amount of time. There is nothing special about the ¾" size other than it is what I got used to. Because the size is small, there is even less shellac in each brush load. The less shellac to spread in one instance, the easier it is. However, it takes more brush loads, so it takes more time. In addition, if I make a mistake with a small load, it will be a smaller mistake than with a bigger load.

The brush technique I use to apply shellac is a quick back-and-forth motion until the load is more or less even in the middle and feathered to nothing on the edges. Because there is not a lot of shellac in a load, five or six back-and-forth motions will do.

When applying shellac, keep the brush moving all the time. That includes initially hitting the surface in motion. If the brush stops, it is very easy to burn through the previous layers. A burn-through can be fixed, but it takes extra time and work.

Also be careful not to hit an edge at 90°. In this case, shellac will come off the brush and drip down the side. When this happens, and it will, brush out the drip quickly. When brushing an edge, either on the case or a carving, the brush motion should be parallel to the edge as much as possible.

In the case of a top edge, the brush motion should be like a plane taking off from a runway. When introducing the loaded brush to the top, the motion should be like a plane landing: touchdown in midrunway and then quick back-and-forth strokes to spread the material.

The next brush load should be placed such that the touchdown is slightly away from the wet previous layer, but close enough that the blend will overlap. Continue in this manner until the surface is complete.

I have no exact number of coats that I apply, but it is probably around ten. A top might get a few more, and a highly carved area a few less. My goal is to use as little shellac as possible to get the sheen and pore fill that I want. If the shellac gets too thick, or the sheen is too high or harsh, it will look like plastic. A plastic look is unacceptable to my eye, and it significantly detracts from the piece.

Surface Preparation

For carved areas there is not a lot of surface preparation after the carvings themselves are complete, but it is important to get the background around the carvings as smooth and uniform as possible. Not only will a smooth background make the carvings look better, but any irregularities on the background will be accentuated when finish is applied, which will further detract from them.

For areas away from the carved ones, blend as many facets as reasonable. Because most if not all final surfaces are touched with hand tools, a few irregularities are okay, even welcomed. It is subtle surface irregularities that give the piece a handmade look and feel, which is desired.

I will try to get horizontal flat surfaces (i.e., flat tops) as smooth as possible. For final surfaces I use mostly scrapers and sandpaper. I quit after 100 grit on most surfaces but will sand to 200 grit on tops.

Another final surface detail that I have adopted is to ease every sharp corner. This includes all corners on all drawer parts, both inside and out, and all case corners, including the quarter-column openings. I do this with a small piece of sandpaper backed by my finger or with a small file. The goal is to take off as little as possible so that the corner looks crisp but is smooth to the touch. This is a small detail, but it adds sophistication and professionalism. A sharp corner is an annoyance because it can cut one's finger. It also looks too harsh and is a sign of less attention to detail.

Apply and Sand a Wash Coat

A wash coat of shellac is a partial sealer, and it is applied to the bare wood before dye. This is to prevent too much dye from being absorbed, which will make the color look almost black. This is especially true on end grain, of which there is a lot on carved surfaces. The most-vulnerable areas for going black are cabriole leg knees and ball-and-claw feet.

Apply the shellac wash coat with a Taklon brush. When it has thoroughly dried—maybe thirty to sixty minutes—sand it with 320–400-grit sandpaper. Be reasonably aggressive and strive for a very smooth surface. The smoother the surface is at this point, the easier it will be to maintain as more coats are applied. Use a small wire brush on the carved areas.

Applying Dye

After the wash coat has been applied and sanded, apply any dyes that are desired. I used a red dye followed by walnut crystal dye. In this case I applied them in layers and let the first coat dry before applying the second.

To start, I use water-based dyes in concentrations of ¼ teaspoon of dye powder per cup of water. This is a pretty dilute concentration, but more coats can be added if more color is desired.

Over the years I have come to like the brown that the walnut dye adds. It negates the orange color that is naturally in mahogany, which I don't like. I have also evolved to liking more brown, so I apply multiple coats of walnut crystals or increase the concentration.

The First Aging Step: Strategically Remove Color

Pieces that are 250 years old have acquired different varieties of wear. The goal is to simulate some of this wear during the finishing process.

One type of wear is color variation, and another is dirt collection. The color varies due to handling, repair, and oxidation. High spots are typically lighter than lower ones due to increased handling. Conversely, low areas are darker because they collect dirt and are harder to clean. This step will remove more color on the high spots and less in other areas.

When the dyes have been applied and dried, remove the color on the high spots and lighten it in others with a 400–600-grit sanding sponge. I like sanding sponges because there is more give to them than sandpaper, so they will conform to the carved surfaces better.

Look at the lighter portions of **figure 13-1**; they are all higher than the surrounding areas. Use the sanding sponge and lightly drag it over the surface. This motion will naturally touch the high spots and miss the low ones. Drawer edges are another high-wear area. Be aggressive in the sanding on the edges, and especially the corners. The fillet above the thumbnail would also get a lot of wear. Vary the pressure behind the sponge so there are even some differences between the high spots. The goal is nonuniform, continuous, and blended variation.

Figure 13-2 shows many high spots. The backbone of the cone labeled "A" is very light relative to its surroundings. The leaf "B" is accentuated because its perimeter is lighter. In general, when the perimeter lines of an element are highlighted, the carving gains visual depth and comes alive.

Fig. 13-1

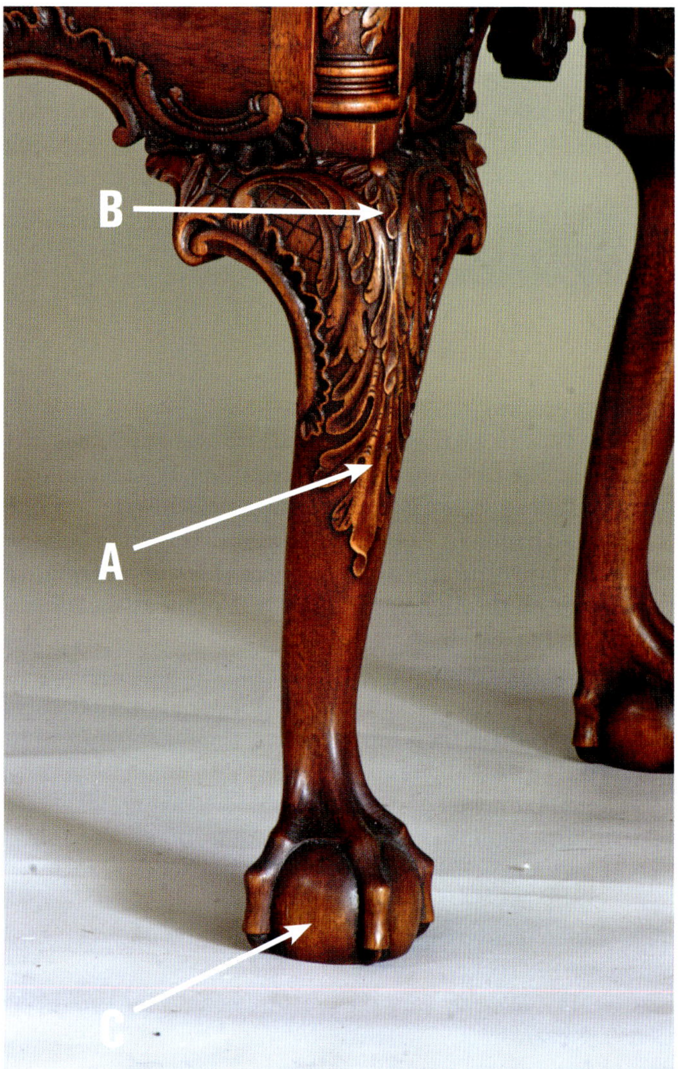

FIG. 13-2. Notice that the lighter colors are on the higher surfaces and lines.

Also note the area labeled "C" in **figure 13-2**. This is the widest part of the ball and is subject to more wear. This is an example of color variation on a smooth surface. Note that the variation is subtle and continuous as it goes from light to dark on the same surface.

This step is subjective because it is not definitive what parts will get the greatest wear. I think it is relatively easy to see that high spots will wear more than others. Use this as a guiding principle when deciding which areas to sand and how much.

Shellac Buildup

Shellac buildup is an iterative process. Apply several coats. Let it dry sufficiently. Sand the surface. Polish with an alcohol rag. The early polishing step is to see if there is enough shellac on the surface. If the buildup is not sufficient, the polished sheen will be dull. This indicates more buildup is needed. If so, apply more coats and repeat.

There is some minimal amount of buildup that is needed to get any gloss. Once this has been achieved, add the minimal needed to achieve the desired sheen. Thinner is better, in my opinion.

I build up shellac with a ¾" Taklon brush. You could use a larger one for the top and sides if you can spread the material in time. Use the brisk back-and-forth technique previously described. Apply several coats in succession. After five to six coats, let it dry for a few hours. This is to let the shellac harden a bit. Now sand the built-up area to diminish the sheen and smooth the surface.

For a top, I have used both wet and dry sanding methods. I have gotten good results with each, but I am slightly partial to the wet method because I think it is a bit more forgiving. That is, the water lubricant provides a less aggressive cut.

For the wet method, use 320–600-grit wet/dry silicon carbide sandpaper backed by a flat rubber sanding grip. The grip is shown in **figure 13-3**. One of my goals is to get a high degree of pore fill by sanding the surface level. Keep the paper and sanding area wet. When it dries so that the paper sticks a bit, add more water. A good way to add water is to use a spray bottle. This will evenly apply sufficient water in a relatively large area.

The sanding will produce a slurry, which is desired. It is the fine particles of shellac in water. After an area has been sanded, wipe it dry with a rag. Sight the surface at a low angle. A uniform gray color indicates that area is level (i.e., pore filled). A speckled gray color indicates a less-than-level surface. The shiny specks are unsanded areas that are below the gray level. With this technique, the fewer shiny specks implies a higher degree of pore fill. This *leveling* is the control for the degree of pore fill.

A complete or high degree of pore fill will probably not be gotten in one iteration. It will take two to three, and maybe more, depending on the level of shellac buildup during an iteration. To understand if the pore fill is to your liking, polish an area with an alcohol-and-oil pad to see what the sheen is. Repeat the buildup and level steps as many iterations as needed.

For the dry alternative, I use 320–600-grit foam-rubber-backed sanding sponges. I like the ones made by Festool because they have a wide range of grits and I can get larger quantities to keep the cost down.

When working with these sponge pads, avoid the edges of the pad touching the surface. The edge can scratch the finish deeper than desired. Hold the pad as shown in **figure 13-4**, so only the middle part of the sponge touches the surface, or use the pad with a sanding block, as shown in **figure 13-5**.

The sanded area will be light gray with high-gloss specks, as with the wet method. The leveling goal is the same, so do as many iterations as needed.

Use a sanding sponge or hand-backed sandpaper to sand the other surfaces that are not carved (the cabriole legs, for example). Sand until the surface is smooth to the touch and uniform to the eye.

For abrading the carved areas, use a small steel- or brass-bristle brush, as shown in **figure 13-6**. Be as aggressive as needed to dull the sheen. This may seem a bit extreme at first, but it is not overly aggressive. If you are nervous, start with a light touch. After a few strokes you will develop a feel for how it works and how much pressure to use.

Repeat these steps until there is sufficient shellac buildup.

FIG. 13-3. Use a flat sanding grip with wet/dry sandpaper to level flat surfaces.

FIG. 13-5. Use the sanding sponge on a sanding block.

FIG. 13-4. Bend the sanding sponge so the edges don't hit the surface.

FIG. 13-6. Use a steel or brass brush to abrade the carving.

Polish the Shellac

After the shellac is sufficiently built up, sand as before to remove the harsh sheen and smooth the surface. The sheen will be brought back by polishing.

I polish with an alcohol-and-oil pad. The pad is one piece of cloth folded into approximately a 2" square by 1" thick. I use old white cotton socks for this. The weave on the foot part is better than that on the leg because it is finer. **Figure 13-7** shows the inner pad. This folded piece is then tightly wrapped in another larger piece of material. I use white T-shirt or bedsheet material for the outer cloth. I like these materials because the weave is very fine and will not leave marks in the shellac. The pad should look like the one shown in **figure 13-8**. Note that it is almost a ball.

When the pad is new, it needs to be dampened with some shellac, but mostly alcohol. I cannot quantify how much of each to use, but it should not be dripping. It should also not drip when squeezed. It should be damp enough to leave a little residue on your hand. When the pad is sufficiently damp and ready to use, put a couple of drops of baby or mineral oil on the contact face of the pad. The oil is needed for lubrication so the pad will not stick as it is rubbed over the shellac.

When the pad is not being used, store it in an airtight container. It will stay damp for years and can be used many times over. **Figure 13-9** shows my storage container.

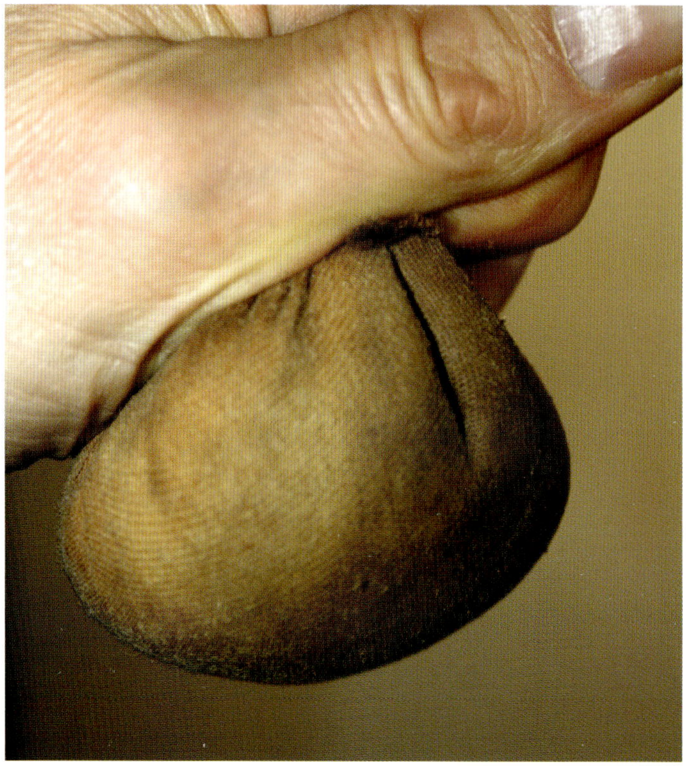

FIG. 13-8. Tightly wrap the internal pad in a piece of T-shirt material.

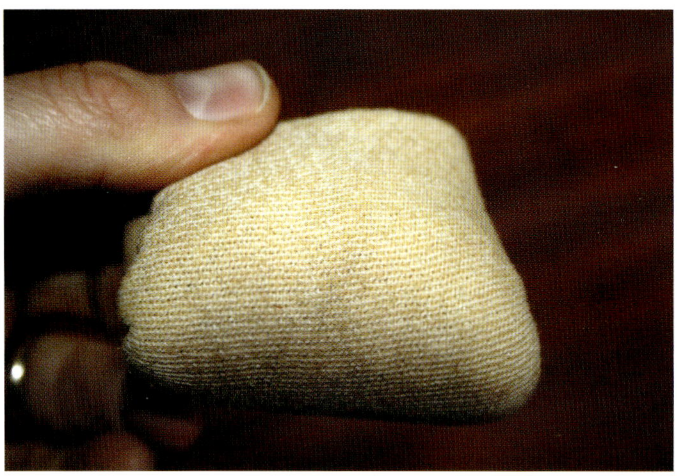

FIG. 13-7. Fold an old sock that will be used as an internal pad.

FIG. 13-9. Store damp shellac polishing pads in an airtight jar. They will stay damp for years.

The Second Aging Step: Simulating Dirt and Wax Buildup with Glaze

Many eighteenth-century pieces of furniture were polished with wax numerous times to maintain their finish. Over the years, the wax would collect dust and get embedded in hard-to-reach places, such as carving depressions. With repeated polishing, the dust and wax darken and become difficult to remove. Today the effect is to produce a dark *halo* around the carvings, and deep shadows within them. **Figures 13-10** and **13-11** point out some of the halos on the original. These effects have a look that is now a featured aesthetic and a characteristic of an antique. They can be created on new reproductions with glazing.

Glazing is a finishing technique in which color is added on top of a fully sealed surface. None of the color penetrates the wood pores; it all sits on the surface of the shellac. The intent is to get some of the glazing material to remain in the deep portions of the carvings and around their perimeters, but nowhere else.

FIG. 13-10. The dark halos highlight the lighter carved areas.

FIG. 13-11. Dirt and wax buildup collects in depressions over the years.

It is important that the glazing solvent be incompatible with that of the shellac. The reason is that the glaze should not dissolve the surface on which it is applied. If the glaze dissolved the shellac, then it would become part of it, and the color would be a muddied mess.

Another feature of having the glaze solvent not impact the shellac is that the glaze can be completely removed without harming the shellac. This is especially comforting for a beginner, who might be alarmed or nervous about ruining their piece with this dark color.

I use a dark oil-based gel stain for a glazing compound. Oil-based gel stain is solvent in mineral spirits, which does nothing to shellac, so it easily wipes off without harm.

Apply the gel stain with a stiff brush. Cover the entire piece and work it into the carvings and other tight areas. Let it dry for five to ten minutes and then wipe off most of it with a clean rag. The idea is to remove the vast majority of the stain, but to leave a little in the depressions and around the perimeters of the carved areas. If the stain dries a little too much, dampen a rag with mineral spirits and wipe the dried area. It will be easily softened and removed.

FIG. 13-14. The color variation and glaze halos give depth to the carved elements.

A good way to leave the proper amount of stain, and in the appropriate areas, is to attempt to wipe the piece completely clean, but don't concentrate on the deep areas and the carving perimeters. As you wipe the surface, the rag will naturally miss the background immediately next to a carved surface, which will leave dark stain in the places it is desired.

When the stain is sufficiently removed, use a clean, dry, natural-bristle brush and lightly brush the remaining stain to feather it into its surrounding area. This is called "dry brushing." This softens the transition line and gives a more natural and pleasant look.

FIG. 13-12. An unglazed drawer front. It looks flat.

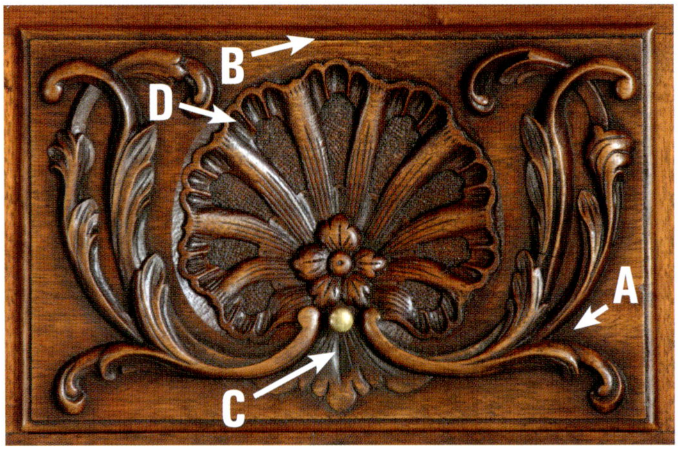

FIG. 13-13. A glazed drawer front. The carvings are enhanced because of the dark halos.

Figure 13-12 shows a carved drawer front without glazing, and **figure 13-13** shows a similar one with glazing. Study the differences between these two treatments. To my eye, the unglazed one is flat and monochromatic. The glazed one is more alive, with a wider color variation. The *halo* frames the carved areas, and the difference between light and dark adds depth. I think the glazed one is much more stunning and visually appealing.

Specifically "A" shows the softening of the halo transition that is created by dry brushing. The fillet portion of the thumbnail molding, "B," would also collect dust and dirt. "C" would be harder to clean because of the drawer knob, and "D" is a deep part of the carving.

Figures 13-14 and **13-15** show two other detailed areas that exhibit color variation and the effect of halos. When viewed at a distance, the carvings are more enhanced because of the light and dark contrast.

Glazing is a significant yet simple step beyond basic finishing that adds a lot to the overall presentation of the piece. It might seem intimidating and frightening at first, but there is little to be afraid of because the glaze can be completely removed with mineral spirits if needed.

FIG. 13-15. The foliage on the quarter column feels light and alive.

I shied away from glazing for many years out of fear and ignorance, but I'm glad I finally decided to give it a try. I will most likely use it on all of my projects going forward.

After Glazing

Let the glaze dry for at least twenty-four hours. On this project I polished with the alcohol, shellac, and oil pad after the glaze dried. I brought the top to a high sheen and let the rest be more matte. I polished the high areas of the carvings so that they were higher gloss than their surroundings.

What parts to polish and how much is subjective; it depends on what looks good to your eye. In addition, what looks good will probably evolve over time. When shiny is next to matte, and light is next to dark, shiny and light stand out more and the contrast gives a dramatic and pleasing look, so strive for variation in color and sheen. Even small differences in the proper places will be pleasantly surprising.

The Third Aging Step: Tarnishing Bright, New Hardware

Brass hardware will tarnish with exposure to oxygen and skin oil, so after 250 years of use, antique brass will not be shiny. Re-create this detail to add authenticity.

When I put bright, new reproduction brass pulls on the aged finish, it did not look right. The brass was too shiny and instantly caught my eye in a bad way. I had to do something.

I soaked the brass in vinegar; that did nothing. I washed it with ammonia; that did nothing. A little internet research pointed me to heated vinegar and hydrogen peroxide.

I heated the vinegar in a microwave oven for sixty seconds. I then added some peroxide. When I put a brass plate in the hot solution, almost instantly I heard the solution sizzle, and I could see the brass color change immediately. After a few seconds I removed it from the solution and washed it with water. The result is shown in **figure 13-16**; **figure 13-17** shows two brass pulls before treatment. I was pleased with the result, although I didn't know exactly what to expect. From my experience, the heat was what made the reaction happen.

Summary and Looking Forward

My attitude has evolved to more fully appreciate the importance of a good finish. I used to think that the quality of the carvings and the strength of the design would overwhelm a mediocre finish, so I didn't spend as much effort on it. I have come to realize that this is incorrect.

A great finish cannot overcome poor carving and craftsmanship, but a nondescript finish can negate excellent woodworking. This project has been a watershed moment for me in finishing. And although I have a long way to go in mastering the finer points of a good finish, I have seen what is possible from me, and I like it.

My two finishing stretch goals were to introduce color variation and highlight carved areas with *halos*. I think I achieved those, and I was pleased with the results. What I wasn't expecting—but is more thrilling—is how the carvings came alive. This is very motivating, and I am anxious to try it on my next project.

FIG. 13-16. The brass pulls after a hot vinegar-and-peroxide bath. Note the color variation.

FIG. 13-17. New reproduction brass pulls lack character and are out of place on an aged finish.

Drawer Dimensions

This chapter will detail the remaining two drawer dimensions and any unique features.

Top Drawer with Half-Mortise Lock

The top drawer dimensions are detailed in **figures 14-1** and **14-2**. The top drawer front has a half-mortise lock; it is the only drawer with a lock. The mortise for the lock is sized to fit the one that I used, so don't cut this mortise until you have the lock you will use. Then cut the mortise to fit.

Typically, a half-mortise lock is not symmetrical. That is, the lock pin is not centered in the lock housing, neither vertically nor horizontally. However, the lock pin must be centered horizontally in the drawer front and positioned vertically so that the top of the outer lock housing is flush with the inside top edge of the drawer front. **Figures 14-1A** and **14-1B** show the lock position. The lock position then determines the vertical placement of the escutcheon on the front face. Because of these constraints, it is a good idea to pick a lock and escutcheon as a pair to make sure the drawer front will look good when complete.

Cutting the lock mortise is a multistep process. Start by measuring the distance from the center of the lock pin to the top edge of the lock housing. This measurement is 11⁄16", as shown in **figure 14-3A**. The lock is shown rotated 180° vertically because this makes the pin visible while keeping the side-to-side lock orientation correct. Locate a point 11⁄16" from the top edge on the drawer centerline. Drill a hole the size of the lock pin through the drawer front.

On the back face of the drawer front, place the lock pin in the drilled hole. Mark the outline of the lock housing and score the lines with a knife and square. This is the red rectangle in **figure 14-3A**.

The thickness of the lock outer housing is 1⁄16". Remove the 3" × 2" × 1⁄16" rectangle (see **figure 14-3B**). Use a flat chisel and a small router plane for this operation.

With a flat chisel, remove the 1⁄16" rectangle on the top edge, as shown in **figure 14-3C**. These depths should be the thickness of the outer lock-housing metal.

Next, remove the section shown in **figure 14-3D**. This is sized to accommodate the inner lock housing. In this case it is 2¼" × 1 13⁄16" × 7⁄16". Use a drill press with an appropriately sized Forstner bit to remove most of the waste. Clean up the remainder with a flat chisel and a small router plane.

Draw the keyhole profile, as also shown in **figure 14-3D**. Use drill bits of appropriate size on the top and bottom circular portions of the profile. Use a small, flat chisel to connect the two holes to approximate the remainder of the profile. Work from both sides to avoid tear-out. Note that this hole doesn't have to be as accurate as the drawing. That is pretty difficult to do. It will be covered on the front with the escutcheon and on the back with the lock. It just needs to be big enough to allow the key to pass through. **Figure 14-3E** shows the theoretical keyhole cut.

Figures 14-4 through **14-10** show some of the techniques and steps. As shown in **figure 14-4**, use a flat chisel to bevel into the scored outline of the outer lock housing. Do this in a few iterations so the cuts will be lighter and easier. When using the router plane (see **figure 14-5**), also make very light cuts. The results will be better.

Install the lock after the finish has been applied.

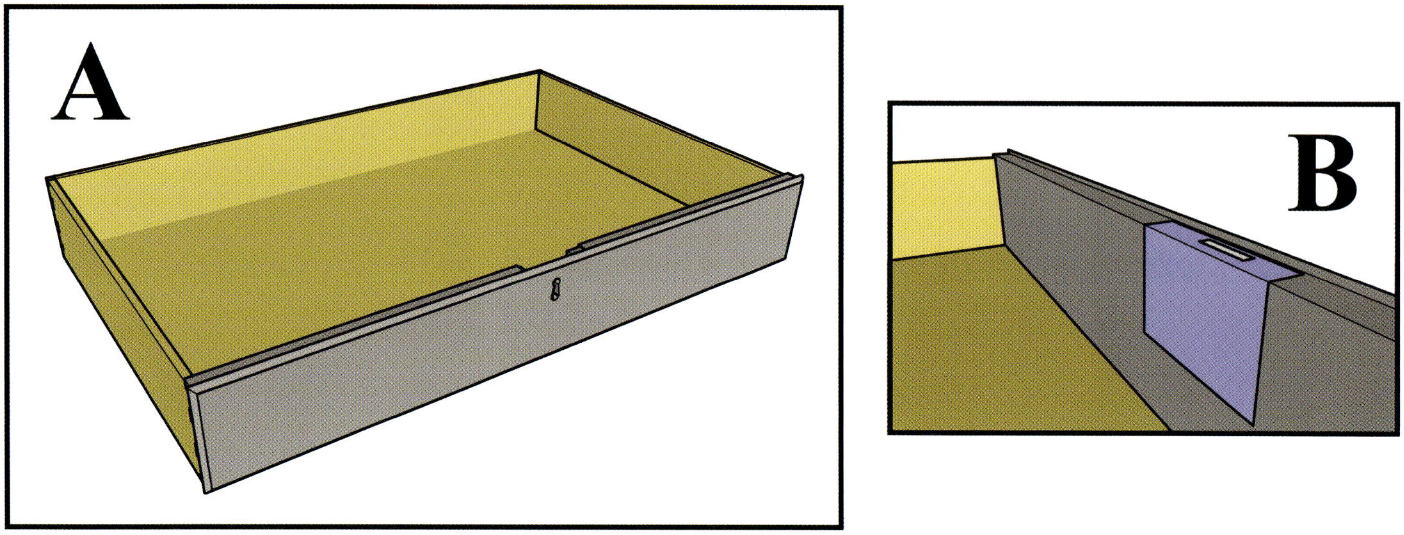

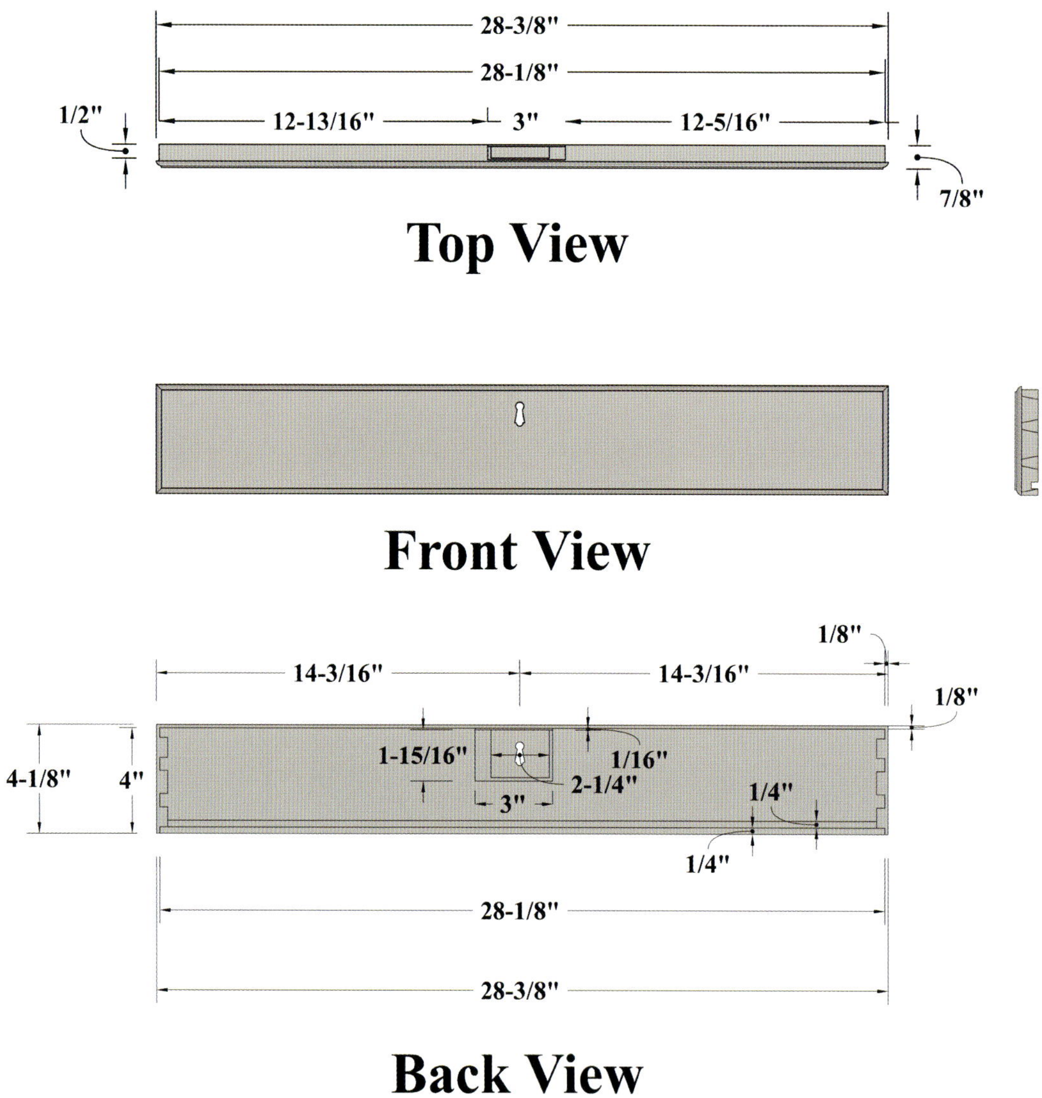

FIG. 14-1. Dimensions for the top drawer front.

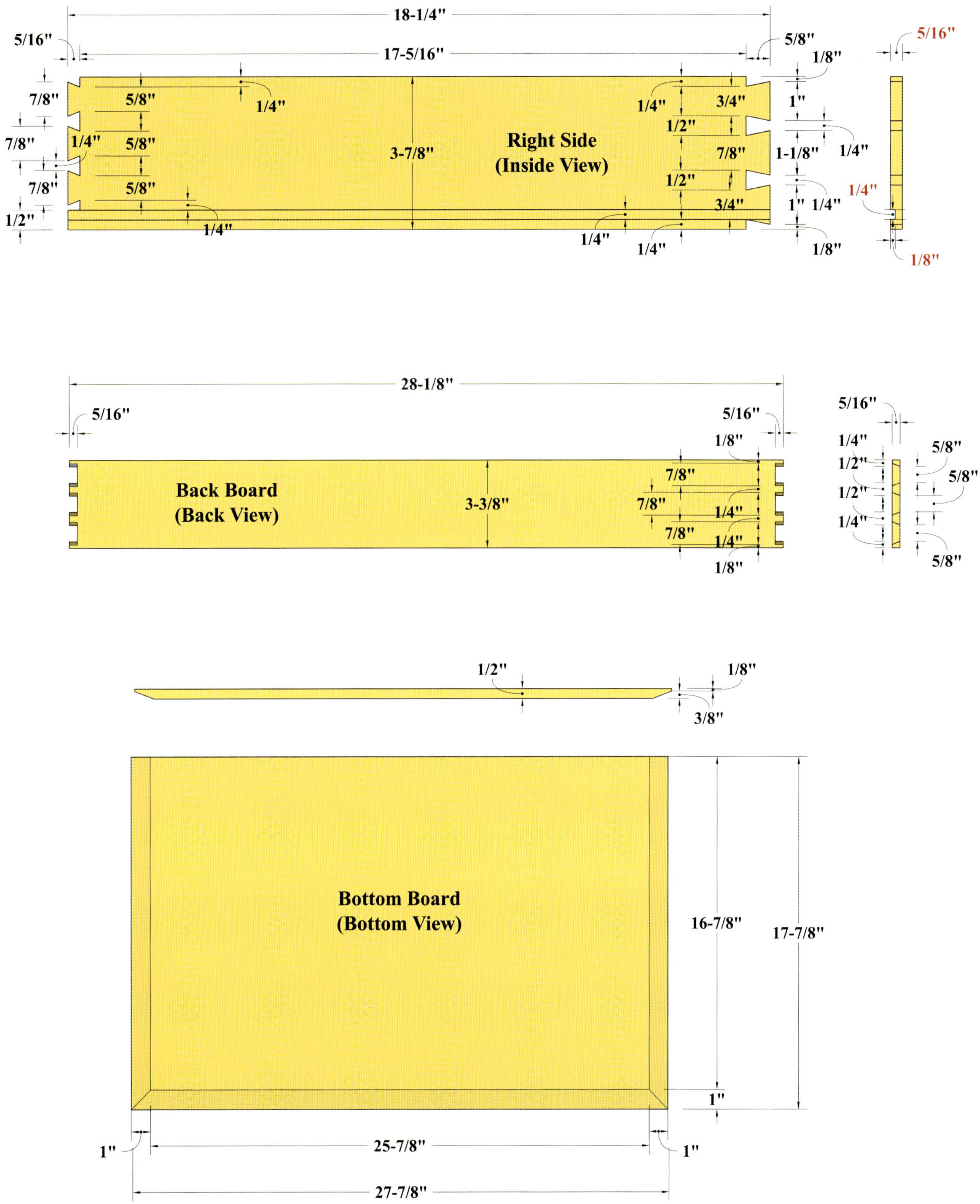

FIG. 14-2. Dimensions for the sides, back, and bottom for the top drawer.

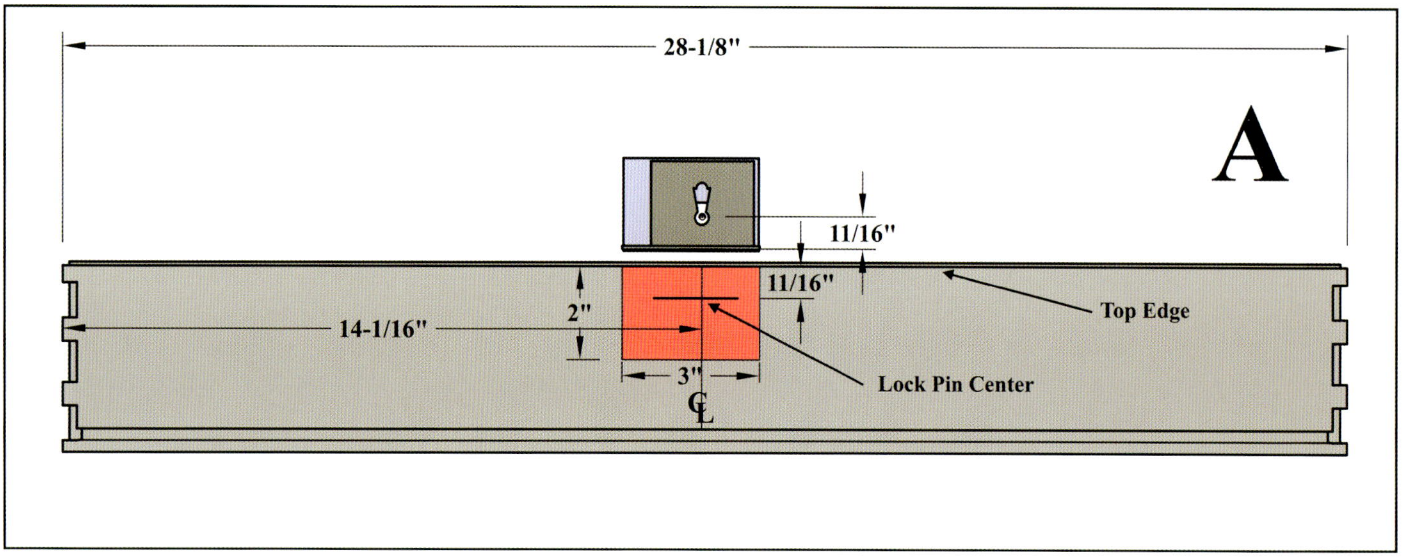

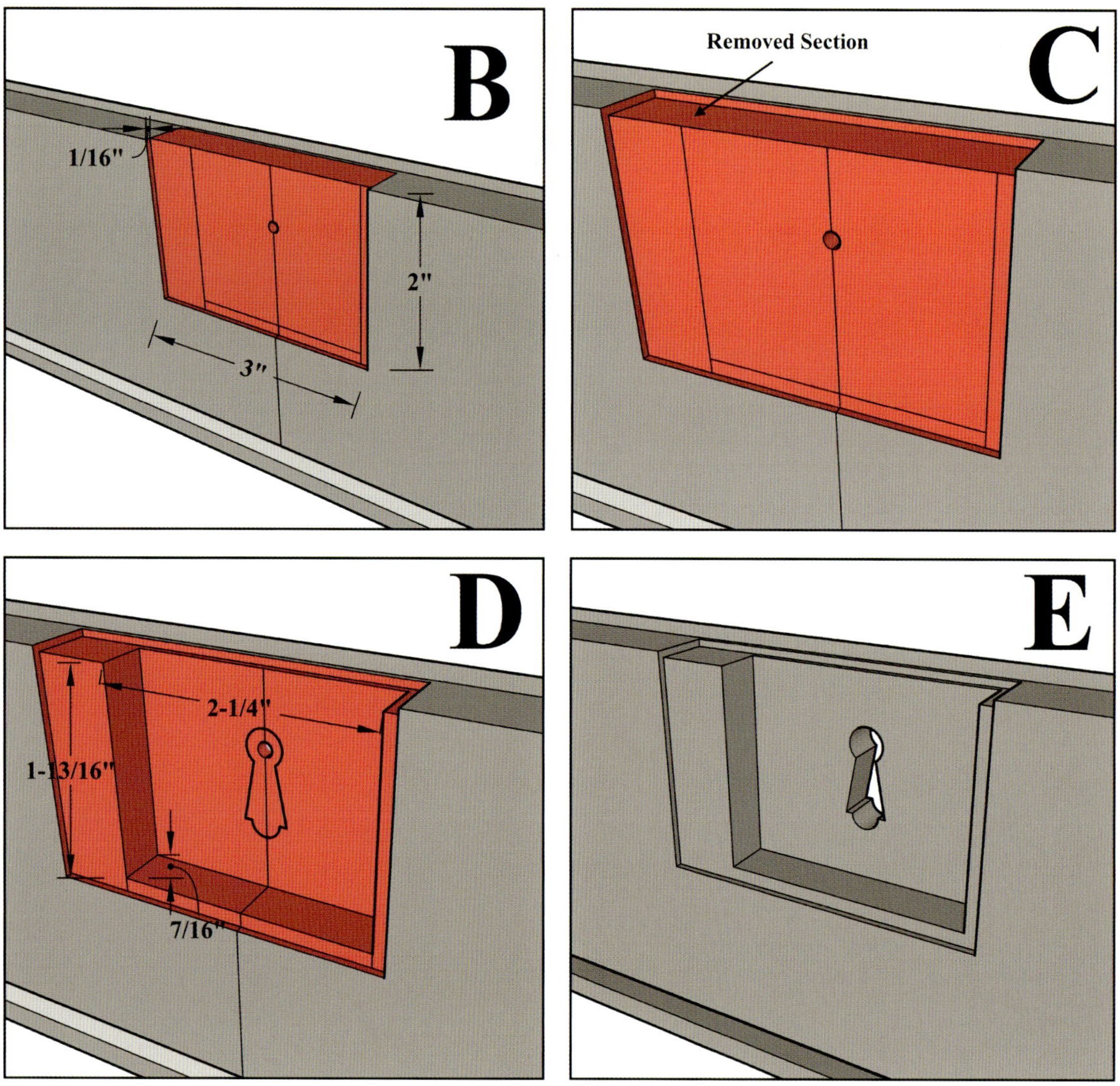

FIG. 14-3. Sequential steps for cutting a lock mortise.

FIG. 14-4. Score the outside lock perimeter with a knife. Cut into the perimeter from the inside.

FIG. 14-5. Use a router plane to remove 1⁄16". This is the lock outer-housing thickness.

FIG. 14-6. Use a drill press with a Forstner bit to remove much of the material.

FIG. 14-7. Finish the opening with a flat chisel and router plane; 1⁄16" has also been removed from the top edge to account for the lock plate thickness.

FIG. 14-8. The keyhole opening is two to three drilled holes that are then connected and cleaned with a chisel.

FIG. 14-9. The completed keyhole as seen from the back. This will be covered with the lock.

FIG. 14-10. The completed keyhole as seen from the front. This will be covered by the escutcheon.

Lower Middle Drawer

The middle-drawer dimensions are shown in **figures 14-11** and **14-12**. The construction techniques are the same as for the others. Cut the joints in the drawer front before carving it; this will reduce the chance of damage to the carved shell and thumbnailed edge while cutting the dovetail pins. The order of operations should be as follows:

1. Cut the joints.

2. Carve the shell.

3. Cut the thumbnail.

4. Assemble and glue the drawer together.

5. Clean up after the glue has dried. This includes removing the pin sections that are proud of the sides to complete the lip.

6. Fit and install the bottom.

7. Attach the applied vines. Use a little glue and small headless brads. Be careful not to split the carved vine.

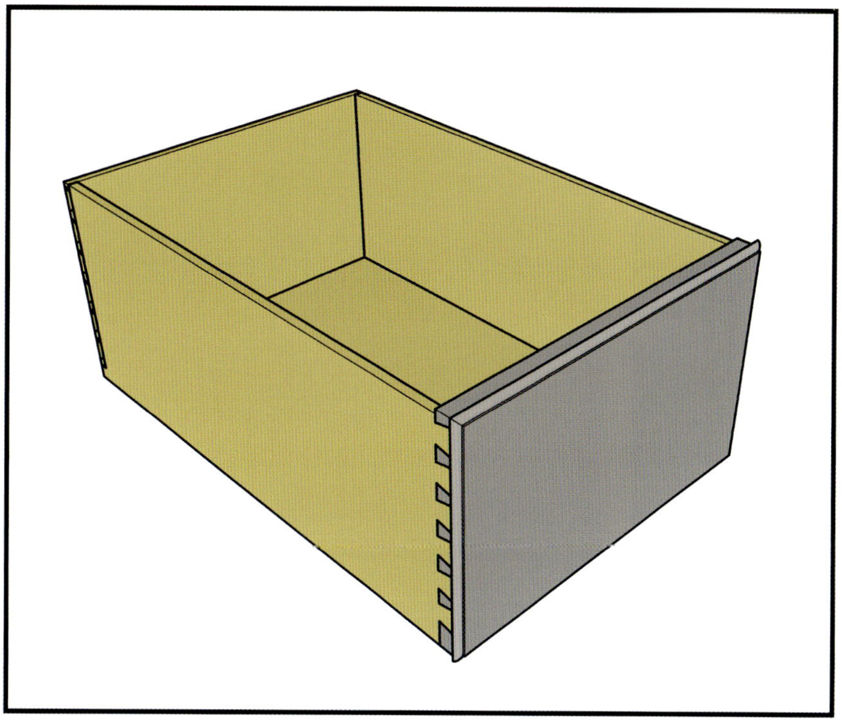

FIG. 14-11. Dimensions for the lower middle-drawer front.

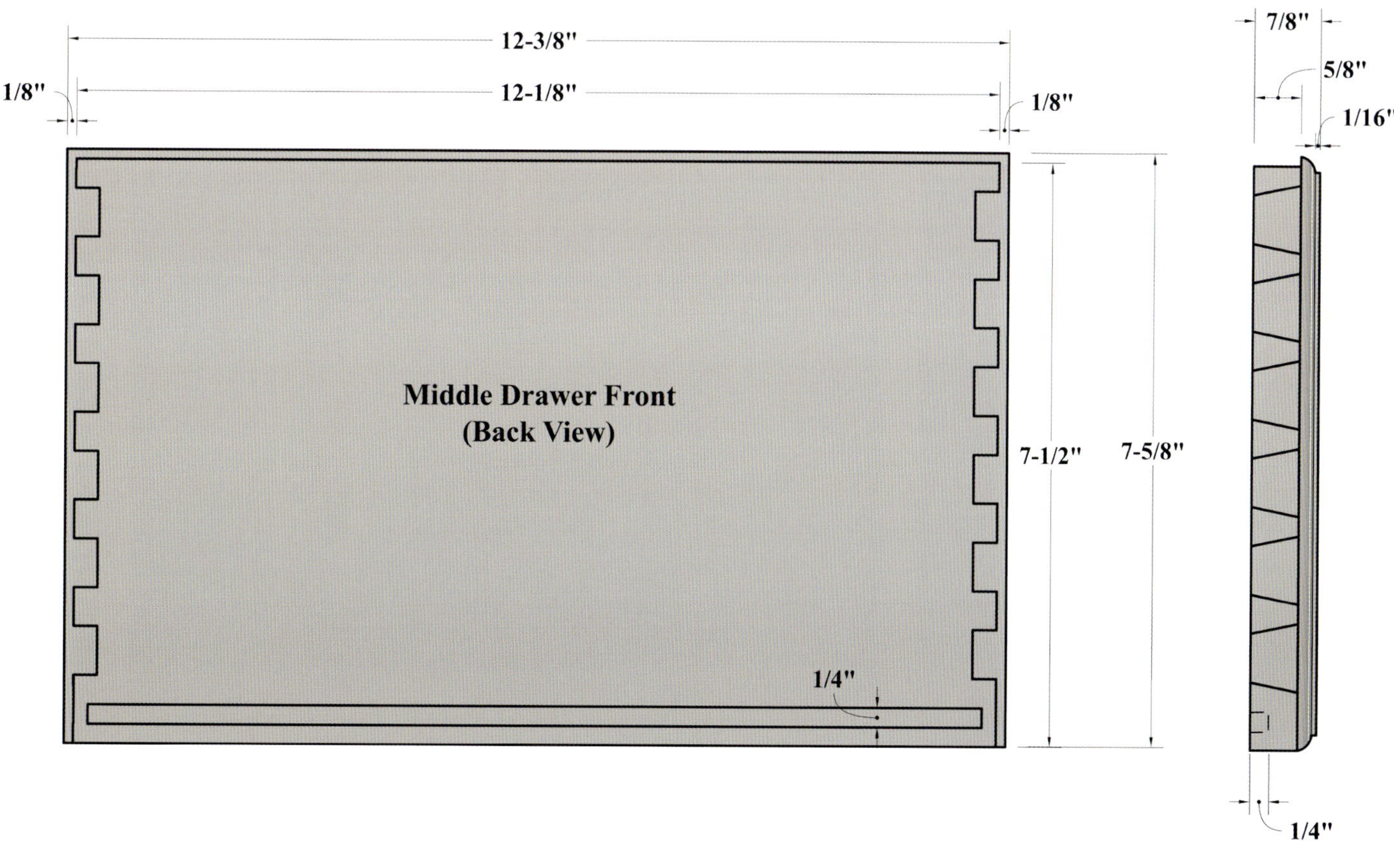

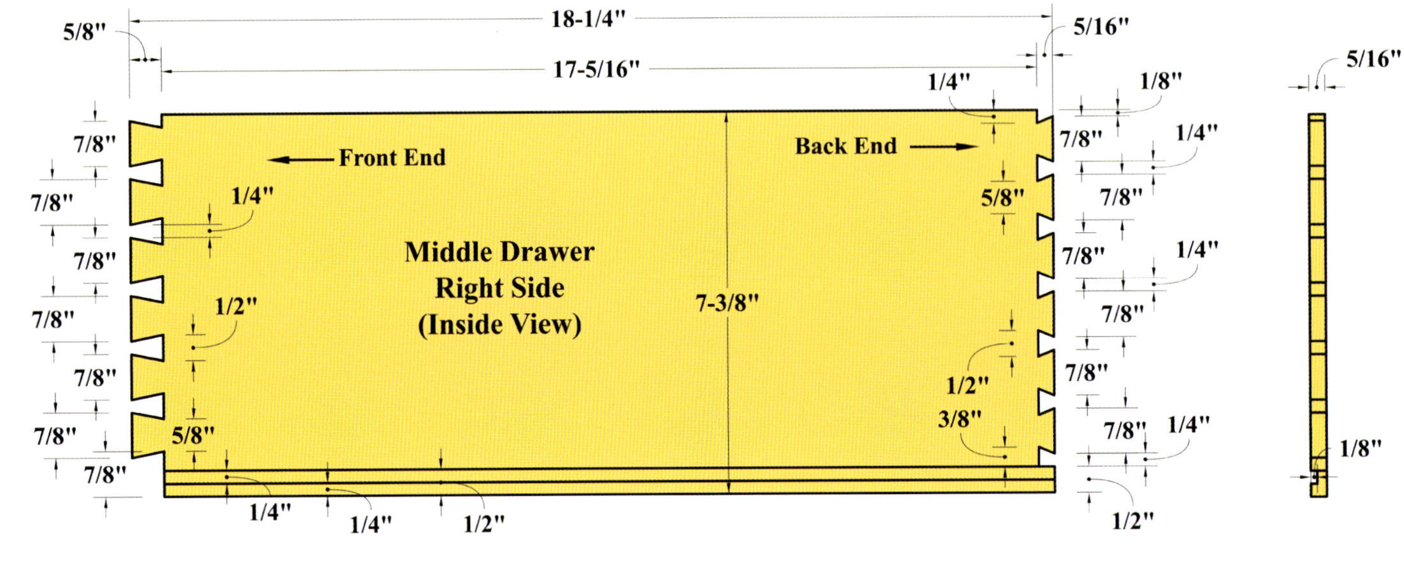

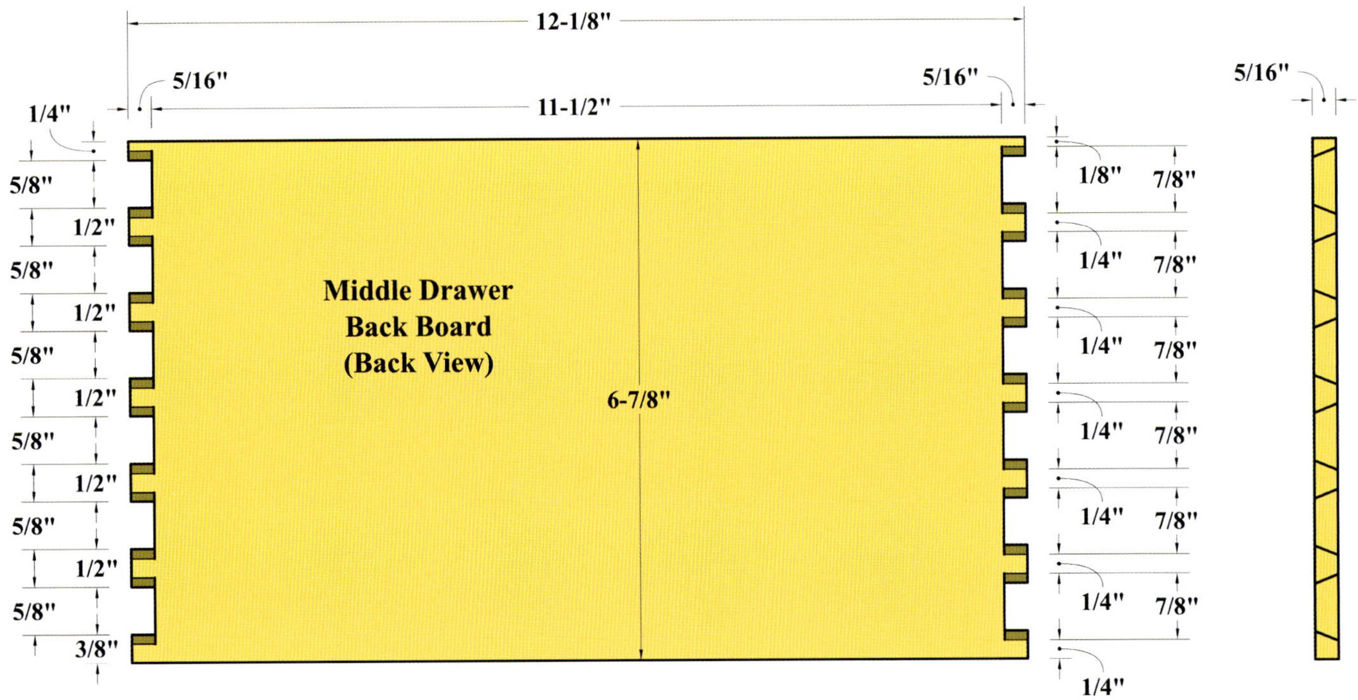

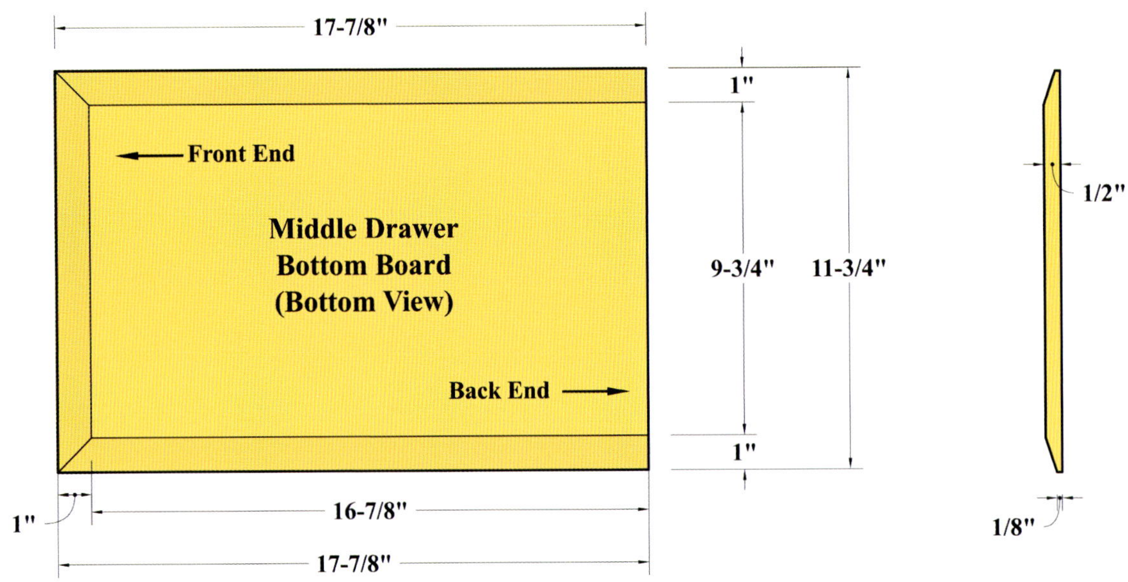

FIG. 14-12. Dimensions for the sides, back, and bottom for the lower middle drawer.

Appendix 1

Drawings

This section contains all the reduced-size drawings needed for this piece. Full-scale drawings are provided in the inside back cover insert. They are referenced throughout the text as needed.

Figure A1-6 is an example of a cut diagram. This is not the only choice; it is just one example to illustrate how to lay out parts with minimal waste.

Garvan Dressing-Table Cut List

Part	Dimensions[1]	Stock	Wood
Top	35 (l) × 21 (w)	4/4	Mahogany
Sides	18 (l) × 17 (w)	4/4 (2 needed)	Mahogany
Front Skirt	30 (l) × 6 (w)	4/4	Mahogany
Top Rail	30 (l) × 2 (w)	4/4	Mahogany
Middle Rail	30 (l) × 2 (w)	4/4	Mahogany
Drawer Stiles	10 (l) × 2 (w)	4/4 (2 needed)	Mahogany
Back	30 (l) × 17 (w)	4/4	Pine
Legs	31 (l) × 3(w) × 3(d)	12/4 (4 needed)	Mahogany
Top Drawer	29 (l) × 4.5 (w)	4/4	Mahogany
Side Drawers	7.625 (l) × 6.25 (w)	4/4 (2 needed)	Mahogany
Carved Drawer	12.5 (l) × 8 (w)	4/4	Mahogany
Quarter Columns	11.5 (l) × 1.125 square	(2 needed)	Mahogany
Molding[2]	34 + 21 + 21 (l) × 7/8 (w)	7/8	Mahogany
Greek Key[2]	34 + 21 + 21 (l) × 1/2 (w)	1/8	Mahogany
Drawer sides, backs, and bottoms	As needed[3]	5/16–3/8	Pine

1. Length is along the grain and width is across the grain, in inches.
2. The three lengths are two sides and one front.
3. The heights and lengths of the drawer sides can vary depending on drawer depth and personal preferences.

Hardware List

I got all my hardware from Ball & Ball, except the lock, which I got from White Chapel. All the hardware is solid brass, in reproduction styles.

4	C57-121	3" boring pull (bright finish)
1	C57-121E	Escutcheon (bright finish)
1	G19-145	1/2" diameter plain knob (bright finish)
1	168L.1	3" × 2" × 9/16" lock

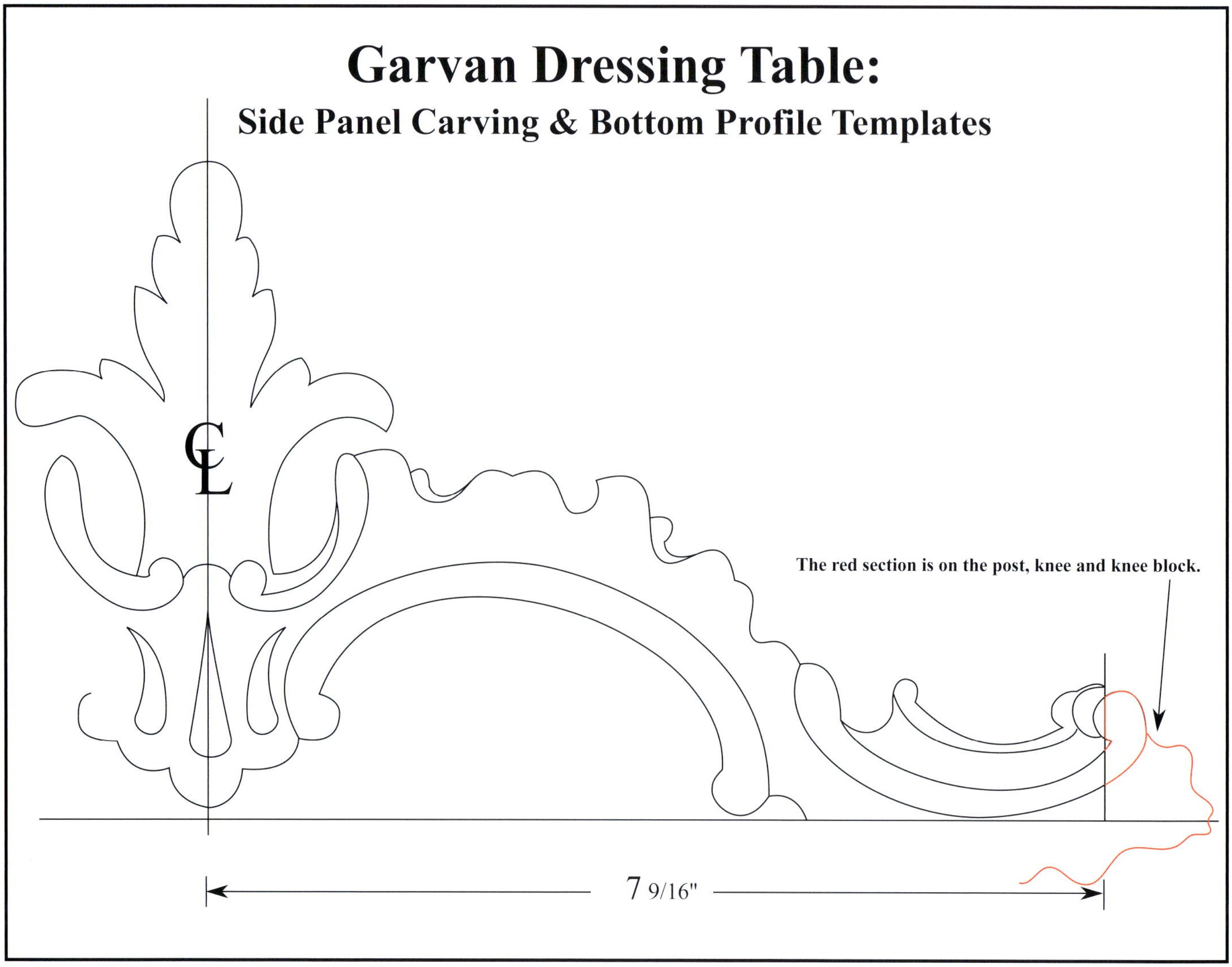

FIG. A1-1. One-half of the side panel carving and bottom profile. The portion of the drawing to the right of the 7⁹⁄₁₆" line is on the leg post.

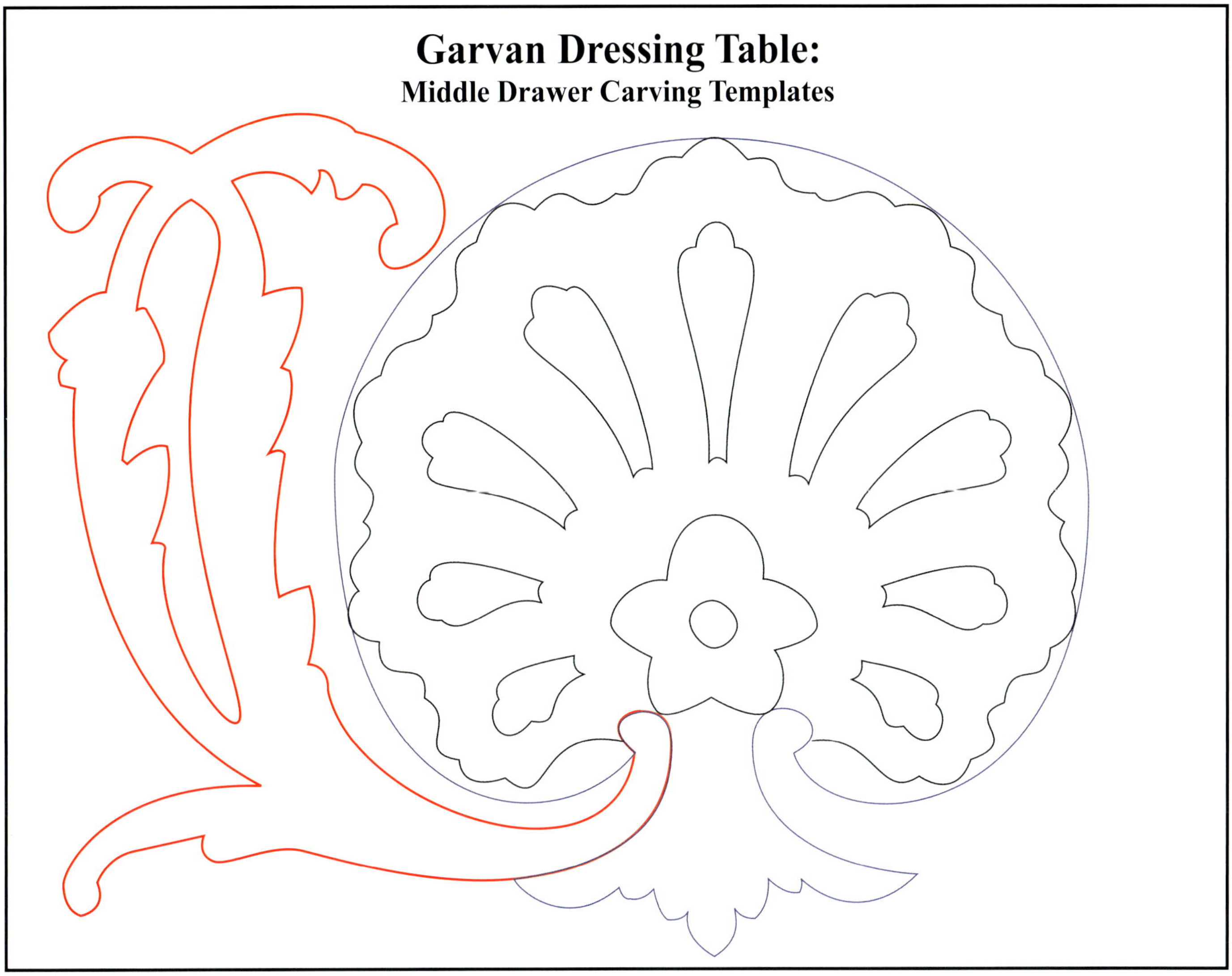

FIG. A1-2. The red drawing is the applied vine. The blue one is the outside shell, and the black one is the inside shell.

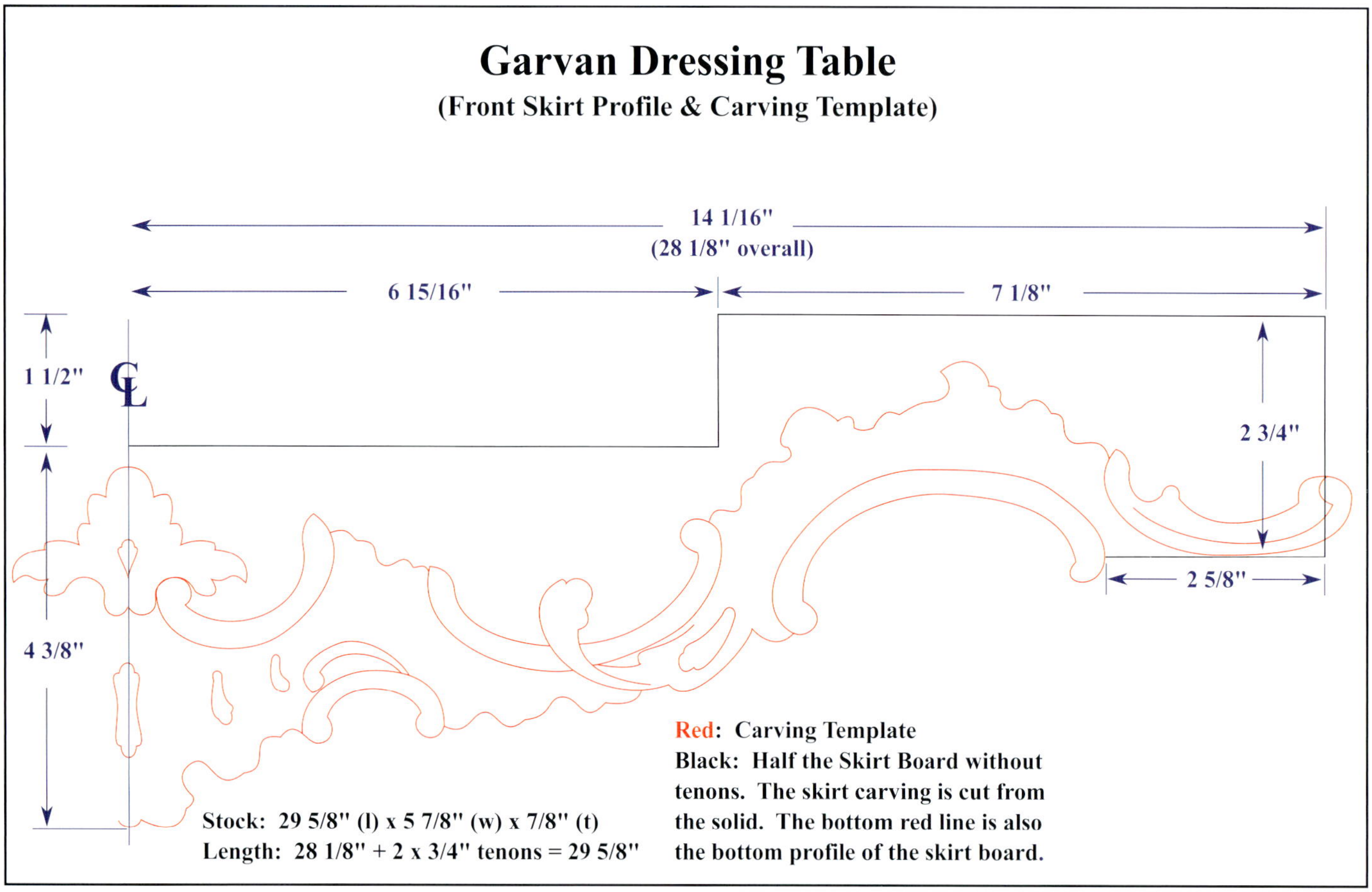

FIG. A1-3. One-half of the front rail carving and bottom profile. The portion of the drawing to the right of the 14⅙" line is on the post.

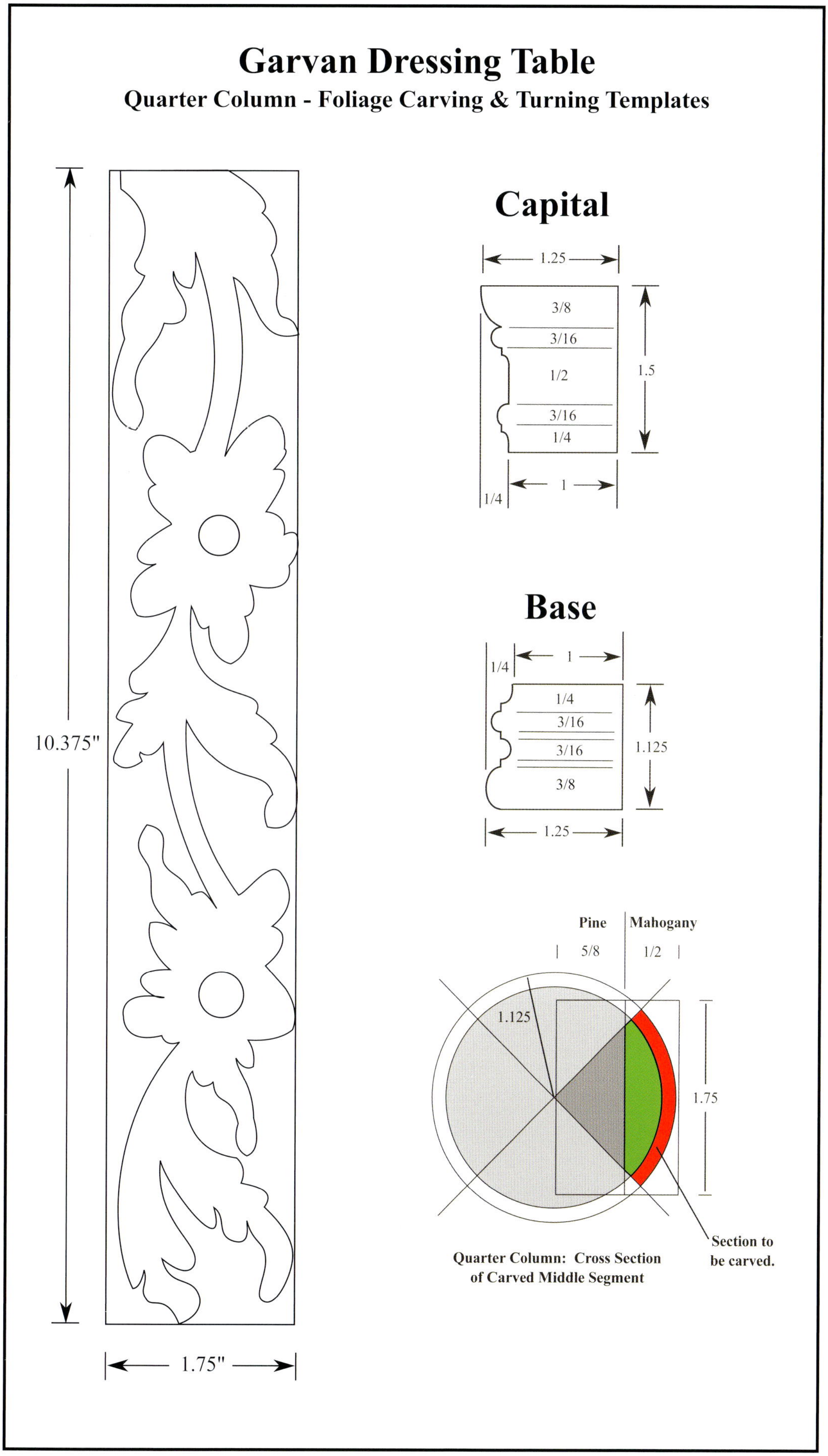

FIG. A1-4. The width of the quarter-column carving is sized to account for the extra distance needed to wrap around the quarter-column blank. Make the capital and base blanks a little longer than needed to give some flexibility when fitting them.

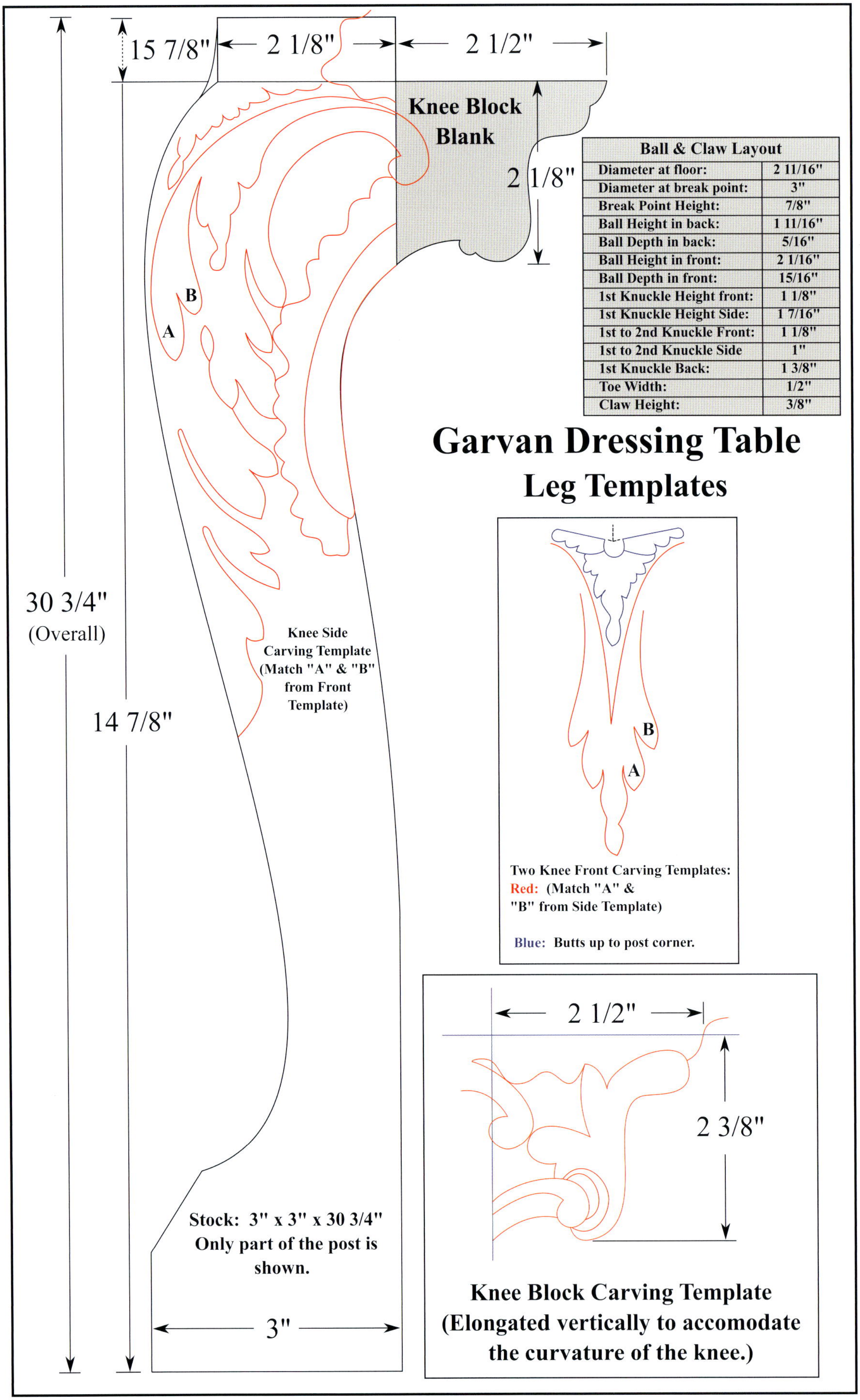

Ball & Claw Layout	
Diameter at floor:	2 11/16"
Diameter at break point:	3"
Break Point Height:	7/8"
Ball Height in back:	1 11/16"
Ball Depth in back:	5/16"
Ball Height in front:	2 1/16"
Ball Depth in front:	15/16"
1st Knuckle Height front:	1 1/8"
1st Knuckle Height Side:	1 7/16"
1st to 2nd Knuckle Front:	1 1/8"
1st to 2nd Knuckle Side	1"
1st Knuckle Back:	1 3/8"
Toe Width:	1/2"
Claw Height:	3/8"

FIG. A1-5. The leg post is shortened to fit the page. The knee carving uses three separate templates.

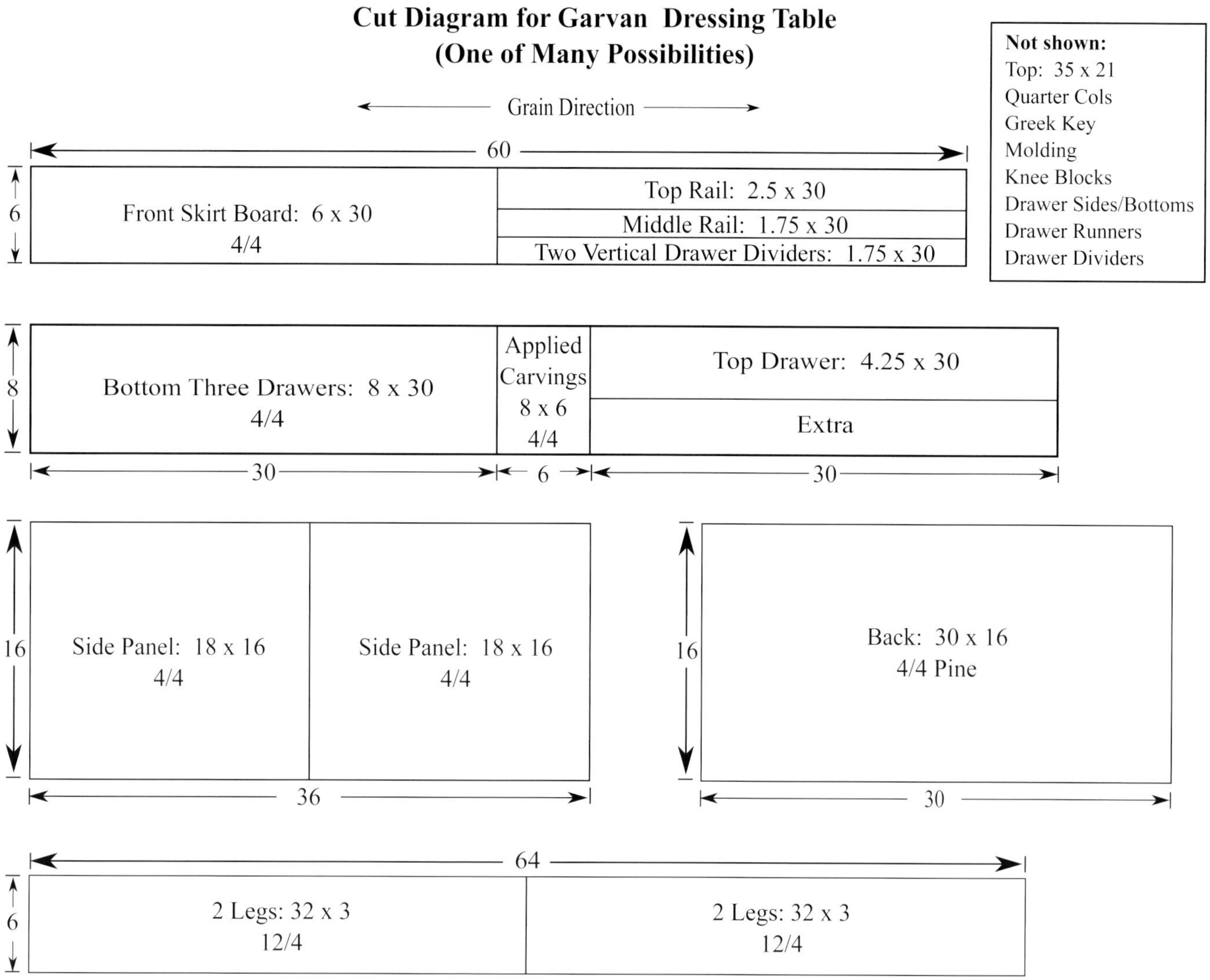
Cut Diagram for Garvan Dressing Table
(One of Many Possibilities)
Not shown:
Top: 35 x 21
Quarter Cols
Greek Key
Molding
Knee Blocks
Drawer Sides/Bottoms
Drawer Runners
Drawer Dividers
Grain Direction
60
6
Front Skirt Board: 6 x 30
4/4
Top Rail: 2.5 x 30
Middle Rail: 1.75 x 30
Two Vertical Drawer Dividers: 1.75 x 30
8
Bottom Three Drawers: 8 x 30
4/4
Applied Carvings
8 x 6
4/4
Top Drawer: 4.25 x 30
Extra
30
6
30
16
Side Panel: 18 x 16
4/4
Side Panel: 18 x 16
4/4
36
16
Back: 30 x 16
4/4 Pine
30
64
6
2 Legs: 32 x 3
12/4
2 Legs: 32 x 3
12/4

FIG. A1-6.

Extra Reference Model Images

This section contains additional images of the original reference model. They are intended to help the reader understand the carvings.

FIG. A2-1. Left corner. Note the pinned joint on the side.

FIG. A2-2. Upper portion of a side view of the knee carving on a front leg

FIG. A2-3. Lower portion of a side view of the knee carving on a front leg

FIG. A2-4. Upper portion of the knee carving on a front leg

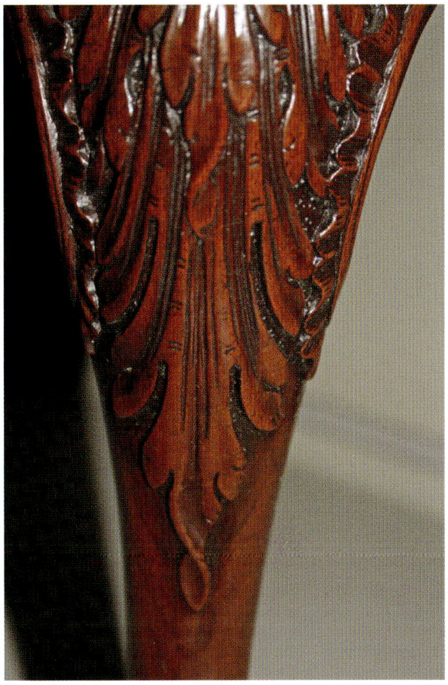

FIG. A2-5. Lower portion of the knee carving on a front leg

FIG. A2-6. Left-side quarter column. The pinned joint on the side orients it.

FIG. A2-7. Upper-left quarter column. Note the line between the capital and middle.

FIG. A2-8. Lower-left quarter column. Note the line between the base and the middle.

FIG. A2-9. Left column, just above the bottom

FIG. A2-10. Left column, just below the top

FIG. A2-11. Upper left corner. Note how the Greek key begins on a full element in front.

FIG. A2-12. Right side. The pinned joints on the side set the orientation.

FIG. A2-13. Carved middle-drawer front

FIG. A2-14. The left side. The quarter column on the right sets the orientation.

FIG. A2-15. Front rail

FIG. A2-16. Case construction details

FIG. A2-17. More case construction details